YOUR DEAR LETTER

Private Correspondence of
Queen Victoria and the Crown Princess of Prussia

1865–1871

The Queen at the unveiling of the statue of the Prince Consort in Coburg, August 1865.

YOUR DEAR LETTER

Private Correspondence of
Queen Victoria and the Crown Princess of Prussia

1865-1871

Edited by
ROGER FULFORD

LONDON
EVANS BROTHERS LIMITED

Published by
EVANS BROTHERS LIMITED
Montague House, Russell Square, London, W.C.1

Set in 12 on 13 point Walbaum
and printed in Great Britain by
Butler and Tanner Limited, Frome and London
237 35187 0   PR1596

CONTENTS

ILLUSTRATIONS

INTRODUCTION

The six years, which are covered by this volume of the correspondence between Queen Victoria and her eldest daughter, the Crown Princess of Prussia, contained critical events in the history of our own country and of Europe. At home those years mark the emergence of Gladstone and Disraeli, the serious difficulties with Ireland over the Irish Church, and the outrages by the Fenians. Abroad they reveal the growth of nationalism, and lead us through the short but severe war between Austria and Prussia in 1866 to the more savage Franco-Prussian War four years afterwards. They were years of exceptional anxiety.

Reading the letters between the Queen and her daughter we are carried back to the old Europe with its civilised traditions, to the multiplicity of German states, with their princes and princesses carefully paraded before us by mother and daughter and to the days when kings, emperors and princes commanded in the field and compassion between victor and vanquished was still possible. Yet for all the charms of this scene drawn for us in the letters we are somehow conscious of darker shadows. We may feel confident that neither the Queen nor the Crown Princess had an inkling of the reality which was to descend on their two countries in the twentieth century but each was uneasy, feeling—as we are told birds and animals feel—the portents which proclaim a storm. With sorrow, amounting at times to despair, the Crown Princess describes the furtive but relentless advance of Bismarck and the way in which he mesmerised her father-in-law, the King of Prussia. The reason for her anguish lies in her realisation of the danger in such a policy for the future peace of Europe. In *Dearest Mama* we saw the strengthening of ill-feeling between Prussia and England resulting from the problems of Schleswig-Holstein. The English felt that they were watching, in the rise of Prussia, the emergence of a new force in European politics—a force which was boastful and ruthless. Relations between England and Prussia were the subject of serious concern and anxiety to both correspondents, and the Queen in particular was greatly distressed when she saw how international rivalries could be reflected in family relationships. Writing to the Prince of Wales the Queen said "What could be more painful than the position in which our family were placed during the wars with Denmark, and between Prussia and Austria? Every family feeling was rent asunder, and we were powerless." (*Letters of Queen Victoria*, Second Series, Volume 1, page 632.) The sympathies of the Queen were naturally in favour of Germany and in favour of Prussia— though it will be remembered that the Germany, which she pictured in her mind from the teaching of the Prince Consort, was fast dissolving. The reader will notice that when the Franco-Prussian War starts, the Queen is violently and vociferously pro-Prussia but as the war develops the humanitarian feelings of the Queen, which were always close to the surface, asserted themselves; she becomes decidedly lukewarm in her sympathies for Prussia when she sees the extent of the carnage on both sides and the dangers inherent in the seizure of Alsace-Lorraine. In March 1871 the Queen writes "the feeling here towards Prussia is as bitter as it can be".

The Crown Princess on the other hand—and this is natural for one writing from a country at war—rebuts the attacks on Prussia, springs to her defence though not to the defence of Bismarck and, as the book closes, offers to return the dowry which she received from England on her marriage. Over and over again the Queen bemoans the divided national loyalties of herself and her daughter, and over and over again she emphasises the sorrow and anxiety which they cause her, and the strains which these impose on family life. Yet neither the Queen nor the Crown Princess masks their differences: neither mother nor daughter ever flinches from expressing her own national point of view. They loved one another too deeply and understood one another too exactly for any concealment of feeling. For this reason the letters, in my opinion, gain enormously in interest because they are exact reflections of the mind of each writer. Unlike the great majority of letter-writers, the Queen and Crown Princess do not consider the recipient; to them a letter is information—not to be blurred or falsified by anxieties over its effect on the recipient. The Queen says, it may be noticed, "if old Mama has a virtue it is that of truth and the absence of all flattery".[1] That indeed was true. But it was also not untrue of her daughter. For instance the Crown Princess evidently did not admire the Scotch with the fervour of her mother and, with her brothers and sisters, she did not altogether relish her mother's publication of her diary of life in the Highlands, because it revealed, they thought, too much about themselves as children. We find ourselves involuntarily exclaiming as we read the letters, "For goodness sake say something friendly about the Queen's book." But nothing comes. As was true of her mother, the Crown Princess could not bring herself to say what she did not truly feel. Indeed some of her difficulties in Germany would have been mitigated if she could have resisted speaking her mind. But it is that quality of frankness which gives both sides of the correspondence its zest.

The correspondence gives a perfectly rational explanation of how the Queen's reliance on John Brown developed. This is a topic which has, in the twentieth century, attracted great curiosity and—it must be added—some silliness. People are perfectly entitled to believe what they like about the Queen and John Brown though remembering that imagination is not always the surest path to truth. From

---

[1] 11 August 1866.

this correspondence the facts appear with force. Brown was, as the Queen says, an ideal servant and, increasingly relying on him, the Queen found someone who, at every turn, eased her path. "He was the child of nature." Those are the words of Sir Henry Ponsonby who probably saw Brown almost every day for twenty years, and he was among the most sensible and perceptive of Queen Victoria's advisers. The Queen contrasted the simplicity and truthfulness of "the child of nature" with the artificiality—for so she deemed it—of the conventional upper classes; her sustained criticism of the fashionable world and of the aristocracy is one of the most constant themes of this book. Her reliance on Brown is explained by the simple truth that she was refreshed by a human being untrammelled by convention or the wish to please. The reader can hardly fail to notice that the Crown Princess is not enthusiastic about Brown, and Lady Longford, in her convincing portrait of the Queen, tells us that the Crown Princess advised against the Queen appointing him her Highland servant. The reason for this— and all the Queen's elder children felt the same—was not of course from fear of gossip but because the Queen, with her particular nature, was a prey to excessive influence by individuals; Lehzen, Melbourne, the Munshi and John Brown are all in point here. This was a danger against which the Prince Consort had repeatedly warned her. In justice to Brown it should be added that although he may have made himself unpopular with the members of the royal family and possibly with some members of the Household, he never intrigued for himself or his family and was to live his life limited by the boundaries of faithful service.

There are two further points about Queen Victoria which deserve emphasis in this foreword. Although the Queen would certainly not have laid claim to being highbrow, she reveals that her reading was by no means trivial—especially when it is remembered how often she complains of the little time which she had for leisure-reading. While we may not today share her fondness for Scotch novels or the limpid works of Mrs. Oliphant her enthusiasm for "Aurora Leigh" and the trouble which she took to master the more difficult poems of Tennyson are unexpected. The other point lies in considering who were the people who influenced the Queen's thought at this time, that is to say both her political thinking and her taste in reading. This is obviously a difficult field but we can probably say that when she writes "we think", "people think" or "they think here" she is no doubt expressing the views of General Grey and her secretariat and perhaps of the Household in general. But over such things as books she was probably much influenced by Countess Blücher as she had been influenced earlier by the Duchess of Sutherland. Not a great deal is known of the Countess, and what I have been able to discover is on pages 53 and 54. She evidently became an intimate friend of the Queen after the Prince's death. She was rather doleful because of her unending series of bereavements, and to her might be applied the remark of the Scottish lady, which so much amused the Queen, "When my good man died he made such a hole in the ground that all the others fell through it." We know that Countess Blücher read out loud to the Queen in the evenings, and it was during these readings that the Queen's son-in-law, Prince Louis, disgraced himself by falling asleep. The Queen's friendship with the Countess, coupled with discussions with members of her Household at dinner, kept the Queen far more in touch with events and opinions than the conventional picture of the recluse at Windsor would imply. Throughout the correspondence her comments are extraordinarily pertinent so that often we feel in the main stream of mid-Victorian life.

Turning to the Crown Princess we see more clearly the emergence of the culminating tragedy of her life. Although she does not welcome it—rather the reverse—and although she certainly does not boast of it, she is obviously conscious of the importance of her position—rendered more important by the defeat of Austria and of France and by the assumption by Prussia of imperial emblems. She was the only one of Queen Victoria's daughters to make a dynastic marriage. Princess Alice's marriage to Prince

Louis of Hesse was, from the point of ambition, disappointing and became more disappointing as Hesse waned and Prussia grew. The three remaining daughters of the Queen made marriages which, from the political and worldly angle, are scarcely worth noticing. There are frequent allusions during this period to the expectation that the Crown Princess must shortly move to the front as Queen of Prussia and German Empress. Indeed this was natural—for her father-in-law was seventy-three at the time of the Franco-Prussian War. When the Crown Princess is discussing whether it would be right or otherwise for the Crown Prince to go to the opening of the Suez Canal at the end of 1869 she writes, "and then I doubt whether it would be prudent in going so far away at the King's age". Who could have foretold that the Emperor William I would live to be over ninety and that his son would follow him to the grave within a hundred days? Had the Emperor and Empress Frederick come to the throne in the 1870's, which was the natural expectation, they would have changed Germany and they might have changed the history of Europe. This is the particular tragedy of the Crown Princess.

Although it has been whispered and, by some writers, too readily assumed that the Crown Princess was a severe mother, there is absolutely no evidence for this in this section of the correspondence. She constantly praises the future Kaiser and shows true feeling for him over his infirmity, and true understanding of his character. We see the beginning of the intrusion into his life of Prussian militarism and discipline which were to disrupt the more civilised beliefs of his father and mother. Was he not first and foremost the child of Prussia?

Similarly the relations of the Queen with her own children become of mounting importance. Readers of *Dearest Child* and *Dearest Mama* will remember how the Prince of Wales was the constant target for the Queen's attack. In this volume all is changed. It is filled with praise of the Prince, of his kindness to all and sundry and of his affection for his mother. The worst that she finds to say of him is that he was "imprudent". It is at once high praise and true when she writes of the Prince of Wales "I am sure that no heir apparent was so nice and unpretending as dear Bertie is". In this volume some of the Queen's other children are causes of vexation and the cynic might argue that they draw the fire from the eldest son. Prince Alfred is the target of his mother's recurring and indignant attack; Princess Alice is in high disfavour throughout these years and Princess Louise is slightly criticised. Prince Alfred, though talented and attractive, was at this time a tiresome youth. He did much to vex his mother—immorality, fondness for London society and, possibly worst of all, he was inconsiderate with the Queen's servants and House-hold. Princess Alice likewise loved smart and intelligent society, a partiality which the Queen did not approve. This prepared the way for an explosion of wrath against Princess Alice over Princess Helena's marriage. The facts can be briefly stated. Of the five daughters of the Queen, Princess Helena was perhaps the least attractive: it is necessary to say this because it was part—though only a part—of the difficulty in finding a suitable husband for her. Religion and nationality were the main stumbling-blocks. As was natural the Queen threw her protection over Princess Helena. She was intelligent and sensible and, as the correspondence shows, a great help to the Queen in family and official matters. Prince Christian of Schleswig-Holstein then came on the scene. He was an agreeable man, be-longing to a distinguished royal house—though an exile. He and his family had been harshly treated by Prussia as a result of the 1864 war, and he was able to offer to live in England. This the Queen hailed with delight because it enabled Princess Helena to continue at hand with secretar-ial help. Princess Alice thought—and hers was certainly no lone voice in this—that it was a mistake for Prince and Princess Christian to agree to an English domicile. She was particularly unwise in warning Prince Christian that "he must not allow himself to be put upon". Such remarks came back to the Queen, and they greatly vexed her. This passing storm reveals for us how painfully easy it was for personal difficulties to arise in so large a family and—principally owing to numbers—how wide were the opportunities for that mischief in the house which the Queen frequently deplores. One of the younger members of the family of George III, alluding to similar difficulties in the Royal Family then, remarked with truth "there were too many of us".

In the case of Queen Victoria these family differences can be easily inflated to the detriment of her true nature. There are three points which it is important that the reader should not overlook.

First—in the nineteenth century—or at any rate in the middle decades of it—severity towards the growing members of a family was general, not particular. Examples to prove the point can be found in novels, diaries, and biographies, and I take one—the letters of the Stanleys of Alderley edited some 30 years ago by Miss Nancy Mitford. This is how a member of that family wrote to his wife about their sons: "with regard to your male cubs I should recommend a wholesome application of the birch". This is Lady Stanley describing her grandson in a letter to the youth's mother: "he is certainly very languid and gives me the idea he has been paying the penalty of his sins, as most young men do. I should not wish to see him too intimate with a very clever Jesuit." Criticism of children, as they grew up, coupled with fears of the Roman Church, were general characteristics of nineteenth century mothers. Possibly it is more noticeable in Queen Victoria because of the delightful vigour with which she expresses herself.

Secondly, after the Prince Consort's death, the resources of the Queen were taxed to the utmost. Her work with Ministers, the supervision of her homes and of the Royal Household and, as we know, correspondence with her relations in Europe filled her working-day. Consequently she was indignant when her children by their behaviour or even, as she explains about Princess Louise, when they saw things in a different light from that in which she saw them, added to the burdens of her working-life. This may not have been an endearing characteristic—but it is under-standable.

Thirdly, in ordinary circumstances, the Queen would have relied on her grown-up sons to advise her and—up to a point—to help her with her work. She did not do this because she placed no real confidence in them. That is why her criticism of the Prince of Wales in previous volumes and of Prince Alfred in this one are important. From this a significant corollary follows. Not relying on her sons she had grown accustomed to leaning on her daughters—first Princess Alice and after her marriage on Princess Helena. The Queen would have argued that fate had dealt her a mortal blow in the death of the Prince and that she could not carry on without the assistance of Princess Helena. That is the explanation of the quarrel with Princess Alice: it was not merely a personal clash but sprang from something which the Queen, with all the tenacity of her nature, felt to be an integral part of the management of her life.

One point may baffle some readers and indeed strike them as almost unseemly, feeling that the editor should have intervened with his blue pencil. That is the severity of some of the comments on the Roman Catholic Church. Here it is important to notice that both Queen Victoria and the Prince Consort (especially) were strictly Protestant with a strong bias away from the Church of England. The Queen intensely disliked the Oxford movement and greatly feared the spread of Roman Catholicism in England. If we were to analyse her feelings we should find that it was not so much that she disliked the doctrines of Pusey and Keble or of Newman and Manning as that she saw that they were a cause of agitation and disturbance. At the same time the Queen and the Crown Princess were greatly provoked— as were many of the best minds in the Roman Catholic Church including of course Lord Acton—by the misrule of the Papal States by the Vatican and by the doctrines which emanated from this stronghold of reaction. This explains why the Crown Princess, in her letter of 4 September 1869, alludes to "the thraldom of the Roman Catholic Church" as "ruinous to a state". At this time people with liberal opinions, all over Europe, looked on the Vatican as a fortress of absolutism from which might emerge a force to drive back the advance of liberal thought so painfully gained. It is fair to remember that many of the statements issued from the Vatican Council in 1869 to '70 were extremely intransigent and highly offensive to Protestants. It must also be remembered that by Clause 80 of the Syllabus Errorum, which was published in 1864 just as this volume begins, Pope Pius IX condemned as "erroneous the opinion that the Roman pontiff can and ought to reconcile himself with progress, liberalism and modern civilization". This Syllabus had a shattering effect on the most thoughtful English Catholic of the nineteenth century (Lord Acton), all of which is explained in Archbishop Mathew's excellent book published in 1968. It was this kind of attitude in the Catholic hierarchy—admittedly more lustily proclaimed than acted upon—which deeply antagonised the Crown Princess and to a lesser extent her mother. These are ancient and long-buried animosities, which were formidable in their day, and it did not seem right to conceal them.

I should explain that in the letters of these years there is no sudden elimination of grief over the Prince Consort's untimely death. There are naturally many allusions to this on both sides of the correspondence. I have almost entirely omitted them, but the reader will recognise that they still governed the mind of the Queen and to some extent of her daughter. I have left them out because I felt that their dominance—so characteristic of the mid-Victorian mind— was sufficiently reflected in *Dearest Mama*.

I have retained passages even of a private nature such as the Queen's objurgations about her children, the Crown Princess's out-pourings over the death of Prince Sigismund or against the Prussian family, because they seemed to me to reveal the inner characteristics of both writers. They stand before us in this correspondence—sensitive, emotional, capable of deep feeling and righteous wrath. Yet for all that, both writers—the Queen possibly more than the Crown Princess—are shrewd observers of the great events of these years and despite their natures surprisingly restrained in their comments on what they see, from their privileged position, unfolding before them. But if for a moment we were able to divest each writer of her position in the world, we should be left with material of copious interest because it reveals—despite the foibles and prejudices with which it may be filled—the habit of mind and the ideals which lifted the mid-Victorian age in England, for all its short-comings and faults, to the summit of our European civilization.

NOTE ON THE LETTERS AND
METHOD OF EDITING

The correspondence between Queen Victoria and her eldest child, the Crown Princess of Prussia is—judged even by Victorian standards—prodigious. It has come down to us virtually complete. Carefully bound, each year in a volume, the letters stretch across many shelves. The Queen and her daughter wrote to one another twice a week, and in times of family or national crisis more frequently. In this habit of letter-writing they reflected, on a larger scale, what was as much a natural part of life in the nineteenth century as a telephone conversation has become for many women in our own day. In Victorian England, mothers of families, widows and spinster-aunts devoted a great part of their mornings to compiling family letters at their once scorned (but now coveted) little writing-desks known as Davenports. Anthony Trollope tells us, at a terrible moment in his history of the residents of Framley, how after the letters for Framley Court had arrived in the letter-bag, Lady Lufton was away in her own room, as was her wont, writing letters at her little writing-table. No doubt Lady Lufton's letters and those of almost all her contemporaries have made splendid bonfires stoked by executors and the unfeeling hands of descendants. Happily Queen Victoria's letters were spared that indignity.

The history of the correspondence is this. As the Crown Princess received the letters from her mother, she treasured them and had them bound. They amount to some sixty volumes. When the Crown Princess died in 1901—she was then a widow and known as the Empress Frederick—

she had followed the example of her mother, and had made her youngest child her literary executor. This was Princess Margaret of Prussia, who married Prince Frederick Charles of Hesse afterwards Landgrave of Hesse. She and her husband lived at Friedrichshof—the castle in the Taunus hills above Frankfort which was built as a memorial to the Emperor Frederick; in this setting the Landgravine cherished the letters, her mother's remarkable library and all her collections, where they still remain. When Queen Victoria's letters were published in nine volumes in the early decades of this century, it is clear that the source at Friedrichshof was not used. It is true that a very few letters from the Crown Princess or from the Queen to her are included in these nine volumes but they were almost certainly made from copies. When the Queen was writing to her daughter on politics she often kept a copy of what she wrote, and if she thought a letter from the Crown Princess of particular interest or importance she would get one of her younger children to make a copy of it. We are therefore probably right in assuming that the editors thought that the bulk of the Queen's correspondence with her daughter was too private for publication at that time, and they therefore used the copies (primarily on public affairs) which were available to them. In fact, in the period covered by this volume, only a single letter from the Queen was used by the editors—that for 20 July 1870. The letters therefore remained undisturbed at Friedrichshof until 1945, when the Americans took possession of the Castle, behaved towards the Landgravine with scant respect and treated some of the Empress's collections in a fashion reminiscent of the Goths and Vandals. Knowing of the particular interest of this correspondence King George VI asked his Librarian, Sir Owen Morshead, to go out to Friedrichshof and rescue the letters before they fell into unauthorised hands. This was done; the letters were brought back to Windsor, and returned some years afterwards to the Landgravine.

On her side the Queen treated the letters from the Crown Princess with no less care. They were handsomely bound by years, and kept in the Royal Archives at Windsor. Sometime in the 1890's the Crown Princess borrowed her own letters from her mother, probably with the idea of collecting material for a biography of her husband. In 1900, when she realised that she had only a short time to live, she sent the letters back to Windsor, and it is likely that she did this so that they should not be read by the Kaiser, who is much criticised in the later parts of the correspondence—parts which are outside the range of this selection. She asked Sir Frederick Ponsonby, who was in attendance on King Edward VII when he was visiting Friedrichshof, to take the letters back to Windsor. Sir Frederick did this, and published extracts from them some 30 years later. (*Letters of the Empress Frederick*, Macmillan, 1928.)

For the six years covered by this selection I have had to make large excisions. At a rough calculation there are 200,000 words written by the Queen during these years and not less by her daughter. Consequently some three-quarters of the whole has had to be dropped. To an extent this was easy. In a correspondence of this kind there is inevitably a great deal of repetition, a great deal about the weather and trifling matters, with one correspondent often commenting on (though not varying) something written by the other. I have therefore attempted to distil the correspondence and to keep it fairly balanced between domestic matters and public affairs. Some may feel that there should have been more about fashions, food and domestic economy in general. Of such matters I have consciously made no omissions because they do not figure in the letters. From this selection all we know is that the Queen had a great deal to do, that she was never in bed till after midnight, that she sometimes found it difficult to get up punctually in the morning, and that she enjoyed being read to out loud of an evening. Naturally that side of her mother's life was familiar to the Crown Princess so that it was not necessary to elaborate it. For her part the Crown Princess was interested in higher things than the details of the kitchen.

So far as the editing of these letters goes there is little to add to what I have already explained in the previous selections. I have included a few letters which will be found in Queen Victoria's published correspondence and also a few which will be found in Sir Frederick Ponsonby's *Letters of the Empress*. The reason for this is that I thought it would be more convenient for the reader than having to refer back to those books. The same consideration—that is the convenience of the reader—governed such changes as I have made in the text. I have altered punctuation, converted abbreviated words into their full dignity, translated foreign words and phrases where I thought, as in my own case, they might puzzle the reader and, as more has been left out than has been printed, it did not seem sensible to indicate where cuts have been made. Also I have not thought it sensible to repeat the underlinings which were freely employed by the Queen and much more sparingly by her daughter; this trick which was characteristic of the nineteenth century letter-writer, was used by the Queen for vehemence rather than for emphasis.

I wish to explain to the reader what I have tried to do in order to avoid confusion over people named in the correspondence. There are naturally certain family names used by both writers; these cover the Queen's children, members of the Prussian Royal Family and various Coburg relations; the Queen is also fond of referring to people by their titles, e.g. The Baron, The General, The Countess and so forth. At the beginning of the book is a list of all the people referred to by their familiar names or titles with their identification. People referred to in the letters by their own names will be found identified in the index. This has meant that I have been able to keep the footnotes to explanation. I have used them to explain passages which might not be quite clearly expressed or which might refer to occurrences which are likely to be outside the knowledge of the general reader. There are a few occasions when I have identified people in the footnotes, but this is when I have felt that the point of a passage would be missed without such explanation. I have been guided by the wish to avoid a great proliferation of footnotes, which in my opinion are too apt to daunt and depress the reader. The freshness and vitality of a corre-

spondence such as this can be marred by flourishes of erudi-
tion by the editor or by his supposing that his readers
need him at hand to expound and explain each sentence. I
have tried to avoid transmitting to the book what has been
wittily called "foot and note disease".

I express the deep sense of my gratitude to her Majesty the
Queen for her gracious permission to publish this correspondence. To the Landgrave of Hesse, who owns Queen
Victoria's letters to the Crown Princess and who has most
generously allowed me to work on the relevant volumes in
this country, I am greatly indebted. His brother, Wolfgang,
Prince of Hesse, has helped me in countless ways, especially
over difficult points of German royal history and has allowed
me to familiarise myself with the Crown Princess's
collections at Friedrichshof and has steered me away from
innumerable pitfalls both of fact and taste. I thank him
for all his kindness.

Lady Phyllis Benton helped me very much over the
matrimonial tangle of her great-aunt, Countess Hohenthal.
I am grateful to Lord Anglesey for clearing up a difficult
point over the sleeping arrangements for the troops under
canvas at Aldershot. Sir Ronald Campbell and Mr. Thomas
Lyttelton were most patient in helping me to decipher some
German words and phrases used by the Queen. Her hand-
writing is notoriously difficult to read and it is not always
easy to determine when she is using English and when the
German schrift writing. Miss Agatha Ramm has guided me
over the difficult problems of Hanover after that country's
defeat by Prussia in 1866. Mr. Cairns, the Vicar of Gressingham, was of great assistance to me over the burial place
of Countess Blücher and other matters concerning her. The
Warden of All Souls generously spared time to identify
the quotation from Pope on page 38. I am truly grateful
to my friend, Mr. Harold Kurtz, who read the whole book
in proof.

Miss Langton and her staff at the Royal Archives have
helped me throughout. Mr. Oliver Millar, the Deputy Surveyor of the Queen's pictures, has helped me to identify

some paintings mentioned in the correspondence. Mr. Robin Mackworth-Young, as ever, proved himself a guide and friend of constant kindness and understanding. The London Library, of which I am proud to be a member, has proved invaluable in answering a variety of difficult conundrums. I am, for the same reason, much in the debt of the University Library at Lancaster. I am grateful to the Bodleian Library and to Lord Clarendon for permission to use the letter on page 58 from Queen Victoria to the 4th Lord Clarendon. I also thank the Commandant and Librarian of the Royal Military School of Music for their help over "I'm 95"—the Regimental March of the Rifle Brigade.

I especially thank Mr. John Browning and Mr. Robin Hyman of Evans Brothers for all their help and encouragement, and I know how greatly the book has gained from this and also from the judgement and discrimination of Miss Audrey White who has chosen the illustrations, corrected countless mistakes of mine and shares with me an affection for the personages—royal and otherwise—who figure so vividly in these pages.

FAMILIAR NAMES USED IN THE
CORRESPONDENCE

In this list of names, the King is the King of Prussia, and the Queen is Queen Victoria.

ABBAT. Prince Albrecht of Prussia, nephew of the King.

ADA. Wife of Fritz Holstein.

ADDY or ALEXANDRINE. Sister of Abbat, wife of Duke William of Mecklenburg-Schwerin.

AFFIE. Prince Alfred, later Duke of Edinburgh.

OLD PRINCE ALBERT. Brother of the King, father of "Abbat" and "Addy".

ALBERT VICTOR, ALB. V. or A. V. Eldest son of the Prince of Wales. He became Duke of Clarence.

UNCLE ALEXANDER. Alexander Mensdorff, son of the Queen's aunt, Sophie of Saxe-Coburg.

AUNT ALEXANDRINE. Wife of the Duke of Saxe-Coburg.

AMALIE. Daughter of Prince Augustus of Saxe-Coburg.

ALICE. The Queen's second daughter.

ALIX. Princess of Wales.

UNCLE ALPHONSE. Count Mensdorff-Pouilly, brother of Uncle Alexander.

ANTOINETTE. Wife of Prince Leopold of Hohenzollern.

ARTHUR. The Queen's third son, later Duke of Connaught.

AUGUSTUS OF PORTUGAL. Youngest son of Queen Maria da Gloria.

AUNT or AUNT FEODORA. The Queen's half-sister, Princess Feodora of Hohenlohe-Langenburg.

THE BARON or THE OLD BARON. Baron Stockmar (1787–1863). According to context "the Baron" can be his son, Ernest, who was secretary to the Crown Princess.

BEATRICE or BABY. The fifth daughter of the Queen.

BECKER, Dr. Secretary to the Prince Consort. At this time attached to the Queen of Prussia's Household.

BENNETT. Mary Bennett, the Crown Princess's maid.

BERTIE or B. The Prince of Wales.

AUNT CAMBRIDGE. Widow of the 1st Duke of Cambridge.

LADY CAROLINE. Woman of the Bedchamber to the Queen, sister of General Grey, widow of Captain Barrington.

CATT, MRS. Housekeeper to the Crown Princess.

CESAREVITCH. Before 1865 Nicholas (1843–65), there-afterwards Alexander III.

PRINCE CHARLES. The King's next brother.

UNCLE CHARLES. The Queen's half-brother, the Prince of Leiningen.

ARCHDUKE CHARLES LOUIS. Brother of the Emperor of Austria.

CHARLOTTE. Daughter of Leopold I, wife of Archduke Maximilian, Emperor of Mexico.

CHRISTIAN. Prince of Schleswig-Holstein, husband of Princess Helena.

AUNT CLEMENTINE. Daughter of Louis Philippe, married Prince Augustus of Saxe-Coburg, mother of Ferdinand of Bulgaria.

THE COUNTESS or THE DEAR COUNTESS. Countess Blücher.

DAGMAR. Princess of Denmark, sister of the Princess of Wales and afterwards Czarina.

THE DEAN or THE GOOD DEAN or OUR DEAN. Gerald Wellesley, Dean of Windsor.

DITTA. Princess Charlotte of Prussia, the Crown Princess's eldest daughter.

ELISCHEN. Princess Elise of Hohenlohe-Schillingsfürst.

ELIZABETH W. Princess Elizabeth of Wied, married King of Rumania. Wrote under pseudonym of Carmen Sylva.

UNCLE ERNEST. Duke of Saxe-Coburg-Gotha, brother of the Prince Consort.

FANNY. Countess Reventlow. One of the Crown Princess's Ladies.

AUNT FEODORA. See AUNT.

FREDDIE.   Afterwards King Frederick VIII of Denmark, married Princess Louise of Sweden.

FRITZ CARL.   Son of Prince Charles, nephew to the King.

FRITZ H. or FRITZ HOLSTEIN or FRITZ A.   Hereditary Prince of Schleswig-Holstein-Sonderburg-Augustenburg. Married to the Queen's niece, Princess Adelaide of Hohenlohe-Langenburg.

KING GEORGE.   King of the Hellenes, brother of the Princess of Wales.

GEORGE V.   King of Hanover, the Queen's first cousin.

UNCLE GEORGE.   The 2nd Duke of Cambridge, first cousin to the Queen.

THE GRAND DUCHESS or THE OLD GRAND DUCHESS. Grand Duchess of Mecklenburg-Schwerin, sister of the King.

GRANDMAMA.   The Duchess of Kent. She died 1861.

HEDWIG.   Countess Brühl, one of the Crown Princess's Ladies.

HÉLÈNE.   Duchess of Orleans, died 1858.

HENRY.   Prince Henry of Prussia, the Crown Princess's second son.

PRINCE HOHENZOLLERN.   The Prince of Hohenzollern-Sigmaringen.

SIR JAMES.   Sir James Clark, the Queen's doctor.

THE KING.   King William I of Prussia.

LANGENBECK.   Doctor to the Prussian Royal Family.

LEHZEN.   Baroness Lehzen, formerly governess to the Queen.

LENCHEN.   Princess Helena, the Queen's third daughter.

LEOPOLD or LEO.   The Queen's fourth son, afterwards Duke of Albany.

UNCLE LEOPOLD, UNCLE or DEAREST UNCLE.   King Leopold I of the Belgians.

LEOPOLD.   Son of above, Duke of Brabant, afterwards Leopold II. Or, according to context, eldest son of Prince Hohenzollern, married Antoinette, Princess of Portugal.

LEOPOLDINE.   Wife of Prince Hermann of Hohenlohe-Langenburg and daughter of the Margrave of Baden.

LOUIS. Prince Louis, husband of Princess Alice, afterwards Grand-Duke of Hesse Darmstadt.

LOUISE. Fourth daughter of the Queen. Occasionally, eldest daughter of the Prince of Wales or the Grand Duchess of Baden, daughter of the King.

AUNT LOUISE. Deceased wife of Leopold I.

PRINCESS LOUISE OF THE NETHERLANDS. Sister of the King, married Prince Frederick of the Netherlands.

QUEEN LOUISE. Wife of King Christian IX of Denmark, daughter of the Landgrave of Hesse, mother of the Princess of Wales.

LADY LYTTELTON. Widow of the 3rd Lord Lyttelton, and governess to the Princess Royal.

MARGUERITE. Daughter of Duke of Nemours, married Prince Czartoryski.

MARIE. Wife of the Duke of Brabant, daughter of the Prince of Hohenzollern-Sigmaringen. Or, according to context, daughter of Princess Frederick of the Netherlands.

MAROUSSY. Great-niece of the King, married to Prince William of Baden.

MARY or MARY C. Princess Mary of Cambridge, first cousin to the Queen.

MAX. Archduke Maximilian of Austria, afterwards Emperor of Mexico.

MECKLENBURG-SCHWERIN. See the Grand Duchess.

M. DE NORMANN. Secretary to the Crown Prince.

OLGA. Wife of the King of the Hellenes, and daughter of the Grand Duke Constantine.

PEDRO. King Pedro V of Portugal, died 1861.

PHILIPPE or PHILIP. Count of Flanders, younger son of Leopold I or, according to context, son of Prince Augustus of Coburg.

THE QUEEN. Augusta of Saxe-Weimar, married the King of Prussia in 1829.

THE QUEEN DOWAGER. Widow of Frederick William IV of Prussia, daughter of King Maximilian I of Bavaria.

PRINCE SALM. Prince Charles of Salm-Horstmar.

SANNY. Wife of Grand Duke Constantine, third son of

Nicholas I, and daughter of the Duke of Saxe-Altenburg.

SIGIE. Prince Sigismund of Prussia, the Crown Princess's third son.

ARCHDUCHESS SOPHIE. Daughter of Maximilian I of Bavaria, wife of Archduke Francis Charles, mother of the Emperor of Austria.

STEPHANIE. Wife of King Pedro V, daughter of Prince Hohenzollern, died 1859.

TILLA. Miss Hildyard, governess to the Queen's children.

TINA OF OLDENBURG. Princess Catherine, born 1846.

VALERIE. Countess Hohenthal, one of the Crown Princess's Ladies.

VICTOIRE. Wife of Duke of Nemours, daughter of Prince Ferdinand of Saxe-Coburg, died 1857.

WALLY. Walburga, Countess Hohenthal, wife of Sir August Paget. Before marriage one of the Crown Princess's Ladies.

WEGNER. Personal physician to the Crown Prince and Crown Princess, afterwards Deputy Medical Director-General of the Army.

WILLIAM. Prince William of Baden.

WILLIAM OF MECKLENBURG. Husband of "Addy".

WILLY. Prince William of Prussia, afterwards Kaiser William II, the Crown Princess's eldest child.

THE CORRESPONDENCE

1865

From the Queen   OSBORNE, JANUARY 4, 1865

I think you will find Lord Napier very agreeable and clever—but very peculiar.[1] I think he is quite aware of Bismarck's want of principle though from old acquaintance he is rather partial to him personally. I hope you have seen Lady Napier; I think her so amiable and such a *grande dame*.[2]

From the Queen   OSBORNE, JANUARY 11, 1865

I hope you don't spoil Affie with your admiration of him. He has already a good amount of vanity and nothing is worse than that brother-worship of sisters. But he is indeed in many things wonderfully like adored Papa—and his figure is a miniature of that angel! Oh! that he were as pure! Alas that bloom is gone! But in many things he is very like and is very much improved and please God! if he becomes more serious and less worldly he will become a worthy son of that perfect father, and will I hope be able to do good service in his future position to dear Germany. I am not surprised at your being astonished at Lord Napier; he is very odd—and likes to say odd things, but he is very clever, very conciliatory, and what is in my eyes a great merit—a true Scotchman.

From the Crown Princess   BERLIN, JANUARY 11, 1865

Writing of her eldest son the Crown Princess says:

I shall endeavour to make him feel that pride and devotion for his country—and ambition to serve it—that will make sacrifices and difficulties seem easy to him—and maybe I shall be able to instil our British feeling of

---

[1] The 9th Lord Napier (1819–98) Diplomat, the British Ambassador to Berlin at this time. He was at St. Petersburg when Bismarck was Prussian Ambassador there.
[2] She was the only daughter of Robert Manners Lockwood of Glamorganshire.

independence into him, together with our broad English common sense—so rare on this side of the water; the Prussians will not hate me for that in the end—however jealous they may now be of my foreign influence over him and Fritz at present. I am as good a patriot as any one of them—and all the better perhaps for not being a blind one.

From the Crown Princess   BERLIN, JANUARY 18, 1865

We are fast driving into the "whirlpool" of the carnival which I dread![1] Oh the expense of the toilettes—and the fatigue! Eleven balls await us!! None over before three o'clock. I do really think it is most alarming and heartily wish it were all over—then two fêtes with trains—and innumerable quantities of small soirées—and concerts, besides the theatre and audiences. I consider it far worse than the treadmill, it is just as much a punishment to me! You have no idea what a foreign carnival is. We have been giving dinners—to be as civil as possible—and some small dances. But we have to give one huge party of over a thousand invitations, crammed into this small house and our very small reception rooms. The house steams for three days after! In spite of open windows.

From the Queen   OSBORNE, JANUARY 27, 1865

Accept on this day my warmest good wishes for our darling William. That beloved and promising child was adored Papa's great favourite; he took (and he takes I am sure) so deep an interest in him and in his physical and moral well-doing. He is so dear and so good that with care and God's blessing he will grow up to be a blessing to his country and a comfort to his parents! But bring him up simply, plainly, not with that terrible Prussian pride and ambition, which grieved dear Papa so much and which he always said would stand in the way of Prussia taking that lead in Germany which he ever wished her to do! Pride and

---

[1] The Carnival of which the Crown Princess recurringly complains was a series of festivities—fancy-dress balls were prominent—which were held in Berlin before Lent, and corresponded in some degree to our London season.

ambition are not only very wrong in themselves, but they alienate affection and are in every way unworthy of really great minds and great nations! I hope my writing case will have arrived in time and will give the darling pleasure.

Little A.V.[1] is a perfect bijou—very fairy-like but quite healthy, very wise-looking and good. He lets all the family carry him and play with him—and Alix likes him to be accustomed to it. He is very placid, almost melancholy-looking sometimes. What is not pretty is his very narrow chest (rather pigeon-breasted) which is like Alix's build and that of her family and unlike you all with your fine chests. He is decisively like her; everyone is struck by it.

From the Crown Princess   BERLIN, FEBRUARY 11, 1865

I hear to my despair that Countess Blücher is not coming here; it is really a misfortune. I had looked forward to it for so many reasons! My only friend and fellow countrywoman here; she is like a mother to me.

From the Queen   OSBORNE, FEBRUARY 15, 1865

I gave all your news to the dear Countess who did not leave me yesterday on account of the very cold weather in the North, but goes with me to Windsor on 17th—leaves on 19th and comes back for one night then, before she goes to Germany. Her plans later depend entirely on her husband. Her loss to me will be very great—but I have profited greatly by her presence; have seen much of her, and feel as though she were my mother too—though she can only be eight or nine years older than me, and barely that. But she is so wise, so clever, so loving, so straight forward and we agree so entirely in everything that I can't express what a comfort and support she is to me who have no husband, no one intimate friend older than myself—and that is what I require!

---

[1] Albert Victor—the Prince of Wales's eldest son.

From the Queen   WINDSOR CASTLE, FEBRUARY 22, 1865

The Queen is answering a letter from the Crown Princess which was
    written from Berlin on 17 February. In this letter the Crown
    Princess wrote:
"Though you 'hate babies' and I never bore you with accounts of
    my little love as the subject is so distasteful to you, I venture to
    send two photos of him—though they do not do him justice
    begging you to show them to the brothers and sisters."
In her reply the Queen thanks for the charming photos of little
    Sigismund "who must be a very pretty child—also like the
    Prussian royal family".

You know perfectly well that I do not hate babies (quite
the contrary if they are pretty) but I do hate an inordinate
worship of them and the disgusting details of their animal
existence, which I try to ignore. You must know besides how
little reason I have to be pleased with many details of this
baby; as you know what has shocked and annoyed me.[1] For
your sake I have been silent but if you speak of my "hating
babies" I must answer.

From the Queen   WINDSOR CASTLE, MARCH 1, 1865

   I had a reception yesterday of the whole Corps Diplomatique at Buckingham Palace—a great bore. There were
a hundred of them with attachés. The good Bernstorffs[2]
were, as usual, in a sort of porcupine condition which is so
odious. It seems to me such a loss of time to be always
offended and Brown's[3] observation about a cross person
seems to me very applicable here "it can't be very pleasant
for a person themselves to be always cross" which I think so
true and so original. His observations upon everything he
sees and hears here are excellent and many show how
superior in feeling, sense and judgment he is to the
servants here! The talking and indiscretion shocks him.
   I have all along meant to ask you if you have ever read

---

[1] The Queen means by this that she was annoyed with the Crown
Princess for having so many children too soon.
[2] Court Albrecht Bernstorff, Prussian Ambassador in London.
[3] John Brown, the Queen's personal servant.

an extraordinary poem by a lady now dead a Mrs. Browning (Augusta Stanley knows her) called "Aurora Leigh"? The Countess read it to me. It is very strange, very original full of talent and of some beautiful things—but at times dreadfully coarse—though very moral in its tendency—but an incredible book for a lady to have written. It would interest you, we both thought, as there is much genius in it.

From the Crown Princess   STETTIN, MARCH 4, 1865
     I have read "Aurora Leigh" and dislike it extremely. I had heard it so much praised and called so curious and interesting that I took it up. I cannot understand or follow the strain of thought at all. I looked for the genius and found nothing but eccentricity and most disagreeable coarseness, which I suppose is meant to be force of language. I think it thoroughly without taste and poetry. The feeling is very crude and does not touch me—in fact I put it down with disgust. How different from the pure simplicity of Miss A. Proctor's poems—the grace of the language and the tender yet passionate feeling expressed in such earnest and yet childlike words.
     I do not think a style overloaded with adjectives (quite misplaced ones too) a proof of genius and I never liked Mrs. E. Browning's. I wonder at their being so much liked; and for a woman I think her turn of mind very disagreeable and was quite disgusted with some of her descriptions; she does not seem to possess the instinct of the beautiful or to have an elevated imagination.[1]

From the Crown Princess   STETTIN, MARCH 7, 1865
     Talking of books, I always forget whether you have read "Le Maudit" and "La Religieuse"; if not you really should

---

[1] *Aurora Leigh* was published in 1857 and Mrs. Browning died in 1861. The poem is written in blank verse, and it has been called by a distinguished critic something of a choke-pear for the modern reader. Much of the best side of Victorian humanitarianism is to be found in it, and this may explain the Queen's fancy for it. Adelaide Ann Proctor was the writer of many popular sentimental poems including *The Lost Chord*.

because they are so remarkable and are two blows dealt at the Roman Catholic religion—or, rather I should say, at the abuses of the Roman Catholic church and at the corruption of the clergy—which are of great force. The said author has published another which I think beats the two first and is called "Le Jesuite". I am sure it could not fail to interest you. That the subject touches on a great many topics not fit for ladies' ears cannot be helped; it is to show where the evil lies and to paint the wrong in its true colours that such things are mentioned, and the high moral and religious tone of the whole book makes it worth one's while to overlook what is disagreeable, and read it all through.[1]

From the Queen   WINDSOR CASTLE, MARCH 8, 1865
    I have heard of dear Arthur's safe arrival at Naples. He paid a visit to the Prince Imperial and saw the Emperor and Empress and people were charmed with him. He is very handsome and has peculiarly nice manners.
    I think you judge "Aurora Leigh" too severely; that is I mean you have overlooked the decided genius and some most beautiful passages; but the strangeness and coarseness I quite agree.

From the Queen   WINDSOR CASTLE, MARCH 11, 1865
    I will at once answer your question about "Le Maudit" and the two others. I have heard a great deal about them and if adored Papa were here—I would certainly read them, but now I can't read those books with descriptions of immorality, etc., They distress me—and are so painful that I cannot read them. I have alas! enough that is painful and distressing to go through in reality, and therefore I avoid as much as I can reading those sorts of things. I dislike novels now—unfortunately so much too, and I don't allow the sisters to read any. Poems I am fond of in all shapes. I am reading several books but can get through so little. Have

---

[1] These novels were written by J. H. Michon 1806–81. He was a Roman Catholic Ecclesiastic, and the novels, which were published anonymously, were regarded as immoral.

you seen Lord Derby's translation of the "Iliad"? It is so much thought of.[1]

From the Queen   WINDSOR CASTLE, MARCH 18, 1865

My dress is always the same—as it is the dress which I have adopted for ever, for mine. The only difference was that I had a train to the dress and a very long veil to my cap, which was trimmed with large diamonds, and the last time with large pearls. The sisters were in green and white the first day and in black the last time.[2]

I am so fond of Burns's poems. They are so poetical—so simple in their dear Scotch tongue, which is so full of poetry. Kingsley (who preached here, and afterwards came to see me and dined with us last Sunday) said that English peasantry had not a grain of poetry in their nature whereas the Scotch are full of it! How true that is and that this is what gives them such a charm and makes the Highlanders so high-bred. One does require that to lift us above the heavy clay which clogs our souls.

From the Queen   WINDSOR CASTLE, APRIL 1, 1865

That wretched Lord Desart is dying; he tumbled down stairs and received a violent concussion; he has not recovered his consciousness.[3]

From the Queen   WINDSOR CASTLE, APRIL 5, 1865

I have not, I think, told you that I have taken good J. Brown entirely and permanently as my personal servant for out of doors—besides cleaning my things and doing odd "jobs"—as I found it so convenient and saving me so much trouble to have one and the same person always for going out, and to give my orders to, which are taken by him from

---

[1] 14th Earl of Derby 1799–1869, Prime Minister. His translation of the *Iliad* was privately printed in 1862, and published in 1864.

[2] The Queen had gone to Buckingham Palace for receptions for the Corps Diplomatique.

[3] Earl of Desart (1818–65). A minor Conservative Politician who is described by Greville as "a mere blockhead". His wife, a daughter of the 1st Lord Cawdor, was one of the Queen's Ladies-in-waiting.

me personally to the stables. He comes to my room after breakfast and luncheon to get his orders—and everything is always right; he is so quiet, has such an excellent head and memory, and is besides so devoted, and attached and clever and so wonderfully able to interpret one's wishes. He is a real treasure to me now, and I only wish higher people had his sense and discretion, and that I had as good a maid. He is called "The Queen's Highland Servant" and (like Löhlein—only in a lower position—ranking with the footmen—) is paid by the Privy Purse, and is under none of the other servants. It is an excellent arrangement, and I feel I have here and always in the house a good devoted soul (like good Grant) whose only object and interest is my service, and God knows how I want so much to be taken care of.

From the Crown Princess   BERLIN, APRIL 5, 1865
I do not look forward to having a tutor in the house as my authority is then pretty well at an end, but I think it will be quite time that Willy should be in men's hands when he is nearly seven. And I trust it will all be for the best. He will have the title of governor according to the custom here and there will be a tutor under the other. We have already a person in view. These people are appointed and paid by the King. I was much afraid we should not be allowed to select them, and am therefore much relieved that our choice has been sanctioned by him.

From the Crown Princess   BERLIN, APRIL 7, 1865
I am glad you have made an arrangement with John Brown that suits you and that you find comfortable; a trustworthy servant is of the greatest value.

From the Queen   WINDSOR CASTLE, APRIL 8, 1865
Dear Uncle Leopold we see alas! very little of—as his cold is a very bad one, and he cannot leave his room; but he is decidedly better today, and I hope in a day or two he will be able to get out a little. The heat of his rooms is such that I can not remain in them; it makes me giddy and faint.

I am much interested by all you say of your plans for dearest Willy. I think you could not well keep him longer without a tutor, but two men is a good deal, and I fear you will have a great deal to counteract quietly and unobservedly. There will else be much pride encouraged and engendered, and all sorts of peculiar ideas which they have abroad. Oh! were but beloved Papa here to watch over all this—and to advise and help you. I know how one dislikes one's boys being put into the hands of men! It seems to be the first separation. You will feel that, dear child—more and more as time goes on! The happy time is when children are 6 to 5 and 3 years old.

From the Queen   WINDSOR CASTLE, APRIL 12, 1865

Leopold had his two teeth out just now with chloroform, had no pain whatever and never gave a sound. And they hardly bled at all. I am so thankful for it. Please God! this bleeding is decidedly better and, after all, that is the dangerous thing.[1]

The arrangement with J. Brown is an immense comfort to me; he is indeed one in a thousand for he has feelings and qualities which the highest Prince might be proud of—viz: unflinching straightforwardness and honesty; great moral courage; unselfishness and rare discretion and devotion. This quite independently of his excellence as a good, handy, thoughtful servant; and in this house, where there are so many people, and often so much indiscretion and no real head now, such a person is invaluable.

From the Queen   OSBORNE, APRIL 26, 1865

How tragic is the death of the poor Czariwitch only a week after his young cousin—and how terrible for poor Dagmar.[2] What a blow for the ambitious mother! But the poor parents and bride are most deeply to be pitied.

---

[1] Prince Leopold suffered from haemophilia.
[2] Nicholas, eldest son of the Emperor Alexander II. He was engaged to Princess Dagmar of Denmark, sister of the Princess of Wales. The cousin was Princess Anna of Hesse, sister to Prince Louis.

From the Queen   OSBORNE, APRIL 28, 1865

I have written to the Queen of Denmark and to the Emperor and today I have written to that unhappy Mrs. Lincoln, whose husband was murdered by her side! Poor Monsieur de Bacourt's death I am very sorry for, as I know how it will grieve the dear Queen and the loss of a true old friend is indeed an irreparable one, God knows![1] How beloved Papa and I felt that. But now friends and all (though they are more valuable than ever in my desolation) are swallowed up in that one blow which felled me to the ground. Doctor McLeod told me of a poor old Scotch woman who had lost her husband and most—if not all—her children, and she said to him "when my gude man went, it made such a hole that all the others went through it." So it is with me, but like all Scotch sayings it is so simple and true!

From the Crown Princess   NEUES PALAIS, MAY 3, 1865

I am shut out of my sitting-room because there is a man from London setting a grate and fender—an English fireplace altogether in one of our large empty chimney-pieces. It will serve as a pattern for others later; it is copied from Bertie's fireplace in his hall at Marlborough House.

From the Crown Princess   NEUES PALAIS, MAY 6, 1865

Bertie has sent me the description of Arthur's journey; how interesting they are—what a deal of good it will do him.[2] I think it so wise of you to let the boys travel as much as possible; they learn so much; it forms their character and makes them independent. I hope we shall be allowed to send our Willy all over the world but we are in a difficult position as Fritz's parents interfere so much in all we do with the children. The King dislikes all innovations, as most people about Court here do and think that where the

---

[1] Adolphe de Bacourt was a French Diplomatist under the Orleans Monarchy. He was a close friend of the Duchess of Dino (Talleyrand's niece) and it was through her that the Queen of Prussia met him when he was living in retirement at Baden.
[2] He was visiting Italy, Greece and Asia Minor on board the Admiralty Yacht *Enchantress*.

children are born there they are to grow up and never go away for fear of their becoming estranged from their country. It is such a mistake; the more they move about the happier they are to return, and then value their home all the more. The more they see and learn, the better it fits them for their future position. This is the place of "tradition"; that word is an all powerful argument; what never has been done—never is to be done, and all people who think differently are unpatriotic. This is the opinion. I am quite astonished when I compare myself with most of the German princesses of my age, how faded they look and how they lose their teeth and are obliged to go to baths and watering places, not to speak of the wretched health of the Russian Grand duchesses. Our English way of living is by far the healthiest and most sensible I am sure, and we owe that to our temperate climate because in spite of all that is said against it I do not think there is one in the world like it—the country of white teeth and rosy children!

From the Queen   OSBORNE, MAY 10, 1865
I have been daily on my pony wandering quietly among the splendid fresh, green foliage which is now very forward, all the oaks being out since a week (!!), the birds singing— all lovely but all bereft of joy, for he is not on earth to enjoy it with me as he once did.

I always feel—when I wander about, so kindly cared for, with one of your dear sisters, and able to have all I can wish for, and yet without joy—that it is like a pilgrimage! Soothing—as all breathes of him—but terribly joyless. But when I am out I can rest—and I can think darling Papa is out too. It is the return home with that silent room nearby, and fagged to death with work, which is fearful indeed!

From the Crown Princess   NEUES PALAIS, MAY 17, 1865
The thought that he (Willy) will have to depend so much more on those around him particularly on servants is so painful. I had always hoped to make him as independent as possible. The arm will be a great obstacle in his education, as what has to be done for it not only takes up so much

time but tires him so that he is not fit to learn directly afterwards. He is very backward for his age in all accomplishments in consequence; he can neither read nor write nor spell yet, as we thought the more exercise and air he had here the better as he had been shut up so much all the winter, looked so wretchedly pale, and slept and ate so badly; we thought his health of more importance than his lessons and therefore let him be out whenever he could; he is looking very well indeed now, I am happy to say. He is a dear, promising child—lively and sweet-tempered and intelligent; it is a thousand pities he should be so afflicted; he would really be so pretty if it was not for that; it disfigures him so much, gives him something awkward in all his movements which is sad for a prince; though you know I would rather he was straight in mind than in body but I cannot help thinking of dear Papa who was perfect in both, and it is hard that it should be our eldest that has this misfortune. It would not matter with poor Henry or Ditta.

From the Queen   WINDSOR CASTLE, MAY 18, 1865
    The Duchess of Atholl is in waiting (in her weeds) and a great comfort to me—so wise, so excellent and so pleasant and so truly Scotch.

From the Crown Princess   NEUES PALAIS, MAY 20, 1865
    Fritz returned the day before yesterday from Cologne late in the evening and was at Berlin yesterday. Today he goes to Herseberg. I can feel for the wives of railway guards as I really do not see much more of Fritz than they do of their husbands who live on the train.
    Unfortunately Sophie Dobeneck and Mlle. Douzé do not quite talk to the children of religion in the right way; they speak too much of hell and of the devil and the Trinity; it only confuses and puzzles their little heads; the simpler the notions of Christianity, their pure precepts, and the touching stories of the Bible are told them, the better. Hard words convey no sense, and only fill their little minds with vague and indistinct ideas which often end in total nonsense,

but it is a point upon which both ladies are so touchy and so eager, that I find it best to let it alone and trust to the children's own sense. I talk to them myself whenever I can.

From the Queen   BALMORAL, MAY 23, 1865
Everybody says no Drawing Room without me gave so much satisfaction as the one held by Lenchen. Dear Alix is rather stiff and cold, and not what the people are accustomed to.

Good Alice seems quite Russified. She writes now, since three weeks to me nothing but about "Aunt Marie, Uncle Sacha, Nixé, dear Sachi, Alexi, Miché etc.,"[1] I own I think it is a little too much.

From the Crown Princess   NEUES PALAIS, MAY 24, 1865
I saw Michel and Cecile yesterday—who beg to be remembered to you. The latter is grown so plain, and looks so common that I was quite taken aback when she came out of the train, and really it is next to impossible to doubt of her origin at present, so strongly is the Jewish type come out in her now she is older.[2]

From the Crown Princess   NEUES PALAIS, MAY 27, 1865
Abbat is gone to St. Petersburg for the funeral of the Czariwitch, and to look at Tina of Oldenburg. If she does not please him he is going to Norderney with his sister to look at the Princesses of Hanover. His fine place Cammentz is finished and I think he is now going to settle and look out for a wife. He never was so nice or so good looking as he is now, and I hope he will be as happy as he deserves. I wish

---

[1] The Emperor of Russia and his family. The Empress was aunt to Princess Alice's husband. Queen Victoria disliked the Imperial Family—a consequence of the Crimean War.
[2] The Grand Duke Michael and Grand Duchess Olga of Russia, formerly Princess Cecile of Baden. The Grand Duchess was sister to the Duchess of Saxe-Coburg. There was a 19-year gap between them; any ambiguity in the Grand Duchess's ancestry was likely to be known to the English Royal family through the Duchess of Saxe-Coburg—Aunt Alexandrine.

his sister could find a husband at the same time; she leads a dull life and is such a good creature.[1]

From the Queen
I spun before Grant and Mrs. Grant on Monday, and dear good Grant said "Ye spin as well as any old woman in the country."

From the Crown Princess
On arriving here this morning I found your very dear and kind letter of 26th May. Many thanks for it. I am so glad my letter and the locket pleased you. What can one wish for but to be able to give you even only the most trifling pleasure as a proof of my love and gratitude? Indeed I agree with you about the Scotch—I am sure it must be difficult for you not to spoil them.

Tomorrow dear Willy goes; he is so sorry—he keeps saying "I don't want to go away from you, Mama." He had some vague fear of there being no soldiers in the place he is going to and that is a grief to his little mind. Dear child, he is so precious to me and I grudge giving him up so completely to the rule and care of people who, however good and trustworthy and excellent, are not intelligent enough to be the right companions for him. You are quite right in saying that we are fortunate in having an intelligent "eldest". I feel it to be a blessing of providence and am grateful for it. Oh! were dearest Papa here to appeal to on every question I would not care for two lame arms! Though I cannot deny that it is a cross which makes itself more and more felt as the child grows older. I am going to impart a secret to you, dear Mama, which is that a match is going to come off between Addy and William Mecklenburg (alias Schnapps). Fancy the horror of my Mama-in-Law—who is quite right about it. The King, the old Grand Duchess and the Queen Dowager and old Prince Albert wish it and I do

---

[1] Alexandrine (Addy). The Crown Princess was anxious that Abbat should marry her younger sister, Princess Louise, Queen Victoria's fourth daughter.

The Queen and Princess Louise with John Brown, Osborne,
April 1865.

Left: The Crown Princess of Prussia, 1865.

Below: Princess Louise in the dress she wore at her Confirmation, March 1865.

not doubt that he will propose shortly and be accepted. Please do not talk of it yet.

Politics are in a sad mess, and I fear Fritz A's chances stand less favourably than they did before. Oh how I wish I was a man just for a little bit—not for long!

From the Queen   BALMORAL, JUNE 5, 1865
There is no inclination or fear to spoil our dearest people here, as they won't and can't be spoilt; that is to say Grant and Brown. They might (and dear Papa was so struck with this in Grant—he did not know the other well) be trusted with all the secrets of the universe. As for Brown I never saw such an unselfish servant; he won't take any leave (which I have never seen before in any one male or female, high or low) and my comfort—my service are really his only objects.

From the Crown Princess   NEUES PALAIS, JUNE 5, 1865
Pray by all means give many, many kind messages to all my dear good Highland friends. I am as fond of them as ever I was and always shall be; they are dear people.

If this marriage of Addy's does come off, the wedding will be most likely at the beginning or the middle of November and of course I could not go away in that case. I have the greatest wish to spend Christmas with you if you would like and allow it. If so, when the time comes (not now) it would be very kind of you if you would express it to the King as a wish of yours to have your children and grandchildren with you for Christmas; and then I think he would not say "no". Please do not say anything to the Queen about it yet. I do not feel sure that you will wish it as you prefer being quite quiet, now all is so sad and changed. At the same time I cannot help feeling that the chances of spending Christmas at home in England are so rare; it would be the first time since seven years, and it is not likely that circumstances will favour the possibility again so soon. This year it would seem quite natural and if the marriage does take place in November—which is only a conjecture of mine at present. You have not yet told me whether you expect Fritz and me at Coburg and when; it would not do to bring the children I think, and you would not care about it either as you would see them so soon after in England.

From the Queen   BALMORAL, JUNE 15, 1865
    I have a few free moments to myself and write before leaving this beloved place which, with its wonderful beauty of scenery, and its great solitude and peace, its purest of airs and its simple, dear, devoted inhabitants, is more and more congenial to my broken and bleeding heart, which shrinks more and more from contact with the world and all its irritating trials, noises, troubles and frivolities. Yesterday evening we were up behind Invercauld till half past eight, and nothing could exceed the beauty of the valley of Braemar, with the very blue hills, reminding one so forcibly of Byron's glorious lines beginning "He who first descried or knew 'the Highlands swelling blue' etc.,".[1]

From the Crown Princess   NEUES PALAIS, JUNE 17, 1865
    I see my proposal is disagreeable to you—please do not give yourself a moment's uneasiness about it, dearest Mama. I would not for the world appear so selfish and that we should be a gène or a fatigue. We will give up the idea of Christmas at once if it is unpleasant to you. It was a great wish of mine to be once more with you at Christmas—and that is why I ventured to express the idea at all. We should not be able to come till a week before my birthday and, after an absence of more than two years, four weeks seemed a little short I own. The expense of travelling with so many people for so short a time besides. And I was so anxious to skip our Christmas at Berlin with their eternal sameness

---

[1]   "He who first met the Highlands' swelling blue
        Will love each peak that shows a kindred hue,
        Hail in each crag a friend's familiar face,
        And clasp the mountain in his mind's embrace."
                                        The Island, ii, xii
The Queen was no doubt familiar with this poem because, later in it, the poet refers to Loch-na-gar, the mountain near Balmoral.

and all this family—but if you do not wish it, of course it is another thing. The winter at Berlin is so long and trying that anything which shortens it for me and the children is a great boon most gratefully acknowledged, and, be it ever so short a visit, home is always a great happiness to me. That you know, beloved Mama—and that I never shall cease to feel the hardship of being separated from you for so long at a time.

I wish you would take in the Volkszeitung, a Prussian paper you ought to have, and it is the only good, courageous and honest one, capitally written, of course hated by the reigning party; it is the only one that has stuck to Fritz Holstein through thick and thin. You ought to leave off the Kölnische Zeitung. It has turned Bismarckite since three months, contains many untruths and is really not worth reading any longer; and if you read the leading articles in the Volkszeitung you will know all that goes on better than I could tell you, and I usually agree with all the opinions and criticisms it expresses and is written in a tone of refreshing energy and independence! It never attacks the King personally and improperly, but it valiantly deals with the Ministers and their policies as they deserve.

From the Queen   WINDSOR CASTLE, JUNE 21, 1865
The Queen is explaining why she cannot have the Crown Princess and her family to stay for Christmas.

Do not say that your proposal about Christmas is disagreeable to me, my dearest child; that is not the word—but it would not be possible or feasible as my letter of Monday will explain. You never will believe how bad my poor nerves are, how more and more shattered they become, and how a large, merry family-party tries me; but on days of former festivity and joy—above all—I am quite and totally incapable of bearing joyousness and merriment. And you would not be happy I know.

From the Queen   WINDSOR CASTLE, JUNE 24, 1865
Dearest child, though life is devoid of pleasure and is only one of duty and very irksome duty, I am ready to

submit meekly, to go on bearing my heavy cross, which is very, very heavy. "Heart-bare—heart hungry, very poor" (to quote that beautiful poem "De Profundis" of Mrs. Browning which perhaps you do not know—as it is one of her very last and is very, very touching.)[1]

From the Queen WINDSOR CASTLE, JULY 1, 1865
This afternoon we are going over to Bagshot to see dear old Sir James.[2] Only think of Sir C. Lacock standing for the Isle of Wight and making really (I think) a fool of himself.[3]

From the Queen WINDSOR CASTLE, JULY 4, 1865
You have, I have no doubt, read all the articles etc., on the Lord Chancellor—than which nothing can be more damaging. It has ended the vote of censure, and he has resigned.[4] Such a thing has not happened—I don't know when, and is most humiliating and painful. He ought to have resigned long ago as I told the Ministers—but Lord Palmerston and Lord Granville took a very low tone, which shocked me and all right-minded people. You, I know, will feel as much as I do (and Oh! how adored Papa would have felt it) the terrible effect at home and abroad of the highest office in the State being so damaged! Such a thing has not been known within (as the Highlanders call it) the "memory of man". On Friday I shall have to receive the Seals—and a pleasant audience it will be—and I shall be alone! This will be the first very painful step for me

---

1   "As one alone, once not alone
          I sit and knock at Nature's Door,
          Heart-bare, heart-hungry, very poor
          Whose desolated days go on."
2 Sir James Clark, the royal Doctor. He retired from practice in 1860, and the Queen lent him Bagshot Park.
3 The accoucheur. He stood as a Conservative and was defeated.
4 Sir Richard Bethell, 1st Lord Westbury (1800–73). Through a disreputable son he was implicated in improper appointments to legal offices within his gift. A committee of the House of Commons had reported that the evidence showed "a laxity of practice and a want of caution with regard to the public interest." Lord Westbury immediately resigned.

quite alone, and Oh! how helpless and wretched and un-
protected do I feel then! These are the times, as well as
when I must appear with my Court, which are overwhelming to me.

From the Crown Princess   NEUES PALAIS, JULY 4, 1865
Our two days at Posen were very interesting. I can
never help feeling sorry for the poor Poles, whose nation
was once so mercilessly torn asunder and swallowed up by
different countries. Their love of their own tribe is touching,
but I know little else to be said in their favour, and cannot
feel any sympathy with them; they are so unlike the
Germans.[1]
We were very kindly received—the peasants and the
town population vied with one another in doing us honour;
we could discover no trace of disaffection or discontent in the
comfortable and friendly faces that smiled upon us. But as
for the priests! I never saw such a set of bad countenances.
All through Italy I saw none so repulsive as these. The
aristocracy was only represented by a few gentlemen, not a
single lady appeared to be presented although they were
said to be all in the town. The gentlemen all speak broken
German and very perfect French—but of course we only
spoke German with them as they are German subjects. At
Posen the bands played "Rule Britannia", "I'm 95"[2] and
the "Bluebells of Scotland" at the parade, and there were
several Union Jacks in the town. I did not find the town or
the people half as dirty as I expected—but then it wore a
festive aspect, and the surrounding villages looked very
Irish, the people as tattered as Irish beggars and the pigs
treated as members of the family. We saw some rich and

---

[1] The Crown Princess means that historically she sympathises with the
Poles, but does not feel the same about their contemporary hostility to
Prussian occupation.
[2] This was the Regimental March of the Rifle Brigade. The words
describe the desire of an old lady of 95 to remain single, and not to be
some man's "mere toy and wedded wife." Queen Victoria first heard it
played after the Crimean War. The Rifle Brigade was, for a time, the
95th Foot.

tidy villages which looked already very German. Polish sounds so soft and pretty and the costumes of the richer peasants are very gay and picturesque. The regiment of Hussars is very fine indeed, we rode out with our very large suite to see them exercise and rode back with them into the town. I wore my uniform jacket to my riding habit.[1]

My belief is that Prussian Poland will in time become as good, quiet and rich a province of this kingdom as any other. The middle and lower classes are happy enough (which they are not in Russian Poland). It is only the aristocracy (and chiefly the ladies and the priests by whom they are ruled) who are the elements of disturbance, and it wants time to get the better of them and of course all difficulties are increased by our unfortunate, illiberal government at home, the ill effects of which are felt everywhere and in every branch of administration. I wish you had seen Wegner in full uniform on horseback, on an animal that almost pulled his arms off!

From the Queen   WINDSOR CASTLE, JULY 8, 1865
The Poles are an attractive, talented but thoroughly immoral people. They have been cruelly used—but still they are quite unfit to govern themselves.

From the Crown Princess   NEUES PALAIS, JULY 11, 1865
I am sure you will understand all this.[2] To you it will perhaps hardly be a disappointment as in your sorrow all the smaller wishes and considerations of life must disappear like molehills, making you feel indifferent to them, but to me it is a great privation. Loving my home as I do and, as I have already often said, from living abroad being able to appreciate what England is, in so many things so far ahead of other nations, I look upon every visit I spend there as a source not only of pleasure and refreshment but of instruction and benefit to myself. I know that the older we get—the more children and duties we have—the rarer my

---

[1] She was Colonel-in-Chief of the 2nd Regiment of Prussian Hussars.
[2] She is writing about her disappointment at not coming to England.

visits home must be, and I have quite given up expecting to go home every year, and I try to look philosophically on what appears sometimes hard to me. There is so much to be thought of and done here that there ought to be no time for homesickness—and yet I do feel it very often and always shall! Certainly not from want of love to this country—for I love it very much indeed, and would never wish to leave it or belong to any other under the sun. It is a love mixed with a great deal of anxiety and hope too. I know what it is capable of and what it might be, grieve over the lost time, but hope for the future which is in the hands of God.

From the Queen   OSBORNE, JULY 12, 1865

You felt—as I was sure you would—about the Lord Chancellor. It is indeed most unfortunate. I am afraid we must entirely except our lawyers from the rule of integrity, for with rare exceptions they have almost all been terrible jobbers. Lord Chelmsford has just been shown up; it is a terrible worry—then Lord Brougham, Lord Lyndhurst, Lord Cottenham—never Lord Cranworth, and the present Attorney General Sir Roundell Palmer, bears the very highest character.

From the Queen   OSBORNE, JULY 15, 1865

Though there is not one political cry—the elections seem to have been particularly violent—and people have lost their elections when it was least expected. Lord Alfred Paget after 25 years has been turned out. Mr. Gladstone also—at Oxford—Lord Bury (my comptroller) and that foolish little Lord Amberley (which is a good thing as he is so very bumptious). Still on the whole the Government have gained.

From the Crown Princess   ISLE OF FÖHR, JULY 15, 1865

We left Berlin on the evening of the 12th intending to embark on board the *Grille* at Hamburg, but when we came there the cupboard was bare, that is to say on arriving at five in the morning at Hamburg we heard that there had been a violent gale from the west, that the *Grille* had got damaged and had been obliged to run into some port or other to get repaired. The *Grille* is about the size of the *Fairy*.[1] The *Lorelei* was at Hamburg, she is not much larger than the *Elfin*[2] and has no accommodation for a party such as ours. At Hamburg we saw dear Fritz H. and Ada and Christian. Fritz really is most touching, so calm noble and dignified and so firm. Politics stand as ill as possible and we could give them no comfort; in this case there is really nothing to be done but to hope for the best and to prepare for the worst. We only saw them for a few minutes.

From Hamburg to Husum we passed through the theatre of war of last year—and saw the Danewerke and Rendsburg and could see the monument to the Austrians. At Husum there was a Hungarian regiment. Fancy our horror on finding the packet (which was not as big as the *Fairy*) so crowded that there were not seats enough for us; we were crammed on two benches on deck—with the children and all—with more than sixty other passengers who kept eating and drinking and smoking nasty cigars. There was such a smell of melted butter—it was horrible. So we sat for hours. The children almost drove us wild— they would not sit still one minute, but kept slipping and fidgetting about for everlasting. Henry, who cries and grumbles more than any other child I ever came near, screamed and roared the whole time and was not to be pacified by coaxing or threatening, slapped May's face and shouted "No, no" to everything that was said.[3] You never saw such a business. The passage only lasted four hours, and thank God no one was sick—what that would have been I cannot think of; there was nothing in the shape of a basin on the ship! I hear we have two gun-boats and the *Lorelei* (*"Cameleon"* and *"Comet"*) but they cannot come further in than the big yacht does to the pier at Osborne.

This is a charming quiet place; a dear little town of about nine hundred souls, quite close to the seashore. We

---

[1] The steam-tender to the Royal Yacht in the 1840's.

[2] The steam-tender to the Royal Yacht (from 1849). She was used daily between the mainland and the Isle of Wight, when the Queen was at Osborne.

[3] May was the under-nurse.

have three little houses with rooms about half as large as cabins on board a ship. One for us two and the children— one for Count Fürstenstein, Hedwig, and M. de Luccadon —and another for the servants. The eating and drinking we get from the hotel.

There is a nice beach a stone's throw from our window so that one can breathe the pleasant sea air all day which is a great luxury to us. The Island is quite flat and there is not a single tree except for a few little objects so-called stuck in a row along the beach.

From the Queen   OSBORNE, JULY 26, 1865

Your account of the simple people at that little Island is pretty and touching, but to me nothing is really poetical without mountains. Still it reminds me of our dear High- lands, though nothing can equal them or their noble inhabitants!

From the Crown Princess   ISLE OF FÖHR, AUGUST 1, 1865

Your kind words gave me so much pleasure. A parent's love is unlike any other, and a word of affection from you touches and delights me more than I can say.[1]

I am glad my letters amuse you, and am much flattered you say I write well. I do not fancy my own style at all and always fear my letters must be very stupid and tiresome to read.

I fear politics are in a worse mess than ever. If you are furious at the way these unfortunate Elbe Duchies and Fritz Holstein are treated what do you think we are! I had a conversation before he left with Lord Napier and found him taking Bismarck's part as he always does.[2] I cannot under- stand a clever man as he is being dazzled by B's balderdash (an expressive word for stuff and nonsense). I think all the trash B. talks not even amusing. I had rather not talk of the B. or rather the wasp, it makes me too angry and Heaven

---

[1] In her letter of 29 July from Osborne the Queen had written, "without a particle of flattery I must say you write beautifully".
[2] The Crown Princess means—before he left on holiday.

knows what other foul proceedings he is meditating. I wish we and the nation were rid of him and all that are like him. If my letter is opened by the Post Officials I shall be accused of high treason—but I am as loyal as anyone as I love the King and would do anything to serve him but as Pope says "my Country's ruin makes me grave"—and more than grave.[1] One resents the injury done to a noble nation by being so badly governed by one reckless adventurer such as B. is, and one deplores that so good a man as the King should lose his popularity in so sad a way. But no more of politics we breakfast, dine and sleep on the same sad subject and are unable to change it in the least!

I see Mr. J. S. Mill, whose magnificent writings I so much admire, is elected.[2]

From the Queen   OSBORNE, AUGUST 3, 1865
I am indeed much alarmed and shocked at the outrageous and I must say shameful and barefaced conduct of Bismarck about S. Holstein! It is monstrous. But how can the King consent to it? That is very wrong.[3]

From the Crown Princess
                    ISLE OF FÖHR, AUGUST 14, 1865
Yesterday we were in your Dominion of Heligoland—a strange, little, red island rising up out of the sea with a flat, green surface on the top of red clay, slate rocks. We paid the Governor a visit (Major Maxey),[4] and were mobbed by

---

[1]   "You're strangely proud. So proud, I am no slave:
          So impudent, I am myself no knave:
          So odd, my country's ruin make me grave."
                              Epilogue to the Satires. Dialogue II.
[2] He had been elected for Westminster at the General Election in spite of telling the voters that the English working classes were "generally liars".
[3] Bismarck was industriously trying to Prussianise the Schleswig-Holstein Duchies through manipulating the Press and advertising the benefits of Prussian rule compared with independence under the Augustenburgs.
[4] Sir Henry Maxse (1832–83) He abolished the gaming-tables on Heligoland.

the immense quantity of tourists. I am very glad to have seen it but I should not like to stay there; it has a sort of fashionable look which I hate. Our quiet Wyk I like much better.

I wrote to the King to tell him we wish to go to England in the autumn to pay you a visit, and that I was anxious to be once more at home after two years' absence etc.—a long and very affectionate letter. He not only let three weeks pass without taking the slightest notice of the letter but he wrote to Fritz yesterday—he did not see why I wanted to go to England, he was surprised to hear of my wishing to take the children, I could see you at Coburg and take the children there. After all I said and the way I put it, I think this very heartless and unkind. Formerly he and the Queen never interfered with the children, it is only lately this has begun. I shall never forget the way in which they treated me last year on that subject. If I had not felt that it was necessary for my health to go to Switzerland last year I should not have left them. We reproached ourselves all last winter and last spring.

The King says at the end of his letter we are to settle it with you. It therefore now rests in your hands; if you tell him you wish to have us and the children and you reckon upon it, he will give way to you—as I see all my arguments and sentiments are of no use. The Queen is very kind about it—she wishes us to go and will do all she can to facilitate it I know. We must again repeat—we cannot separate from the children and leave them alone in the winter in Berlin. We do not think it safe. We have always taken them to England before and no objection was raised. I think you wish to see them too do you not, dear Mama? I know you do not care so much about the little ones—but still I cannot help thinking you would like them to come too and prefer seeing them to our staying away altogether. It would be a bitter disappointment to me not to be able to go to England I own—I have looked forward to it for so long. If I saw any sensible reason against it I should not be childish enough to wish to go—but it is really so simple, and a mere whim of the King's who might see how natural it is that children and grandchildren should wish to be once again with their parents.

From the Crown Princess

KRANICKSTEIN, SEPTEMBER 1, 1865

You will have heard what a state the Queen was in when she heard you were not going to see the King, and I am very anxious to hear what you have decided to do. If I may venture an opinion at all, it is—not to make her angry. You do know how very difficult it is to deal with her when she is once up in arms.

You know that from the beginning I hoped it would be possible for you to see the King as I know how attached to you he is. Your letter was however so amiably worded that I am certain he would not have taken it ill. But the Queen was already very cross at not having seen you at Coblentz, at not having been invited to the ceremony at Coburg[1] (which is very strange she could expect). She seems to take your refusal of the King's visit as a slight to him and her— and it is impossible to argue on that point with her and tell her it is not meant so. I am not quite without self-interest in what I say, as most likely she would get the King to prevent our going to England, as she got him to prevent the children's travelling last year, and then she would be very unkind to me all the winter, as she would fancy that it was by my advice (as I was there at the time) that you refused to see the King.

I quite see what a bore and fatigue it is to you to see people on your road when you want to be quiet, but in this case—as I know what will be the consequences if it is not done in some way or another—I hope and trust there will be a possibility found. How would it be for instance if you left Darmstadt in the afternoon, ask the King to dinner in the hotel at Mayence—and then dressed and prepared

---

[1] The inauguration of the statue to the Prince Consort at Coburg on 26 August. Members of the English Royal Family and relations of the Prince were present.

yourself for the night after you had seen him? Would that tire you so much? Forgive my making a suggestion.[1]

In her next letter of 11 September 1865 from the Neues Palais the Crown Princess says:

The King seemed much pleased with the interview and I had a letter from the Queen in which she does not mention the visit but seems quite pacified.

Miss Durant is here—doing my medallion for the Wolsey Chapel—it will be very successful I think. I am so anxious to see how the Mausoleum has got on—and also the work of the Wolsey Chapel which was not begun when I last was there.

Prince Charles told me Bertie had been civil to him, and Alix very rude, that she had turned her head when he was presented to her, and had hardly answered him when she spoke, and he really could not say whether she was pretty or not. (Please do not tell Bertie.) Then that Uncle George had been very civil but Aunt Cambridge and particularly Mary so rude—that if he ever came to England again he would not visit them.[2] He was quite furious. It amused me so much that I could hardly help laughing when he told me the ladies of the Cambridge family can be so rude and ill-bred when they determined to set about it.

From the Queen   FROGMORE, SEPTEMBER 11, 1865

I must now tell you in the very strictest confidence what I could not before, as after so many disappointments and difficulties, I could not speak till I was sure—but what I have no doubt will please you and what you very likely suspected—viz. that there is a prospect of Lenchen's marrying Christian Holstein. You know that Lenchen could not

---

[1] The real reason why the Queen wished to avoid seeing the King was political. The Convention of Gastein between Prussia and Austria had been signed on 10 August, and the claims of the Augustenburgs were ignored. To her uncle she wrote: "Odious people the Prussians are, I must say." Eventually the Queen gave way, and she met the King at Darmstadt on 6 September, but she wrote: "we talked of nothing but *pluie et beau temps*". *Letters of Queen Victoria*, Second Series, Vol. I, page 275.
[2] They were showing their Danish sympathies.

and would not leave me, as in my terrible position I required one of my daughters to be always in England. Well—dear Aunt Feodora kindly undertook to ascertain all this and the result—since Christian's visit to the Rosenau—has been all that I could wish; I heard from you and others of his excellent qualities and good character, and so—though I rather objected originally to the difference of age—I wished he should see Lenchen, and she and I should see him. Dear Aunt Feodora wrote to me the impression was very favourable and so it was on Lenchen (to whom however I had mentioned nothing.) But it was only three or four days ago that I heard from Aunt F. who copied me a letter from Fritz H., that he had no doubt of his brother's feelings, and that his brother would willingly come to England when I asked him (which I mean to do at the end of December) and above all that he entirely accepted my conditions, and I enclose a copy of part of the letter that you may see what a noble and right view Fritz and Christian take of my very forlorn and difficult and almost unbearable position. I spoke to Lenchen on Friday and she is much pleased, feels no hesitation but great respect and confidence—which no doubt will become firmly strengthened when they meet again and see more of each other. You will both I know rejoice at this—and at the great relief and feeling of security which this gives me. This of course you may all tell dear Fritz—but not another soul, excepting Alice to whom I have written it today—equally in strictest confidence. Bertie and Alix will of course be much annoyed, but that is of no consequence and it is but a fair return to the poor Augustenburgs who saw their rivals fêted in so mad a way as Alix and her family were in March '63.[1]

---

[1] The objections to Princess Helena's marriage, within the Royal Family, were vociferously proclaimed. The political reasons which annoyed the Prince and Princess of Wales and might have annoyed the Crown Princess are obvious. The bridegroom was younger brother to the Augustenburg claimant to the Schleswig-Holstein duchies. But Prince Alfred and Princess Alice also objected strongly, presumably on the ground that Prince Christian lacked any territorial connexions and would become a foreign dependent on the English Royal Family.

From the Crown Princess

MERSEBURG, SEPTEMBER 21, 1865

The Crown Princess was here for the autumn manoeuvres and she
writes:

Bismarck is made much more of than the King and is
fêted in every way. I think it disgusting. Two days ago he
was raised to the rank of Count.

From the Crown Princess

BURG FALKENSTEIN IM HARZ, SEPTEMBER 26, 1865

I am much relieved to hear that Bertie and Alix have
taken the announcement kindly, and I hope and trust that
in time they will become reconciled to it so that there may
be no coldness or discord in the family, which would be so
sad. To us it is also a great comfort to think that we know
Christian so well and are his friends. We have been throughout, from conviction, the warm supporters of his brother's
cause—and it will not be our fault if things are brought to
an end which we shall ever deeply regret, as it is in our eyes
against the real interests of Prussia and we have no others
in view.

The wisest course for us is always the most honourable
and the most generous, what makes us respected and trusted
not what makes us feared and disliked, but it is at the latter
at which the present Government aims with all its might,
ruining the paths which Fritz will have to tread. But it is not
the country and the people who are in the wrong—much
as all those who blindly hate us in England and the rest of
Germany would wish to make it appear. No—it is the small
but powerful party which now reigns, which does the
damage and the mischief to present and future, and which
merits the just censure of the whole of Europe. Forgive my
digressing into politics—I seldom do it. But at present they
are mixed up with the fate of the family to which Lenchen
is to belong and can therefore not improperly be alluded to.

From the Queen   BALMORAL, SEPTEMBER 30, 1865

It is midnight and I must go to bed—I am hardly ever
in bed before ten to one or one now!

From the Queen   BALMORAL, OCTOBER 21, 1865

When I wrote to you on the 18th I had not heard of Lord Palmerston's death. It occurred at eleven that morning. One can hardly realise it! Poor Lady Palmerston—it is the end of everything. Both were very worldly and how the vanity of earthly things is again strikingly shown! That strong, determined will and hard head, that energetic, courageous man, who possessed great qualities with many bad ones, is gone!

From the Crown Princess   COBLENTZ, OCTOBER 23, 1865

Lord Palmerston's death is a great event; I cannot think of it without melancholy. He was always very kind to me, and I think of poor old Lady Palmerston, who was such a tender wife—how she must feel it. I telegraphed directly to her, but having received no answer I fear she did not get it. For you, it will be a source of much trouble I fear. I hope Lord Russell will do all he can to save you as much of it as possible. You disliked Lord Palmerston and had indeed serious reason—but since our misfortune it always seemed to me as if he did all in his power to behave well to you—it was nothing more than his duty, but it touched me—because it showed that age had softened him and awakened his conscience which had been dormant for the whole of his life before. One can never forget that he was a true patriot at heart and was not eaten up by small personal vanity as so many are. He was very wonderful for his age, and I cannot help feeling an interest in him, he was one of the most remarkable men of his age.

The day before yesterday we were at the immense cannon foundry at Essen belonging to the famous Mr. Krupp —who supplies almost the whole of Germany and Prussia with steel rifle-guns. He employs from nine to ten thousand work people; the noise was enough to drive one wild.

From the Crown Princess[1]

SANDRINGHAM, KING'S LYNN, NOVEMBER 7, 1865

Bertie and Alix are most amiable hosts, and seem so

---

[1] At the end of October the Crown Prince and Princess came to stay at the Prussian Embassy in London and later at Windsor.

The Prince and Princess of Wales with Prince Albert Victor and Prince George, July 1865.

The Crown Prince and Princess of Prussia with their children, November 1865. *Left to right*: Prince William, Prince Sigismund, Princess Charlotte and, seated on the foot stool, Prince Henry.

happy here at Sandringham. The improvements made about the place are charming, and I am so glad to see Bertie taking so much interest in these things, and showing so much taste for building and planting—occupation of that kind is so good for him and he really has a great turn for it. He has a capital gardener—Mr. Carmichael.

From the Queen   WINDSOR CASTLE, DECEMBER 5, 1865
I mean to write properly tomorrow but I must write a few words to thank you for your dear letter and to say how much and with what love, I think of you both! Words cannot express how deeply I have felt your love and affection, your help and understanding on this very eventful occasion—when others behaved so ill![1] May God bless and reward you both for it. And may the thought of this cheer you in many a trying hour I grieve to think you will have to go through. Fritz's conduct to Christian was beautiful, and he was so dear and affectionate to me. When one is in such a sad and desolate position as I am, love, affection and sympathy is doubly felt, and so is the contrary. Your love and affection, our own beloved child, did my poor heart so much good. I must tell you how much improved I found you in every way and yet always the same, simple, unspoilt child. God bless and protect you.

From the Crown Princess   BERLIN, DECEMBER 7, 1865
I plunged yesterday all at once into the freezing depth of the family circle here. It began with a pail of cold water being poured upon my head in the shape of a visit to Charlottenburg where I found the three aunts together, viz the Queen Dowager, the Grand Duchess of Mecklenburg and Princess Louise of the Netherlands. The conversation was neither amusing nor cheering to one's spirits, consisting in cross little remarks about nothing. I was not asked after Lenchen by any of them; neither has the King mentioned the subject to me as yet. It wants a deal of heroism to take

---

[1] The discussions in the Royal Family following Princess Helena's engagement to Prince Christian.

the life here kindly after having been at home (and so much spoilt) and I am afraid I have not got it.

I have just received your dear and kind letter which made me cry. I do wish, dearest Mama, I could in any way pay off a small part of the debt of gratitude I owe you—or could give you pleasure, that you might know how deep is my love—how deep too my compassion and sympathy. I know I am unworthy of so much kindness and that you think better of me than I deserve; it more than makes up to me for the many that think less well of me than I deserve. No love can replace a parent's and yours warms and cheers us both far or near. I have not thanked you half enough for the kindness to the children. I hope they will some day be able to understand how great a blessing and advantage they possess in having so kind a grandmama.

From the Crown Princess   BERLIN, DECEMBER 12, 1865

I have not thanked you for your dear letter of the 9th—how well I can imagine all you feel, dearest Mama![1] You are so kind to ask about the marriage.[2] It was celebrated with the greatest pomp but had something of the solemnity of a funeral about it—nothing gay, festive or bridal. Perhaps my own sadness made it appear even gloomier to me than it did to others. The only thing that made a pleasing impression on me was dear Addy herself, who although she cried the whole time, had such a dignified and touching appearance that I never saw her look so well. She went through it all (and a very trying ceremony of four hours it was) with the most perfect *tenue*—though I never saw her smile once. She did not look a bit like a bride but I must say very elegant and *distinguée*. She had a heavy, silver gown and train without any trimming—only embroidered—and all the crown jewels.

I will give you an account of it all later when you will feel more disposed to hear about it. At present too my heart is too confused and I can only think of dearest Uncle!

---

[1] King Leopold was dying when the Queen wrote, and he died on 10 December.

[2] Princess Alexandrine, Addy, niece of the King married Duke William of Mecklenburg-Schwerin on 9 December.

The other thing which pleased me was Abbat's fackel-tanz;[1] it was so fine—more like a very solemn march but it suited the occasion under the peculiar circumstances. The bridegroom's countenance looked as evil as possible the whole time. I looked in vain for a trace of softness of feeling. Addy has pleased me much throughout. She is not what one would call "happy" but she seems contented, and takes it all in a serious light, and is very unselfish.[2]

From the Queen   WINDSOR CASTLE, DECEMBER 15, 1865

We went to the dear Mausoleum at half past ten—a splendid morning as it was four years ago—and there the good Dean read some beautiful selections and a beautiful prayer in which he alluded most touchingly to dearest Uncle with adored Papa. In the evening the Dean of Westminster read to us and addressed a few very fine words to us. Bertie came to luncheon and, after it, I saw him and he was nice and affectionate and amiable (and what I know will give you both the greatest pleasure) all is quite satis-factory as regards Lenchen. He spoke most kindly and affectionately to her—sent Christian a kind message—and all is right. This happening yesterday on that solemn day gave me great satisfaction. Bertie has a loving, affectionate heart and never could bear to be long in disagreement with his family. Towards me also he was very dear and nice. He felt dearest Uncle's loss deeply! I thank God for all this—for the spirit of love which he passed into Bertie's and our hearts, and which brought us all together.

I must tell you how touchingly my poor faithful Brown spoke to me yesterday. He was there at the Mausoleum (of course for the first time) in the morning and when he came to my room later he was so much affected; he said in his simple, expressive way, with such a tender look of pity while the tears rolled down his cheeks; "I didn't like to see

---

[1] A dance with torches in which only members of the royal and princely families took part.

[2] This not very cheerful marriage was to prove "most unhappy", see *Memories of Forty Years*, by Princess Catherine Radziwill.

ye at Frogmore this morning; I felt for ye; to see ye coming there with your daughters and your husband lying there— marriage on one side and death on the other; no I didn't like to see it; I felt sorry for ye; I know so well what your feeling must be—ye who had been so happy. There is no more pleasure for you, poor Queen, and I feel for ye but what can I do though for ye? I could die for ye:" I wish you could have heard it. In that beautiful sermon of Robertson's called the "Irreparable Past" he speaks of this—the relief there is "to see the honest, affectionate face of a servant lighting your suffering. His sympathy in your dark hour is worth a world. . . . Very little can be done when the worst does come, but yet to know that the pulses of a human heart are vibrating with yours, there is something in that —let the distance between thou and them be ever immeasurable—which is exquisitely soothing."[1] I have felt this so strongly in this good, tender, devoted, and truly noble-hearted creature. It does my poor heart good to see such simple and touching appreciation of my grief and loneliness and there is something peculiarly touching in seeing this in a strong, hardy man, a child of the mountains. When he wished Lenchen joy the evening of her engagement he said "Only one thing; I hope you'll never forget the good Queen; . . . I hope you'll never forget and always be good to the good Queen." Few would think of that and fewer would say it.

From the Crown Princess   BERLIN, DECEMBER 16, 1865

It seems that no attention is going to be paid to his wish of being laid in his last resting place by the side of Princess Charlotte at Windsor. Is that right?[2] The descriptions of

---

[1] "The Irreparable Past." A sermon preached at Brighton on 8 May 1853 by F. W. Robertson based on St. Mark XIV, verses 41 and 42. "There is a past which is gone for ever. But there is a future which is still our own."

[2] Three days after the funeral of Princess Charlotte, King Leopold had gone down to the vault in St. George's and arranged for its alteration to take his own coffin (see *A Biographical Memoir of Princess Charlotte,*

dear Uncle's last moments are most touching, his end seems to have been so quiet and peaceful. Marie meant well no doubt in announcing to him that he was about to die and calling upon him to confess his sins, but to our Protestant ideas it seems cruel to trouble the last moments of the dying, and useless too. I should not have had the heart to do so. How admirably the Belgians behaved, and how satisfactory and gratifying it is—proving to the world how dear Uncle was appreciated, and is a triumph of constitutionalism which always gives one so much pleasure and is so encouraging. Dear Uncle's career has closed in a way so worthy of his public life—and he leaves a name behind him which will always form a bright exception from other sovereigns of his day on the continent, whose lives are spent in useless struggles for prerogatives which are in themselves not worth having.

From the Crown Princess   BERLIN, DECEMBER 19, 1865

I am indeed delighted at all having come right with Bertie.[1] I was sure it would; he has much too kind a heart and is too fond of you to keep up a long opposition to anything you have so much at heart. Fritz said he (Bertie) had spoken in the same sense to him, and had made up his mind to be quite kind to Christian. He had only added that he and Alice had been much provoked and very angry with me for taking up a different line from what they had. Fritz explained to him that he had no right to be angry with me on the subject, and he promised he would forget it all. This, dear Mama keep quite to yourself, but I was pained to think that those two—brother and sister should be against me and excite one another for nothing at all, and surprised too because Alice had never shown the slightest displeasure towards me and being as amiable as usual. However it is not

---

1817). The new King of the Belgians explained to the Queen that although his father's wishes were known, the Belgian people would never have consented to them. The Queen wrote "I could say no more, but feel it very much." *Letters of Queen Victoria*, 2nd series, Vol. 1, page 288.

[1] About Princess Helena's marriage.

worth troubling one's head about—and is over and done with.

I consider that from the 14th the whole thing has passed into a new phase altogether which is one of mutual goodwill and contentment, and I consider it a great blessing that it is so and am thankful for your dear sake above all.

Fritz had a great deal to tell me about Brussels. The public seems to have behaved so well and showed so much feeling. But I hear the end of the funeral was dreadful. Fritz was shocked; he said he never saw anything worse done; indeed he thought it disgraceful. I am sure the details would be as painful to you to hear as they were to me; it seems it was all the fault of the Roman Catholic clergy who behaved so ill. Fritz was delighted with Leopold's speech and said that the ceremony of taking the oath was very fine and striking, and that Leopold had been enthusiastically received.

From the Queen   OSBORNE, DECEMBER 23, 1865

All you tell me of the funeral is very painful and caused by that atrocious Catholic clergy. Nasty "beggars" as Brown would say—who dear Papa detested and beloved Uncle spoilt, and who never were very much attached to him.[1]

I do think it most shameful that it was expected you should take the same undutiful and disrespectful and heartless line as nameless people did about L's. marriage. If I could ever think that our own children would join in a clique against me I cannot tell you how I should resent it! You may all have your opinions—and so every reasonable and independent person ought to have—but when your parent and your sovereign settles a thing for her good which interferes with none of your rights and comforts, opposition for mere selfish and personal objects—indeed out

---

[1] The explanation here is that King Leopold was a Lutheran and was given a Protestant funeral-service. The difficulty arose over the interment; this took place in the Catholic church at Laeken where the Protestant service was allowed to be conducted but only within a temporary structure.

of jealousy—is monstrous. I cannot tell you what I have suffered.

You have also never said one word about my poor little Highland book—my only book. I had hoped that you and Fritz would have liked it.[1]

From the Crown Princess   BERLIN, DECEMBER 26, 1865

If you will recollect, dear Mama, both Fritz and I spoke to you out walking at Windsor about your little Highland book, which we had read at Sandringham, and said how glad we should be if you would give us each a copy, which you were kind enough to do the day we left and which we thanked you for then; but we repeat our thanks today.

The King allows no mourning on Christmas Eve nor Christmas Day—so I had to take mine off yesterday much *à contre-coeur*. I think it so whimsical to be continually finding an excuse for going out of black (the last sign of respect for a loved relation).

From the Queen   OSBORNE, DECEMBER 30, 1865

The Queen is referring to a visit paid to her by the Prince and
    Princess Leopold of Hohenzollern-Sigmaringen.

I must speak of Leopold and Antoinette. I must now say how charmed with her we are. How lovely she is and what a look of dear Aunt Victoire she has. How like her she is —only handsomer perhaps. And so simple and unaffected— and dear Leopold I am so fond of.[2] Oh! if B. and Al: were

---

[1] This is the privately printed edition of *Leaves from the Journal of Our Life in the Highlands*. The Queen had lent her journal to Sir Arthur Helps, Clerk to the Privy Council, when he was at Balmoral. He had shown a great interest in it, and the Queen thought that extracts might be made into a book for members of the Royal Family and for the Queen's private friends. Three years later the book was published for general circulation.

[2] Prince Leopold was the eldest son of the Prince of Hohenzollern-Sigmaringen. His wife was the daughter of Maria da Gloria, Queen of Portugal and King Ferdinand who was Queen Victoria's cousin.

like them! Oh if Antoinette was in Al:'s place! She is so much more *sympathique* and *grande dame*. Our good Al: is like a distinguished lady of society but nothing more![1]

---

[1] Answering this letter on 2 January 1866 the Crown Princess says, "I am so glad you are so charmed with Antoinette. I knew you would be— she has something like a Dove in her expression, and is a great darling, but if you were to live long with her you would not find her wiser than Alix—for she is still very childish and has been so superficially educated."

1866

From the Queen   OSBORNE, JANUARY 3, 1866

I send you today an admirable speech of good Dr. McLeod's which has produced a perfect revolution and the greatest violence in Scotland.[1] He is here, the dear good man, on a visit of three nights which is a great treat and he says since the great movement in '43 there has not been such excitement. Dr. Muir, one of my Chaplains, and a stupid, affected man, says what Dr. McLeod has said must be from satanic inspiration!! He told us wonderful things.

From the Queen   OSBORNE, JANUARY 6, 1866

What you say about dear Antoinette is I think quite just. I did not mean that she was cleverer than Alix but she is softer, more affectionate, and a real Princess—which the other is not.

From the Crown Princess   BERLIN, JANUARY 6, 1866

I am sure you will have been as grieved as we are about poor Count Blücher. Our dear Countess how sad for her! What a life of sorrow for her! One after another those nearest and dearest to her depart and leave her more lonely than before. She will be quite overwhelmed by this; she was such a devoted wife, and he was, in spite of all his oddities, such a kind husband and appreciated all she was. It is very, very sad. He was such a strong and healthy man without a grey hair and, never having ailed a thing, he might have lived for twenty-five years longer without feeling really old, and she, poor Countess, who has such frail health is now left quite desolate.[2]

---

[1] At a time when there was much feeling in Scotland over Sabbath desecration—especially the running of trains on Sunday—Dr. McLeod spoke against this feeling arguing that it derived from the Jewish Sabbath and had little in common with the divine sanctions of the Lord's Day.

[2] Count Gustave Blücher, grandson of the celebrated Field Marshal. He was born in 1800, and married in 1828 Madeline, younger daughter of

I send you today, dearest Mama, what I know will be very valuable to you and what I would not have parted with for anyone else but you, some letters written by dear Papa as a young man, and one of Uncle Leopold's to dear Papa; they are so pretty and so interesting; it was quite by chance that I heard of them and the person into whose hands they had come by accident, gave them to me.

May I trouble you about something which I mentioned at Windsor? Now poor Sir Charles Eastlake is dead will you not use your influence to prevent a person quite unfit for the place being put in his stead? The Director of the National Gallery is appointed by you I believe or at least you have a voice in the matter and it is so important it should be somebody of a scientific education who is acquainted with all the Galleries of Europe, and who can give up all his activity and time to the one pursuit, and not an artist who must be more or less absorbed by his own works. The person ought to have a thorough knowledge of all matters and periods of art, and experienced in managing affairs which are most difficult (i.e. finding and buying works of art). Sir Charles Eastlake will be most difficult to replace. The only person in my humble judgement fit for it is Mr. Robinson[1] of the Kensington Museum (who rather clashes with Mr. Cole[2] as he is very independent). Forgive

---

Sir Robert Dallas, who was Lord Chief Justice of the Common Pleas. As a younger woman Countess Blücher is alluded to in the journal of that outspoken diarist the last Lord Holland who met her in Italy. He says that she had married the grandson of "that old barbarian" Blücher, that "she had a large fortune, and has rather a pretty face and pretty manners, but is not very clever or agreeable". Later he refers to Lady Dallas "and a tribe of unmarried daughters, Countess Blücher being the only one among them at all *presentable*". The tribe of unmarried daughters later married and it is their deaths to which the Crown Princess is alluding when she writes of the Countess's "life of sorrow". See *Journal of Henry Edward Fox*, edited by Lord Ilchester, 1923.

[1] John Charles Robinson (1824–1913). He was first superintendent of the art collections at the South Kensington Museum. He was Surveyor of the Queen's pictures from 1882–1901.

[2] Henry Cole 1808–82. One of the principal promoters of the Great Exhibition. He was head of the Department of Science and Design of which the South Kensington Museum was an adjunct.

my meddling in such a thing. I feel dear Papa is no longer there to protect the interests of art; and it is a question which constantly occupies me here—as old Waagen[1] will most likely not live much longer, the Director of the Museum is quite unfit and our Academy is without one at all. I know that what qualifies a person for being President of an art academy is quite a different thing from what is necessary to be a good Director of an art collection. Sir Charles Eastlake united all this in one—that made him so invaluable a person but I do not think you would find that again; connoisseur, good man of business and artist at once. Will you think it over again, dear Mama, and not take offence at my mentioning it?

From the Queen   OSBORNE, JANUARY 11, 1866
    I am so thankful for all you say about art, and hope that Mr. Robinson will be appointed. He has already been recommended by several people to Lord Russell. I hope you will always write to tell me of anything of this kind, because I do not understand these things well, having always placed implicit reliance with adored Papa, but you have inherited that from him, and he talked to you so much about it that I feel the greatest confidence in you.

From the Queen   OSBORNE, JANUARY 13, 1866
    I fear Mr. Robinson has no chance, but I send you here the copy of two letters from Lady Eastlake which I think will reconcile you. Besides he[2] is old and Mr. Robinson might succeed him. I have urged Mr. Robinson very strongly but Lord Russell and others seem so anxious for Mr. Boxall that I fear I cannot resist it.

From the Crown Princess   BERLIN, JANUARY 13, 1866
    Christian was here yesterday, looking very well, but coughing. I wish you would make him talk to Dr. Jenner

---

[1] G. F. Waagen (1794–1868). Professor of Art History at Berlin University; author of *The Treasures of Art in Great Britain.*
[2] William Boxall 1800–79. He was a portrait painter, and was Director of the National Gallery from now until 1874.

about that nasty cough—he has had it for two years now—and does not attend to it. Then I wish someone could persuade him to get Mr. Saunders to see to his teeth. I was too shy to say anything to him, but know how much good it did Fritz and Louis. Here one does really not pay enough attention to these little auxiliaries of life, and really they have a deal to do with health. How meddling and interfering you will think me become!

From the Queen   OSBORNE, JANUARY 17, 1866
I shall see to Christian's cough and teeth. Both are important, Aunt feels just the same.
Mr. Layard[1] is to be made temporarily Director of the National Gallery—and I hope later Mr. Robinson will.

From the Crown Princess   BERLIN, JANUARY 23, 1866
I must tell you that Bismarck is furious that Lord A. Loftus is coming, and his whole party, *à la tête* Prince Charles, say the rudest things on that subject. They have succeeded in disposing the King as ill as possible towards poor Lord Augustus which is a great shame. And I have no doubt he will be very ill received. We shall however do all in our power to support him and are very glad he is coming.[2]

From the Queen   OSBORNE, JANUARY 24, 1866
On Monday was Christian's birthday. Alas! his 35th. If only he looked a little younger! We think him looking older this time even than last December! And his manners and movements are so old. It is such a pity. Saunders has seen

---

[1] Austen Layard (1817–94), the distinguished excavator, was Under Secretary for Foreign Affairs, at this time. Lord Russell felt that he could combine both posts but then decided that the jealousy of artists made it an impossibility. See *Layard of Nineveh* by Gordon Waterfield.
[2] Lord Augustus Loftus (1817–1904). He succeeded Lord Napier as British Ambassador in Berlin. He was, by no means, an admirer of Bismarck and was sympathetic to the Danes over the Schelswig-Holstein dispute. He was described by the Foreign Secretary, Lord Granville, as "having some merits" but "wanting in tact and a great bore". *Letters of Queen Victoria*, Second Series, Vol. II, page 85.

him and will do what he can. Doctor Jenner also—who recommends less wrapping up and coddling and less eating —and I think when he has been here sometime he will look fresher and younger.

From the Queen   OSBORNE, JANUARY 31, 1866
   Many, many thanks for your dear, long letter of the 27th—the contents of which I shall keep entirely to myself. Christian looks already younger and better since he came, eats less—coddles himself less, and is more out in the open air. He has plenty of good sense—and will, I am sure, in time take plenty of interest in many things. He and Lenchen seem thoroughly fond of each other, which is a great comfort—much as it tries me to feel my own child's affections are now entirely divided.[1]

From the Queen   OSBORNE, FEBRUARY 2, 1866
   Your little ebullition about children and the exquisite delight of having them (certainly a thing very few share in) I will not reply to—except to say that you will find the pleasure less great when they grow up, and the sorrows and anxieties of one kind or another overwhelm you—and hardly counterbalance the pleasure. My trials are greatly increased by the number of the children. To have none must be very sad in one's old age—but to have a great many is a great trouble and a great anxiety. I have worries and bothers and am driven half wild with all my work. I shall certainly break down.

From the Queen   WINDSOR CASTLE, FEBRUARY 7, 1866
   The King's letter is a gross insult and as such I resent it and all my people do.[2] I shall write a letter which Fritz is

---

[1] The Queen herself destroyed parts of the Crown Princess's letter of the 27th which, almost certainly concerned the hostility of the Prussian family to Prince Christian.

[2] Not of course the public as the correspondence was private: the Queen means by "my people" the members of her Household. This correspondence has not survived, but it concerned a suggestion that Prince Christian might use Gravenstein Castle—a property which belonged to the Augustenburg family in the Duchies. Presumably it was intended that Prince Christian and Princess Helena should spend a part of their

to show his father. His conduct I can only call ungentleman-like—painful as it is to me to say this of one I had much liked and respected.

From the Crown Princess   BERLIN, FEBRUARY 27, 1866

We are all in the greatest alarm here.[1] I can speak of it openly as I know no more than anyone else from an authentic source, and gather all my information from hearsay and the newspapers. I am sadly afraid the bad man B. will succeed in his plan of driving us into a war with Austria! Quite setting aside how sinful and horrid it is, my hair stands on end at the dangers it will plunge not only our unfortunate country but the whole of Germany into. My hope is in the great foreign powers, that it may be

---

honeymoon in the Castle. On 5 February the Queen wrote to Lord Clarendon, the Foreign Secretary,

"The Queen thinks that Lord Clarendon ought to see these two private letters—the more so, as Prince Christian will speak to him upon the subject tomorrow. The King of Prussia's letter and his conduct in this affair are most improper and most rude to say the least. The C. Princess is dreadfully hurt and shocked.

Of course Prince Christian and Princess Helena will not expose themselves to an insult—but it is monstrous in the King of Prussia to pretend to forbid a Prince who is not even the Heir to go to his private property." (Clarendon Papers in the Bodleian Library.)

Replying about Gravenstein the Crown Princess wrote: "If he (the King) was left to follow his own better impulses, how different things would be! He is by nature so kindhearted, easy and amiable and was so beloved by those around him. How that wicked and mischievous man B. has poisoned all—even the very sources. One often finds it hard to recognise the King's former self. The talent B. possesses in working him up, irritating him—in short speculating on his weak points—is diabolical".

[1] This letter is the first allusion in the correspondence to the developing storm between Austria and Prussia. By the Gastein Convention of August 1865, Austria and Prussia ended their joint control of the Schleswig-Holstein Duchies following their victory of the previous year. The Convention assigned Schleswig to Prussia and Holstein to Austria. Prussia made it obvious that she would annexe Schleswig, while Austria made it plain that she only held Holstein as a pledge that ultimately she would grant it independence. She allowed agitation in Holstein on behalf of the Augustenburgs, and this was the cause of trouble between her and Prussia in the early months of 1866.

possible for them to interfere and save the peace of Europe, though one may be pretty sure that it will suit France best to look on quietly at a Civil War in Germany and then step in and take for herself whatever bit she covets the most.

From the Queen   WINDSOR CASTLE, MARCH 5, 1866
    Before I say more let me tell you that good Sir T. Biddulph, from his experience, position, age, etc., is the successor of poor dear Sir Charles—but, as the stupid Ministers will not adopt the natural, simple and right precedent of General Grey's being called my P. Secretary (and considering his long and faithful service he must have some mark of distinction) he and General Grey are appointed joint keepers of the Privy Purse, a most absurd invention of Lord Russell's!! And Sir J. Cowell becomes Master of the Household.[1] He will then be brought gradually forward.
    I am greatly distressed and perturbed about your state of affairs. Louise suggested that Lenchen like Herodias should ask for B's head![2] I think it a clever idea of hers. She is so very amusing and original.

From the Crown Princess   BERLIN, MARCH 9, 1866
    We are more and more alarmed at what we can pick up about the state of politics; officially we know nothing. Fritz is kept quite out of it all, the King does not speak to him

---

[1] These are important changes in the Royal Household. Sir Charles Phipps (1801–66) had been private secretary to the Prince Consort for 14 years: thereafter he acted (not always in complete harmony) with General Grey (1804–70) as private secretary to the Queen although the position was unproclaimed and unrecognised. Sir Charles died on 24 February 1866. As the Queen explains Sir Thomas Biddulph (1809–78), who had been Master of the Household, was made joint Keeper of the Privy Purse with Grey, but their duties were distinguished. Grey was to act as private secretary—and his post was recognised by the Government in the following year—while Biddulph was responsible for the financial side. Sir John Cowell (1832–94) described by the Queen as "young, very steady and intelligent to whom she is deeply indebted for all the difficulties that he has encountered throughout his career with Prince Alfred" was appointed Master of the Household.
[2] As a wedding present from the King of Prussia.

on the subject and the Ministers never communicate anything to him. I have no words to say what a calamity I would consider a war with Austria in every point of view —for us in particular, for Germany and for Europe. No one can tell where it would end and the only gainer by it would be the Emperor Napoleon. The Queen is much alarmed, and fears the King will be provoked into it. I do not know, but it is useless to judge what the King would or would not do now by what he used to say or think, since he is in Bismarck's hands—one has no guarantee, nothing and nobody is safe! I cannot say how Fritz and I suffer under the state of things. In my bad nights I lie and think of all the sad and dangerous eventualities which we are running so close—thanks to Bismarck's madness, and sigh for something or somebody to deliver us out of the hand of the Amalekite! I am so convinced that no second person exists who would be so pernicious; old Manteuffel would not be half so dangerous.

From the Crown Princess   BERLIN, MARCH 13, 1866
We are still in great suspense between war and peace. The King looks preoccupied and disturbed; the Queen thinks it bodes nothing good, but we know nothing of the real state of affairs.

I have so many ladies to see and audiences to give which is the greatest bore I know; it makes one feel so stupid talking about the weather etc., that I get quite absent, and nearly go to sleep before the ladies. Most ladies are bores; I suppose that is what makes the exception so very charming and valuable.

From the Crown Princess   BERLIN, MARCH 16, 1866
The last days I have spent in most anxious—I may say cruel—suspense and many tears. War seemed coming on like a hideous monster to devour all one's happiness, one's security and one's future. But today I feel hopeful! You will see by a letter which Fritz writes to you by the King's desire that he is anxious to accept an offer of mediation if England will mediate between Austria and Prussia. I hail this as a

possible prevention of the much dreaded calamity of war, and as perhaps productive of much good. You again, dearest Mama, may be the means of averting a European conflagration, and it now rests in your dear hands. Lord Clarendon will I am sure know what to do and be glad of this opportunity of being a peacemaker in the best sense of the word. England's interference has often been so untimely and unlucky in Continental affairs, and her influence so much suffered, that I am doubly thankful to think she can now achieve a place—and the first place—among the great powers without any damage to herself—and most likely with every chance of success. I fancy Bismarck knows nothing of what the King intends and would be most likely against it as he is bent on war for his own wild mad purposes. The quarrel with Austria is a very strange one as in my idea Austria has done nothing to offend us whereas the measures, with regard to the Duchies, the Prussian government has taken, are most arbitrary and violent and provocative. I trust Austria will remain quiet and not take M. de Bismarck's bait; it will be in her own interests in the end, though her patience is put to a hard trial. The consequence of a war would be so serious that no one could tell where it would end. It would upset the whole of Germany—in short I dare not think of all that would or might happen. The feeling in the country here is strongly against war and thankfully would any opening be received (Bismarck and the Kreuzzeitung party always excepted). I hope no time will be lost in considering what can be done, and look to you as our good genius.

From the Queen   WINDSOR CASTLE, MARCH 21, 1866
     Austria has done nothing but keep to the Gastein Treaty and I cannot understand how the King can say the contrary. Lord Clarendon is unfortunately so irritable and cross that it makes everything very disagreeable; he is excessively jealous of General Grey which is most abominable and very trying for me. However I think all are most anxious to prevent war, but none feel about the poor Augustenburgs as they ought—and that makes it all so

tragic and difficult for me. Oh! how helpless I do feel at these moments without adored Papa! I can only pray to God (and that I can ever do, and find a strength and comfort in it which no one, who has not felt the want of help and has been bowed to the earth with sorrow, can know and feel) for guidance and to be directed to do the best! But it is a feeling which overwhelms me at times! You may both rely on my doing everything I possibly can to prevent the war.[1]

From the Queen   WINDSOR CASTLE, MARCH 24, 1866

Many thanks for your kind letter with the important intelligence which I at once conveyed to Lord Russell; for I think we have fallen into the trap laid for us by Bismarck, for Lord Clarendon (who is most disagreeable, and un-

---

[1] The reason why this intervention by the Royal Families was unavailing is clear. The original proposal of arbitration by the British Government seems to have come from the British Ambassador in Berlin but after the King had spoken to the Crown Prince (alluded to in the Crown Princess's letter of 16 March) the Ambassador saw Bismarck who drily said that the British "should address themselves to Vienna, for Austria was the party who threatened to be the disturbers of the peace". The Ambassador adds that Lord Clarendon foresaw that the task would be hopeless (Lord Augustus Loftus, *Diplomatic Reminiscences*, Second Series, Vol. I).

On 28 March, after consulting with the Government, the Queen wrote to the Crown Prince that it was difficult for England to interfere with the course pursued by the Prussian Government "under the influence of Count Bismarck". *Letters of Queen Victoria*, Second Series, Vol. I, page 311.

The following letter of 31 March from Lord Clarendon to the Prime Minister helps to explain the difference between him and the Queen.

"The Queen thinks of nothing but the Duchies and with reference to the Augustenburgs getting back that which they were handsomely paid never to claim; but the idea of our spending one shilling or one drop of blood in the banditti quarrel which is now going on in Germany is simply absurd." After describing certain steps which he has taken with the French he adds of arbitration. "I know it will be useless, and as we are now aware of the real object of Prussia and the only basis upon which she would negotiate, the less we have to do with it the better." *The Later Correspondence of Lord John Russell*, Edited by G. P. Gooch, Vol. II, page 345.

manageable) spoke of a long letter of B's to B-f[1] and that it would all end in smoke! Lord R. is however very amiably disposed and if anything can be done he is most anxious to effect it; but there are many troubles at home and I fear a Ministerial crisis is impending on account of this wretched Reform which I fear has been brought too hurriedly and carelessly forward.[2]

From the Crown Princess   BERLIN, MARCH 24, 1866

 I am not astonished at what you say about Lord Clarendon for it is just as I found him when I spoke to him at Windsor—so touchy and irritable and cross, not well-disposed to General Grey—of whom he seemed jealous and suspicious. Heaven knows it is very unjust and unreasonable of him. It is surely best to ignore it and take no notice of it as it is a weakness in his temper which I fear one cannot reform. But I am sure it makes things much more difficult and complicated for you which I grieve at—as you have trouble enough—and without dear Papa's help it is a nervous business. But thank God you are surrounded by devoted and trustworthy people, and at least you can trust to the common sense and moderation of your ministers even if you know they are not so perfectly informed on the state of Continental affairs as they ought to be, and particularly do not quite understand the Schleswig-Holstein question with regard to the poor Augustenburgs. I must say Lord Augustus L., like a good, honest and well-intentioned man as he is, does what he can to keep matters straight and has shown tact and sense, but I sadly regret Morier's[3] absence. Lord A. is now in the phase of Prussian politics and has not

---

[1] Bernstorff.

[2] The Reform Bill on which Russell's government resigned in June of this year.

[3] Sir Robert Morier (1826–93), diplomatist. He had held appointments at various German courts since the early 1850's, and the Crown Princess had much wanted him to be given the Berlin Embassy. In later life he described his work as "the political and heart union of England and Germany".

one human being in his Embassy who has enough knowledge or head to keep him as well-informed as he should be. Bismarck relies on that too and plays his desperate game with desperate energy and blindness. If he would only break his own neck and not run the chance of breaking ours too. I should say it does not matter what he does; the worse he fares the better for the good cause.

From the Queen　　　WINDSOR CASTLE, MARCH 31, 1866

I think you might like to hear what I saw at Landseer's the other day. Such beautiful unfinished things. A "Lady Godiva" most charmingly treated, on a dun pony (of course nude but, so simply arranged—you see her back and she has her arms outstretched, offering up a prayer to be supported in this terrible ordeal), an old Duenna standing by, closing her eyes.[1] Then another, but merely rubbed in, the idea of which struck me so very much—as being so beautiful and novel. It is to be an altar piece and represents an old carved stone font with doves flying down upon it— in a glory, and beneath gathered round it are lambs including a black one. Is it not a pretty and novel idea?[2]

I am, as you may well think, terribly anxious at the state of affairs and trying what I can to prevent war which is entirely the fault of Prussia. It is too, too, wicked. Good kind Christian, I have asked him to come over sooner (only for 10 days) as I am anxious to speak to him about many things.

What you heard is a complete fabrication from beginning to end.[3] There was never the slightest question of

---

[1] Lady Godiva's Prayer. Exhibited at the Royal Academy in 1866 and afterwards bought by Mr. H. W. Eaton, later Lord Cheylesmore, for 3600 guineas.

[2] The Baptismal Font, stated to have been Landseer's last picture. It is now at Buckingham Palace.

[3] The Crown Princess had written to her mother saying that she had heard "in a round-about way" that Count Bernstorff had reported to Berlin that the Queen had had differences with her ministers which had caused her many tears "about the keys of dear Papa to the ministers' boxes, which they want to have back. I don't know whether it is true, but it seems to me not unlikely on account of Lord Clarendon's jealousy of General Grey."

anything of the kind. The only trouble there was, was the general tone of Lord C. about politics but he has been put in his place by good Lord R. who behaves extremely well. He has a personal affection for the King and always laments over his having been misled and ruined by that monster. If you could tell me positively of any of these lies ('lees' as Brown calls them) of Bernstorff's I would bring them home to him and a stop could be put to his odious and mischievous reports. Dear Alix I don't think improved. She is grown a little grand, I think, and we never get more intimate or nearer to each other. I am much more intimate with Leopoldine and dear Marie than with Alix; it is not a sympathetic nature, good, and kind as she is. I think that Lenchen's marriage and a stoppage which I have put to her hunting (which shocked everyone) has made her a little embarrassed and may make her appear grand. Little Alb. V is a great darling but a fairy.

From the Crown Princess   BERLIN, MARCH 31, 1866
   How matters stand I do not exactly know. Five of our forts have orders to be armed. This does not look peacable, but I cannot yet give up all hope; time gained is much gained. I hope and trust the Austrians will remain firm but not allow themselves to be carried away by the irritation, which is most natural. Bismarck waits for an opportunity of war; if none is given him he is beaten, and much evil prevented. The worst of it is the French play a double game. They want us to go to war—and yet they want to appear friendly and peacemaking.

From the Queen   WINDSOR CASTLE, APRIL 4, 1866
   I really think that the danger of war seems blowing over, and that this last wise move of Austria's will frustrate Bismarck's plans and, even perhaps, break his neck.[1] Lord Clarendon has held firm and energetic language to Bernstorff and when he brought him a dispatch from Bismarck

[1] The Queen is probably referring to the Austrian withdrawal of reinforcements from Bohemia.

with the accounts of all the aggressive preparations of Austria he said he did not believe a word of it!

I fear the poor Queen is much disappointed in not coming here in a fortnight but it really never would have done at this moment and would have put herself and me, in a most painful and awkward position.

I think I told you poor Mr. Turnbull was dying. He died on Tuesday and today I saw him in his coffin, looking like a fine old knight. It is the fifth lifeless form, I have stood by within five months. I have no fears or horror of it now—death seems so familiar to me! He is a great loss.[1]

From the Crown Princess   BERLIN, APRIL 4, 1866

We are still midway suspended between peace and war; not a day passes without some little incident which might be easily laid hold of to turn the scales on the side of peace; and not a day passes that the wicked man does not, with the greatest ability, counteract and thwart what is good and drive on towards war, turning and twisting everything to serve his own purpose. The tissue of untruths is such that one gets quite perplexed with only listening to them, but the net is cleverly made and the King, in spite of all his reluctance, gets more and more entangled in it without perceiving it! The Queen's humour is quite dreadful, makes my nerves so shaky and agitated—partly politics and partly her health—and I think her not going to England now which she was bent on, though she never mentioned the subject to me, has made her so cross that one can hardly get on with her. You don't know what a trying thing it is or how she can lose her temper. Sophie Dobeneck is going to be married to a Monsieur de Jagow; the bridegroom elect is a widower, well-off and has five children. She was a friend of his wife and knew him all her life. She seems very happy.

I quite understand what you say about Alix. When Lenchen is once married it will wear off you will see. To be intimate with her, one must see much of her; she never

---

[1] John Turnbull who was Clerk of the Works at Windsor Castle. He was highly regarded by the Queen and Prince Consort.

makes advances of her own and has nothing overflowing or warm and tender about her relations with others and yet she is kind and good and affectionate, and one cannot be in the house with her without loving her. She is never *maussade* or out of temper or cross and impatient; her household are very fond of her.

From the Crown Princess   BERLIN, APRIL 6, 1866

Of politics I know nothing except (which I suppose you have already heard) which is that the Emperor of Russia has sent a General to Vienna with a letter to the Emperor, of which Monsieur de Schweinitz brought a copy to the King yesterday. What the letter contains we do not know.[1] Uncle Ernest has also sent some letters to the King, I believe from the Emperor of Austria and Uncle Alexander, but I fear they have no sort of impression on the King, who is furious against Austria for her aggressive armaments and exasperated at her denying this fact, which he declared to be double perfidy.

It is most difficult to find out what is true about the armaments; from many sides one hears it so positively affirmed with so many details that it seems hardly possible to doubt it. Then again one hears it flatly denied by people who ought to have means of knowing the truth. For my part I think it is exaggerated on purpose to irritate the King which has certainly succeeded. Bismarck goes on unceasingly, untiringly working at getting us into the war by every means in his power and, as no absolute monarch could be more powerful than he is, my fears are still as great as they were two weeks ago.

---

[1] General Hans Lothar von Schweinitz, soldier and diplomat, was at this time Prussian Military Attaché at Vienna. He had been A.D.C. to the Crown Prince. He was afterwards German Ambassador in Vienna (1869–1876) and in St. Petersburg (1876–92). He was an old friend of the Czar. The letter, from the fact that it was sent to both sovereigns, was evidently written to urge a conference. The Czar and Francis Joseph had been on bad terms since the Crimean War, and the Czar had a great admiration for his uncle—the King of Prussia.

From the Crown Princess   BERLIN, APRIL 10, 1866
A thousand thanks for your dear letter and for the telegram I received yesterday. So the engagement between Mary and Prince Teck has really come to pass![1] I am very glad for her sake if she is happy. I have heard he is an amiable and agreeable young man. The worst of it is his having no position and no money—but Mary has enough to live upon I suppose. Uncle George is so rich he can help her; besides, when the Duchess is no longer alive, I suppose she will inherit all she has. I think it is a blessing that somebody has been found as I fear after all that passed between mother and daughter they would never have been comfortable together again.

From the Queen   OSBORNE, APRIL 11, 1866
I send you here, a copy of a letter which I, of my own accord, wrote to the King, feeling I could not do otherwise. [2] I have sent it to Lord A. Loftus to take himself at once to the King. Show it dear Fritz. The stories of Austria's armaments are base fabrications. I think her conduct admirable and dignified. Really I cannot find words to say what I think of the conduct of Bismarck. It is too, too, fearful. Fearful will be the retribution if innocent blood is shed!

From the Queen   OSBORNE, APRIL 18, 1866
Though it is very naughty of me to show dearest Fritz's English up to you I must tell you, as you will laugh so, he telegraphed you were "Happily delivered *from* a strong and healthy daughter!"—and the telegraph clerk corrected it, putting an x and "of" below.[3]

---

[1] Francis, Duke of Teck (1837–1900) married Princess Mary of Cambridge. He was the son of Duke Alexander of Württemberg by his marriage to an Austrian Countess.
[2] This fine letter is printed in *Letters of Queen Victoria*, Second Series, Vol. I, page 317. It contains the sentence "You are deceived, you are made to believe that you are to be attacked, and I, your true friend and sister, hear your honoured name, attacked and abused for the faults and recklessness of others—or, rather more, of *one* man."
[3] Princess Victoria was born on 12 April.

Queen Victoria's children, August 1865. *Left to right*: Princess Louise, Princess Beatrice, Princess Alice, Prince Alfred, the Prince of Wales, Prince Arthur (*seated*), Princess Helena, Prince Leopold, the Crown Princess of Prussia.

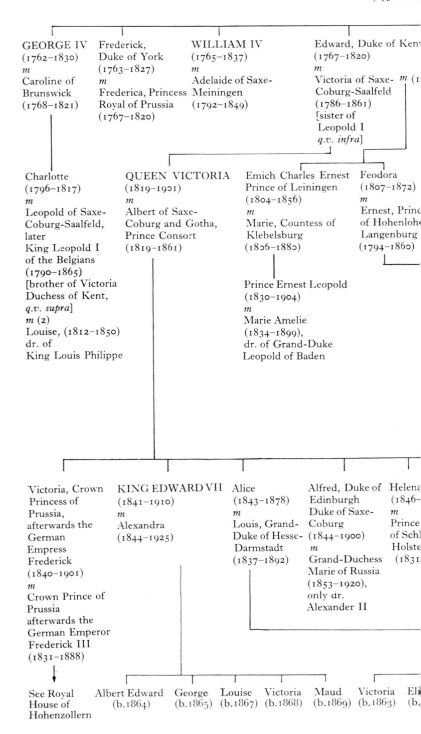

GEORGE IV
(1762–1830)
m
Caroline of
Brunswick
(1768–1821)

Frederick,
Duke of York
(1763–1827)
m
Frederica, Princess
Royal of Prussia
(1767–1820)

WILLIAM IV
(1765–1837)
m
Adelaide of Saxe-
Meiningen
(1792–1849)

Edward, Duke of Ken|
(1767–1820)
m
Victoria of Saxe- *m* (1
Coburg-Saalfeld
(1786–1861)
[sister of
Leopold I
q.v. infra]

Charlotte
(1796–1817)
m
Leopold of Saxe-
Coburg-Saalfeld,
later
King Leopold I
of the Belgians
(1790–1865)
[brother of Victoria
Duchess of Kent,
q.v. supra]
m (2)
Louise, (1812–1850)
dr. of
King Louis Philippe

QUEEN VICTORIA
(1819–1901)
m
Albert of Saxe-
Coburg and Gotha,
Prince Consort
(1819–1861)

Emich Charles Ernest
Prince of Leiningen
(1804–1856)
m
Marie, Countess of
Klebelsburg
(1806–1880)

Prince Ernest Leopold
(1830–1904)
m
Marie Amelie
(1834–1899),
dr. of Grand-Duke
Leopold of Baden

Feodora
(1807–1872)
m
Ernest, Princ
of Hohenlohe
Langenburg
(1794–1860)

Victoria, Crown
Princess of
Prussia,
afterwards the
German
Empress
Frederick
(1840–1901)
m
Crown Prince of
Prussia
afterwards the
German Emperor
Frederick III
(1831–1888)

KING EDWARD VII
(1841–1910)
m
Alexandra
(1844–1925)

Alice
(1843–1878)
m
Louis, Grand-
Duke of Hesse-
Darmstadt
(1837–1892)

Alfred, Duke of
Edinburgh
Duke of Saxe-
Coburg
(1844–1900)
m
Grand-Duchess
Marie of Russia
(1853–1920),
only dr.
Alexander II

Helena
(1846–
m
Prince
of Sch|
Holste
(1831

See Royal
House of
Hohenzollern

Albert Edward
(b.1864)

George
(b.1865)

Louise
(b.1867)

Victoria
(b.1868)

Maud
(b.1869)

Victoria
(b.1863)

Eli|
(b.

Charlotte Sophia of
Mecklenburg-Strelitz
(1744–1818)

Ernest, Duke of Cumberland King of Hanover (1771–1851) *m* Frederica of Mecklen- burg-Strelitz (1778–1841)	Adolphus, Duke of Cambridge (1774–1850) *m* Augusta of Hesse- Cassel (1797–1889)	three other sons and six daughters

:iningen

⟨,	George, Duke of Cambridge (1819–1904)	Augusta (1822–1916) *m* Frederick, Duke of Mecklenburg- Strelitz (1819–1904)	Mary Adelaide (1833–1897) *m* Francis, Duke of Teck (1837–1900)
Hanover ⟩8)			
rincess of enburg ⟩7)			

e Victor, t Gleichen –1891)	Adelaide (1835–1900) *m* Frederick of Schleswig- Holstein-Sonderburg- Augustenburg (1829–1880)	one other brother and sister
a Seymour Admiral -eorge Seymour		

Augusta Victoria
m
William II,
German Emperor

ise .8–1939)	Arthur, Duke of Connaught (1850–1942) *m* Louise of Prussia (1860–1917)	Leopold, Duke of Albany (1853–1884) *m* Helen of Waldeck (1861–1922)	Beatrice (1857–1944) *m* Prince Henry of Battenberg (1858–1896)
quis of Lorne e of Argyll 5–1914)			

THE ROYAL FAMILY TREE

Ernest ⟩6)	Frederick William (b.1868) (b.1870)	2 others

Prince William of Prussia, 1866, outside the Neues Palais.

From the Queen   OSBORNE, APRIL 21, 1866

You will I know like to hear about Prince Teck, who came here yesterday evening, and leaves by the Messenger's boat today. I must say he is very nice and amiable, thoroughly unassuming and very gentlemanlike and certainly very good looking. His profile (only with a much better mouth) is like his cousin Sanny, and his colouring and eyes are like Uncle Alexander Mensdorff's. The eyes are very fine with a pleasant, kind expression. I should not think he was very clever but still he is very sensible and all he said to me about Mary (and he spoke very openly) showed me that he knows her character, her fine qualities and her faults, and is attached to her and knows what he undertakes. I think we must be thankful to have got such a person into the family, who evidently is most anxious to be civil and kind and sensible. He was very civil to Christian and naturally they were thrown a good deal together. I do wish one could find some more black eyed princes and princesses for our children! I can't help thinking what dear Papa said that it was in fact a blessing when there was a little imperfection in the pure royal descent and that some fresh blood was infused. In Prince Teck's case this is a very good thing and so it is in Christian's—only I wish his mother had been dark for that constant fair hair and blue eyes makes the blood so lymphatic. Dear Alix has added no strength to the family. If only for Affie (if he does not choose Elizabeth Wied) one could find some dark eyed, handsome and amiable Princess in a mediatized house!— someone who he would really fall in love with. Can't you find him one? I must end for today my somewhat odd letter, but it is not as trivial as you may think for darling Papa— often with vehemence said "we must have some strong dark blood" and really all the Protestant Royal Families are related again and again.

From the Queen   OSBORNE, APRIL 25, 1866

I am much pleased and touched that the dear, new baby (and long may she remain the baby!) is to be called after me, as I cannot deny that it pained me very much that four children were born without one being called after either of your parents. However I know that you could not help that. I love my poor old name, though so sad a blight has fallen on her who bears it, but it was my precious Mother's name and is one which I know the people love here, and which I hope will at any rate be recollected hereafter as one of peace and love, and as united for ever to a great and blessed one, who will live ever more.

The state of affairs is very alarming still, for I am certain that monster leads on to war, even when peace is seemingly within one's grasp! The best news was Fritz's saying that Bismarck was really very ill. May he remain so!

Alluding to Prince Arthur's confirmation, the Queen writes:

Dear Boy! he is so good, and innocent, so amiable and affectionate that I tremble to think to what his pure heart and mind may be exposed! There is no blemish in him, no fault like there was in poor Affie—no falsehoods and want of principle, nothing but real goodness! Oh may God keep him so and may he at least wear "the lily of a blameless life".

From the Queen   OSBORNE, APRIL 25, 1866
Here are copies of the King's two letters. I leave it to you to say what you think of them![1]

From the Queen   OSBORNE, APRIL 28, 1866
I hope you will ask Louise to be god-mother too; she nearly cried when she heard Arthur (two years her junior) had been asked and, as she is very sensitive, thinks no one likes her (and Alice makes such a fuss with her). I should be very sorry if you overlooked her. She is decidedly cleverer

---

[1] These were the answers to the Queen's letter quoted on page 68. Clarendon, when he read them, told the Queen that "in nothing is his Majesty's power of deluding himself more strongly displayed than in his belief that he is not influenced by his Minister". *Letters of Queen Victoria*, Second Series, Vol. I, page 321.

(odd though she is) than Lenchen and has a wonderful talent for art.

From the Crown Princess   NEUES PALAIS, APRIL 28, 1866
Dark-eyed Princesses I know none. The mediatized families I know almost all, the most of their number being queer sorts of creatures in mind and body, and very little use—Salm-Salm, Hohenlohe, Wittgenstein, and many of them Roman Catholics. By the time Affie means to lead a settled life and to marry—there may be some more grown-up stock. Princess Louise of Sweden is fair—but her family, on the father's side, are very dark—and that might reappear in a future generation. It is a great pity that Sanny's charming daughter is a Greek—she would do so well.[1]

From the Crown Princess   NEUES PALAIS, MAY 1, 1866
Many thanks for the copies of the King's letters. They made me quite sad. I think the tone is very nice; it touched me, because I know he felt what he said. But the *exposé* he gives of his policy is a mess indeed; it is the often repeated, illogical, inconsistent confusion—which he has reasoned himself (or been reasoned into by others) into believing all right. I know it all by heart, and you will see by it how useless it is to combat the errors it contains, how hopeless to expect he will ever see things in their true light. I do not think it will do any good now your writing again to him—indeed I almost regretted your last letter, fearing it would not be in the least understood. It is so difficult to know in England exactly how matters stand here and events and phases of policy change so often, rapidly and suddenly that by the time a letter arrives it is no longer to the purpose. Things look blacker and more threatening than ever till yesterday when a telegram arrived which revived one's hopes of peace again. Bismarck is "dangerously well" again, and his audacity rises with his spirits.

---

[1] The Crown Princess refers to the Greek Orthodox Church. The daughter in question married King George I of the Hellenes in the following year.

From the Queen   BUCKINGHAM PALACE, MAY 5, 1866

Affairs look worse and worse. God grant that wickedness will not prevail—but one knows not what to say. But
the sin of their provocation and the vaunting of what is
going to be done (if war does break out) will be upon the
heads of B. and the K.! My letter was written solely by my
own wish—and on the spur of the moment and because I
could not, *pour l'acquit de ma conscience*, remain a passive
spectator of the horrible sin of shedding so much innocent
blood gratuitously—without at least lifting up my voice
against it as a friend of the poor deluded King!

From the Queen   WINDSOR CASTLE, MAY 9, 1866

I see what anxiety you are in, and I can do nothing!
I and the Government (and Lord Clarendon behaves
extremely well) have done all we can, but the Emperor N.
will do nothing—and he could! This is very distressing!
But what is to be done? I hope against hope—and have a
sort of feeling as if after all war would not break out—but
still one knows not why. This state of suspense is fearful.
I wish Fritz would be firm and say he refuses to take part in
such an iniquitous war! It would raise him in the eyes of
all the world.

Poor Alice writes in terrible trouble. I fear it may hurt
her.[1] Poor child, it really is terrible for her now! How
thankful I am that Lenchen at least will never be exposed
to these dreadful eventualities! I wish I had you all safely
established here!

From the Crown Princess   NEUES PALAIS, MAY 9, 1866

Here all is in the greatest excitement and confusion.
I hardly see my Fritz who has so much to do now—his corps
is "mobil". I sit and cry all day (not very useful or very
sensible) but what every other poor wife, mother and
daughter is doing at Berlin. I sleep badly in consequence

---

[1] Her third daughter was born in July. Hesse-Darmstadt sided with
Austria against Prussia.

and my nerves are rather shaky. How can it be otherwise with such a prospect before one?

The poor, well-meaning but mistaken and short-sighted wretch who shot at Bismarck is dead. It is better so—better that he should live to see what the consequences of his reckless madness is than that he should die a martyr pitied by all. "Vengeance is mine saith the Lord" and that I believe, and I think it a pity that poor creature did not think of that before he sacrificed his own life and committed a sin! The temptation is great.[1]

The Queen is gone to Baden for a short time, which I thank God for; she was so irritated and excited that she vented it on whoever came near her and especially on me, and every time I saw her I have been quite ill after—my knees shaking and my pulse galloping. It is a little early for me to stand scenes as yet, and it seems the Queen must make them to relieve herself; so I am thankful that I shall be left in peace for a little from that quarter at least. You will laugh at the catalogue of my troubles which to stronger-minded people than I am would appear so small. The *coups d'épingle* are very depressing sometimes.

From the Queen WINDSOR CASTLE, MAY 12, 1866
I write today to say how constantly my thoughts are occupied with you both (you and Alice) and the awful prospects of a war—which is in fact a civil one. The poor, innocent, peaceable inhabitants don't wish to cut one anothers' throats, and how they will hate those who have driven them to it!! I can't quite agree that it is better that B. was not shot. Here people think it was got up on purpose and don't believe that the man really tried to shoot B.— else why did he not succeed? What will be the end of it all? I am deeply grieved to hear by your dear letter of 9th that

---

[1] On 7 May Bismarck was shot while walking along Unter den Linden after seeing the King. His assailant was Ferdinand Cohen, step-son of Karl Blind, the extremist who was a German exile living in England. He fired five shots, but their effect was weakened by the muzzle of the gun being embedded in Bismarck's coat. Cohen cut his throat immediately afterwards.

you are so worried and distressed, and full of troubles and anxieties. Put your trust in God! Pray and trust in him, pour out your troubles to him, as I do mine and you will find yourself strengthened and supported to bear the heavy, heavy trials—which are oppressing you. It wrings my heart to think of you and to be unable to help you! And that your own Father-in-law should be the cause of this is indeed terrible. The poor Queen is much, much to be pitied, but I can well imagine how trying she must be to you, knowing myself so well what it is to be irritated and worried by people when I am weak, low and nervous, and knowing what a comfort it is to have about you kind, calm, soothing people and I fear you have not this in your servants even—for devoted though Hobbsey is—she is a violent-tempered woman.[1]

From the Crown Princess   NEUES PALAIS, MAY 16, 1866
The King's adoration for B. grows every day; he told us he did not go to the theatre on the day B. was shot at (who by the way wears a breast-plate of silk and wadding which seemed to have saved his life!)

From the Queen   WINDSOR CASTLE, MAY 16, 1866
Your dear, sad letter of the 12th went to my heart. Oh! my darling! could I but clasp you in my arms and shield you from all grief and sorrow! Oh! if adored Papa was still near us, all this would never have happened. I am convinced of that! Since that dreadful 14th of December '61 we are as sheep without a shepherd. Then on the 10th of last December followed the loss of beloved Uncle Leopold and now there is no longer any one sovereign or statesman in Europe left whose opinion, whose wisdom and calmness can any longer have any effect. God leaves us to ourselves and we must work hard to fight the good fight. Lord Clarendon (who really behaves uncommonly well) has advised me to

---

[1] Mrs. Hobbs—the nurse to the Crown Princess's children.

write the letter (which I enclose) to Fritz, and which I ask Fritz to show to the King. I was asked to write another appeal to the King, but that, I and Lord C. felt would be utterly useless—and therefore I abstain and have written the letter to Fritz which you will see.

You will be pleased and interested to hear that there is every reason to hope that the Royal Academy is going to come to South Kensington and to build there! This would be a great triumph and a very great satisfaction.[1]

The state of affairs being so critical I have been obliged to give up for the present going to my beloved Balmoral, which is a terrible annoyance to me as I require rest and quiet so very, very much. I am going to spend my poor sad birthday here and on the 26th we shall all go for 10 days to Cliveden which the dear Duchess of Sutherland has kindly lent me, so that I shall be away from here during the noise and turmoil of Ascot. In case I should not be able to write to Sophie Dobeneck myself (which I still hope to do) say how much interest I take and ever shall take in her welfare and happiness for I know how devoted she has been to our dear grandchildren and that I send her a tea-set for her new home—which I hope she will often use. It is Stafford-shire.

From the Queen   WINDSOR CASTLE, MAY 19, 1866
I must say I think Uncle E. ought never to have asked for a command! He might have agreed to neutrality—for that might be necessary, but to change colours I cannot think right.[2]

Imagine that suddenly the most atrocious calumnies

---

[1] Both the Royal Academy and the National Gallery were at this time in Trafalgar Square. The removal of one would have enabled the other to expand. Parliament decided that the Gallery should stay and the Academy move. In the event the Academy did not, of course, move to Kensington.
[2] The Duke of Saxe-Coburg had done his best to persuade the King of Prussia not to go to war with Austria, but his fighting with Prussia was generally criticised—though perhaps less criticism was heard when Prussia was victorious.

have been spread of poor Christian—that he was a lunatic, had 15 children—one of whom was going to live with Lenchen. Another report is that the King of P. had written to warn me, and that the marriage is going to be broken off and the people in the shops all ask if it is true! Poor Lenchen is much vexed and annoyed at it, though as General Grey says it is utterly contemptible. Still why, Oh! why is the world so wicked? I can't really understand it.

From the Queen   WINDSOR CASTLE, MAY 25, 1866
This afternoon I am going to give a tea to all the servants' families in the Orangery—and they will dance a little afterwards—the first time since five years that I have allowed anything of this kind, but for dear Lenchen's last unmarried birthday (which ever seems so sad to me) and being here I wished to do it.

From the Crown Princess   NEUES PALAIS, MAY 19, 1866
We hear nothing talked of all day but war and preparations for it. The command which Fritz has received is very fine and very honourable—but a most difficult one; he will have almost exclusively Poles under him who you know are not so pleasant as Germans. He is busy forming his staff —and has been lucky enough to get some very good officers.[1]

Mary C. has not written to us yet. You know they call her marriage the "Polly-Teck-nic" marriage.

*   *   *

Sometimes from the superior heights of the Twentieth Century we tend to look on the little graves of Victorian infants as the symbols of momentary sorrow for parents, soothed by the numerous children still remaining to them but the Crown Princess's letter telling her mother of the death of her son Sigismund shows that such a point of view is but superficial.

---

[1] He was in command of the Second or Silesian Army—nearly 120,000 men. General von Blumenthal (1810–1900) was his chief of staff.

From the Crown Princess   NEUES PALAIS, JUNE 19, 1866

Your suffering child turns to you in her grief, sure to find sympathy from so tender a heart—so versed in sorrow. The Hand of Providence is heavy upon me. I have to bear this awful trial alone without my poor Fritz.

My little darling, graciously lent me for a short time to be my pride, my joy, my hope is gone—gone where my passionate devotion can not follow, from where my love can not recall him! Oh spare me the details—spare me telling you how—and when—and where my heart was rent and broken; let me only say that I do not murmur or repine. God's will be done.

What I suffer none can know—few know how I loved! It was my own happy secret—the long cry of agony which rises from the inmost depth of my soul reaches Heaven alone.

I wish you to know all—you are so kind, darling Mama —that you will wish to know all about the last terrible days —I cannot describe them.

I am calm now—for Fritz's sake and my little ones'— but oh! how bitter is the cross.

I kiss your dear hands and wish I could be in your dear arms.

Your broken hearted child
Victoria

Look at sweet little Beatrice—and think if you had seen her as I saw my precious angel—and you will feel what I am now going through.

Prince Sigismund, who was not quite two, died from meningitis— rather suddenly on 16 June. Full details were sent to the Queen by Wegner and Hedwig Brühl. The British Ambassador, who attended the funeral, contrasted the melancholy event with the brilliant gathering at Potsdam only four weeks earlier for the christening of Princess Victoria. He was greatly struck by the sight of "Papa" Wrangel—the octogenarian Field Marshal—bareheaded in attendance on the little coffin.

Queen Victoria, sometimes regarded as a rather Roman mother, was most painfully distressed. To begin with—before the news came—she was anguished by thinking of the Crown Princess alone at Potsdam, the war having started. On 13 June she writes:

Beloved Child, my heart is very heavy in thinking of you, my own poor Darling—left with your dear little ones at Potsdam. Oh! it is shocking, wicked, awful to have brought all this about. Fearful will the retribution be!

The news of Prince Sigismund's death reached her at Balmoral. Her letter on hearing the news has not been kept. On the day of the funeral she wrote "Oh could I but have you in my arms But I am ever with my precious child in thought and prayer." It was during this time that John Brown pleased her with a simple expression of his loyalty. She wrote in her journal that she was in great trouble about the Princess Royal, and Brown said to her, "I wish to take care of my dear good mistress till I die. You'll never have an honester servant."[1]

The letters for the next few weeks are completely occupied by the death of the Crown Princess's child, though the Queen continues her invective against Prussia for its "monstrous behaviour" in starting the war with Austria. Writing from Windsor Castle on 7 July 1866 the Queen gives a short description of Princess Helena's wedding. She says:

Lenchen looked extremely well, and so did Christian, but certain relations (an old Aunt especially) made one uncomfortable.[2] Bertie was very amiable and kind. There were great crowds and great enthusiasm. How I wished to have had dear Fritz by me! I never was so alone. Thank God he is safe, and I am pleased and proud to hear him praised, though you will not be angry if I say no more. I only pray it may stop now.

---

[1] *The Empress Brown* by Tom Cullen, The Bodley Head, 1969.
[2] The wedding took place on 5 July. The Aunt is the Duchess of Cambridge.

From the Crown Princess   HERINGSDORF,[1] JULY 9, 1866
What do you say to all these dreadful battles? Are you not a little pleased that it is our Fritz alone who has won all these victories? You know how hard I tried to help in preventing the calamity of war, and how Fritz did too, but now it is there I am thankful to think that our cause under Fritz's leadership has been victorious!

From the Queen   OSBORNE, JULY 11, 1866
I fear this great victory, which I think of doubtful happiness to you all—has been most dearly bought.[2]
Dear Fritz himself wrote to me for my birthday that success would be almost as bad as defeat—for the sacrifices it would cost and the difficulties it would entail.

From the Queen   OSBORNE, JULY 14, 1866
Though I can't rejoice at the defeat of the poor Austrians, I do at dear Fritz's conduct—and feel proud of him. I only wish it was all in a better cause and against real enemies and not against brother Germans.
I think with your elastic spirits after a time you will be quite gay again—though with a more serious tinge. God knows! my loss has so completely crushed everything and the work I have is so herculean that I wonder how I can live, but I do and can even be cheerful and take more interest and cry much less than I used to do—but to me this is a great grief.

From the Crown Princess   HERINGSDORF, JULY 16, 1866
Referring to her sorrow over the death of her child, the Crown Princess says:

---

[1] On the Baltic.
[2] The Prussian triumph over Austria at Königgrätz or Sadowa was fought on 3 July. The Prussians lost 9,000 men.

I so often think of what Shakespeare makes Constance say in King John.[1]

You know I consider the war a mistake caused by the uncontrolled power of an unprincipled man, that I have no dislike to the poor Austrians in general and that therefore I really can speak impartially. I assure you that if the rest of Europe did but know the details of this war—the light in which our officers and men and our public at large have showed themselves—the Prussian people would stand high in the eyes of everyone, and I feel that I am now every bit as proud of being a Prussian as I am of being an English-woman and that is saying a great deal—as you know what a John Bull I am and how enthusiastic about my home. I must say the Prussians are a superior race as regards intelligence and humanity, education and kind-heartedness and therefore I hate the people all the more who by their ill-government and mismanagement etc. rob the nation of the sympathies it ought to have. My affection to it is not blind but sincere—for I respect and admire their valuable and sterling good qualities.

I know quite well that they can be unamiable and make themselves distasteful (there is no disputing but that they have their little absurdities etc.) but at heart they are excellent, and the amiable, engaging Austrians commit cruelties and barbarities which make one's hair stand on end. Fritz said he never could have credited it had he not been a witness to it himself. It is their bad education and their religion I suppose. Oh! may the war soon cease it is so horrible. I have lost so many acquaintances!

I send you a photo of Miss Victoria—it is not at all favourable she is such a dear, pretty, little thing and so lively; she crows, laughs and jumps and begins to sit up and has short petticoats. If I was not continually reminded

---

[1]
        "Grief fills the room up of my absent child,
        Lies in his bed, walks up and down with me,
        Puts on his pretty looks, repeats his words,
        Remembers me of all his gracious parts,
        Stuffs out his vacant garments with his form;"
        King John, Act III, Scene IV.

of what we have lost I should enjoy her so much and be proud of her too. I fancy she will be bright and not a little "silly" like Ditta—who has been awfully naughty for the last week. She is a most difficult child to bring up, if she were not so stupid and backward her being naughty would not matter. She is at this moment very pretty.

From the Queen   OSBORNE, JULY 18, 1866

I have excellent accounts from dear Lenchen from Paris. All but the heat which is such as to almost prevent them going about. The Emperor visited her. The Empress only returns from Nancy tomorrow. Yes—Lenchen is fortunate indeed, I think, to be able to live in this blessed and peaceful land, safe from all wars and troubles. I miss her very much for it is not only the help but the power of telling her everything which is such a great comfort. She was quite invaluable during the Ministerial crisis when I was so exhausted from the heat and the worry I could often do nothing but lie on my sofa, and she saw General Grey for me and told him many things which no one else could —and helped (poor child) in arranging everything for her own wedding. She really was admirable in her entire unselfishness and anxiety for me—forgetting herself. She was so full of confidence in Christian—and certainly (though I wished he looked younger, for he really looks older than dear Papa did at 42) now that your sisters have no beloved Father and now that they are to live here—it is far better that he should be as old as he is.[1]

From the Crown Princess   HERINGSDORF, JULY 20, 1866

Fritz praises Colonel Walker so much and seems great friends with him, and gives him an opportunity of judging all that goes on in order that you may know.[2] His reports go to the War Department and Uncle George—but I hope

---

[1] They started married life at Frogmore in Windsor Great Park, moving six years later to Cumberland Lodge in 1872.

[2] Sir Charles Walker (1817-94). He was at this time military attaché at the Berlin Embassy.

they are sent to you or at least General Grey to read. I am so anxious you should know the part Fritz has taken as the newspapers only mention Fritz Carl which is not fair, as my Fritz has the largest share of all the difficulties and ought to have the most glory.

From the Queen   OSBORNE, JULY 21, 1866
    I fear I must end today as my head is like a lump of lead. I have too much anxiety, too much worry and work, and I miss Lenchen terribly as I can't speak *à coeur ouvert* to Louise (though she does her best) as she is not discreet, and is very apt to take things always in a different light to me.

From the Queen   OSBORNE, JULY 28, 1866
    How could dear Fritz believe or even think I would ask Bertie or Affie to give away Lenchen! If dear Papa and Uncle Ernest were not there I was the only one to do it, and even if Uncle Ernest had come I was determined to do it, as you know. I never would let one of my sons take their father's place while I live! But it is a monstrous invention —like everything else printed at that time.[1]
    What you say of the children's remarks is wonderful— and painful for you. But it is not right in you, dear child, to say you would give up everything, "home, them all" to get little Siggie back. That is really wrong, dearest child! It is tempting providence. Think what is a child in comparison with a husband. Oh! pray don't say or think it—for it is not right.

From the Crown Princess   HERINGSDORF, JULY 31, 1866
    Many thanks for your dear note containing the copy of poor dear Alice's letter which is so distressing. What can I do? Nothing! I have no control or influence over anything of the kind—and have for obvious reasons always avoided

---

[1] The marriage took place in the chapel of Windsor Castle, and the bride was given away by the Queen. This gave rise to the rumour abroad that, owing to their disapproval of the marriage, the bride's brothers declined to give her away.

mixing up any of my family feelings or interests with politics; and I think you will say I am right. The most painful and distressing position darling Alice is in is one of the unavoidable results of this dreadful war. I foresaw not only this but every other sort of sad consequence from it, therefore I tried all I possibly could to prevent it but without any result. I am quite unable by writing to Fritz or the King to prevent the occurrences which are so disagreeable and unpleasant for her, poor dear. I cannot say how it grieves me![1]

Many thanks for your dear letter which arrived yesterday, but I am much grieved to see that from the few words I dropped on the subject of my grief you should have received so false an impression of my state of mind! From the very first moment I felt that it was my duty to try and reconcile myself to what had happened, and I do not think I have ever unduly given way to my sorrow or let it stand in the way of any of my duties, or tormented other people with it. The nature of that sorrow none can judge but myself and, when I said I would willingly give up the house and home to bring my child back, I think I was expressing a most natural feeling and not in any way rebelling against my fate—and I am sorry it seemed otherwise to you, but I will in the future not mention it again, and reproach myself for having let my pen run on just as my thoughts did without reflecting on the impression it would produce on you—who have not seen me since my affliction. I also wish to say that I would not for the world dwell on the last day and last moment as you seem to suppose. I would allow no picture—no representation of any kind to be made. But to witness as I did for five days those most frightful convulsions has given me a shock which is not so easily overcome. I start up in the night with those images before me which by day I try to banish from my recollection. So, dear Mama, do not reproach me with grieving at God's will etc. and please do not fancy me in an unwholesome state of mind,

---

[1] The Prussians over-ran the Grand Duchy which had taken up arms for Austria.

for I feel far from it. From afar things sound and seem so different to what they really are.

From the Queen   OSBORNE, AUGUST 1, 1866
Sympathy with the poor King of Hanover's methods of government I have none, but I hope that for the sake of the honour of Prussia he will not be too harshly treated! He really had no time left him to decide, when his kingdom was occupied, and I trust he will be placed in a *convenable* and comfortable position whatever happens. There is a strong feeling here about it. I won't write to the King and Queen about it, but I mention it to you and Fritz.[1] The riots in London have I hope ceased, but they were very unpleasant.[2] Some of the new Government are clever, distinguished people—amongst others Sir S. Northcote, who worked under dear Papa for the Great Exhibition and he spoke with such emotion of him, and with such admiration and true appreciation that I was quite touched by it.

From the Queen   OSBORNE, AUGUST 4, 1866
I quite understand that you can do nothing for poor Alice or anyone and I think you are quite right, but how dreadful it is! I have had to write to Fritz about Hanover and today I sent him a letter from poor Ada.[3] I cannot refuse sending the letters *pour l'acquit de ma conscience* and I know that dear Fritz will do what he can. I expect no more.

---

[1] George V (1819–78) King of Hanover. He was the son of King Ernest Augustus, Duke of Cumberland and grandson of George III and therefore first cousin to the Queen. He was blind from boyhood, but sympathy for this affliction was diminished because of his reactionary and out-moded political opinions. He had a large private fortune, reported to be £1,500,000; this, with much of the jewellery inherited from George III, he transferred to England before joining the Austrians against Prussia. The question of his rights and property in Hanover, which he never renounced, remained an unsolved problem until, in 1913, his grandson married the Kaiser's only daughter. When the Queen speaks of the King having no time left to decide, she is probably referring to the time between the Prussian ultimatum and invasion in June.
[2] Demonstrations in Hyde Park and the West-end in favour of man-hood suffrage took place on 23 July.
[3] Niece of Queen Victoria, and married to the Augustenburg claimant.

Poor Alice was so worn—without news from Louis and knowing that fighting was going on that she has been quite ill, and Morier and J. Ely wrote quite anxiously about her. But she is better again, still I fear her nerves, which were already so terribly irritated after and before each child was born, will get worse and worse and it will be long before she recovers all she went through just in her confinement —poor child!

From the Crown Princess   HERINGSDORF, AUGUST 5, 1866
Writing of Prince Sigismund's death the Crown Princess says:

I was alone in that sorrow, was quite forlorn in the house as I had neither brother, nor father nor any male relation to make the arrangements for the funeral of which every detail I did myself—which falls to the lot of few women I think and in which I was of course quite in-experienced—the only guide I had was all I recollected of dear Grandmama's. Strange to say Mrs. Hobbs had never been at a death-bed and never mixed up in anything of the kind: but all that devotion can do she did, poor woman, but both she and all the maids and nurses so lost their heads that I thought they would not only go mad but drive me mad also; they quarrelled and fought and gave way to fits of passion and violence and also of grief—which I assure you were quite extraordinary. I had only G. von Normann to rely on—and he certainly behaved most admirably with the greatest tact and delicacy—and was always calm and collected. Hedwig and Valerie were touch-ing in their kindness and devotion. I shall never forget it as I was in a most helpless and painful position, and I had not one married woman about me. . . . How I wished I had had the Dean, or Arthur Stanley or Dr. McLeod with me or Professor Jowett.[1] I sent for the only clergyman I had the least confidence in—from Stettin—a good worthy man, full

---

[1] Benjamin Jowett (1817–93) Master of Balliol. A rather unexpected name as he was under suspicion of heresy at this time. The Crown Princess was proud of her friendship with him.

of courage, and a friend of Fritz's—as there is not one at Berlin who is not odious to me, and whose vulgarity is not repulsive at such a moment. I could not have stood that. You know most of the German clergymen are not gentlemen. If they are very good or very gifted one forgets that —but if not their society is really unbearable.

I am boring you with all this I fear but as you talk of my having borne my trials well I mention some of the minor ones—which made themselves much felt. How kind of you to say so—you cannot think what a word of approbation from you is to me! What I most cared for in all the world was a word of praise or a look of satisfaction from darling Papa; I used to feed on it for days in my heart. Now a word from you has the same cheering, encouraging influence and repays me for oh! so much, so I kiss your dear hand in deep and tender thanks for those words. I have no right to be satisfied with myself in general. I know all my failings, weaknesses and shortcomings, and bitterly reproach myself with giving way to them so often—because my feelings are so impetuous and my imagination so lively —that I pray God to help me to get the better of them more and more as He has helped me to bear the heavy, heavy burden now laid upon me, and I know that whatever leads to improve oneself must be accepted with gratitude be it even suffering and sorrow! To have your approval, dearest Mama, is and must be a very great satisfaction to me.

Pray do not think harshly of dear Alice.[1] She has so many excellent qualities—she is a little too impetuous and says too freely what passes through her head—but that is all. When she grows older, that will soften more I am sure. I think it is more irritability of nerves. I would have nobody's rights upset and yet have the present state of things cease. That this is not Bismarck's ideal (and much less the King's) with his spirit of military despotism you know—but the majority of the Prussian people are of my

[1] On 1 August the Queen wrote "Poor Alice! She has done herself such harm. She has become so sharp and bitter, and no one wishes to have her in their house."

opinion I know. What is going to happen I am quite ignorant of.

From the Queen OSBORNE, AUGUST 8, 1866

The Queen is writing of Fritz:

Everyone speaks in such love and admiration of him, and the admirable behaviour of the troops under Fritz—which is strongly contrasted with Fritz Carl and his *armée corps*. Fritz Carl is said to have been unfeeling and overbearing but we know what Fritz Carl is.

Alice is looking very ill, J. Ely told me; so thin and drawn; sleep and appetite have failed. The poor Hessians were actually in want of food. Louis lived for three days on nothing but a bit of brown bread and slept in the open field for six nights. All this for nothing—it is disheartening.

From the Crown Princess   HERINGSDORF, AUGUST 10, 1866

He (Fritz) thanks you for your dear letter and the enclosure from Ada. No one feels all she says more than he does but he does not see how he can help the poor Augustenburgs in any way. About the King of Hanover he has received a letter from Uncle George, and the Grand Duke of Oldenburg comes here today to express the same wish. At this sad time one must separate one's feelings for one's relations quite from one's judgement of political necessities or one would be swayed to and fro on all sides by the hopes, wishes and desires expressed by those we would be sorry to grieve. It is one of the consequences resulting from this war. Nothing will or can ever shake Fritz's principles of sound liberalism and justice but you know by experience that one must proceed in the direction given by the political events which have come to pass.

Those who are now in such precarious positions might have quite well foreseen what danger they were running into; they were told beforehand what they would have to expect; they chose to go with Austria and they now share the sad fate she confers on her allies. Those who have taken our side or remain neutral are quite unharmed, for example Uncle Ernest, the Duke of Anhalt, the Grand Duke of

Mecklenburg etc. They all believed the untrue statement of Austria about the strength of her own forces and would not see that Prussia was likely to be victorious and so the poor things have broken their own necks. Oh! how cruel it is to have one's heart and one's head thus set at right-angles! A liberal, German-feeling, reasonable Prussian government would have prevented it all! But as it was not to be decided *à l'amiable,* as rivers of blood had flowed and the sword decided the contest, the victor must make his own terms and they must be hard ones for many! I cannot and will not forget that I am a Prussian but as such I know it is very difficult to make you or any other non-German see how our case lies. We have made enormous sacrifices and the nation expects them not to be in vain! I fear this is all the answer I can give you at present.

The Princess now goes on with her domestic difficulties telling the Queen that she thought she would manage very much better if she could have a lady superintendent under whom the governesses and her own ladies would work.

I should so much like to have a copy of the papers drawn up about the relative positions of governesses and lady superintendents, as I do not wish a repetition of what I went through with Sophie, who never left the children for one minute all day and directed their lessons which she understood nothing about—and did a deal of harm. I cannot and will not abandon all right of interfering with the children's education and must reserve to myself to judge of what they are to learn and who is to teach them and also of making remarks to the governess who has charge of them. It is very difficult here as the princesses were given up hand and foot to a countess or a baroness who had the unlimited control over everything—lessons, meals, dress, walks and all and answerable to the sovereign whoever he might be. This is the predicament here and I never could get it out of Sophie's head who was all that was good, honest, right-minded and —obstinate.

In my few, hurried lines I could not tell you what I intended and what I hope to be able to do now. You are so dear, so loving, so simple and warm-hearted that it goes to my heart to hear of all you went through alone! Well can I understand how terribly trying and harrowing for you it must have been to have to order all for the funeral, which is always so dreadful and so revolting to one's feelings, with your own darling, little child and do wonder how you could have gone through it without being seriously ill. But God certainly gives strength to bear what he sends, for else how could I be alive? He fits the back to the burthens though the poor back bends under the cross. But this terrible trial and affliction will leave blessed traces on you, my darling child—as I rejoice to see you even now are ready to accept and you will in time feel how it draws one up-wards, and how little it makes all the ordinary things of this world appear.

12th. You have improved so much within the last year and a half and I see in every letter how our own darling first-born's great mind and large heart develops itself more and more, and becomes more and more mature and en-larged, and more and more what our fondest hearts could wish. Now, dear darling, you know, if old Mama has a merit it is that of truth and the absence of all flattery and a tolerably quick and correct appreciation of character—therefore if I do say this, you know it is exactly what I feel and what it is; and therefore I also sometimes say what may not be palatable from the same sense of truth.

How proud adored Papa would have been of you. How proud of you he was and how dearly and tenderly he loved you! Oh! were he but here to give us advice and to tell us what to do now! Oh! he would have known how to make poor Germany happy and great. And you know and feel what he did. Oh! how much we talked over all those events day by day and hour by hour in '48. Little did I think to see it come to this! But Oh! if only Papa's great maxim of Prussia becoming Germany and a great German empire could be realised—and not merely a large Prussia with annexations and the exclusion of south Germany! Oh! if Fritz and the Liberals would only insist on this.

I should not have thought your women would have quarrelled and fought in that way—but women are uncontrollable and unmanageable, and it is too bad to think and see that in moments of trouble and trial they think of their own passion and jealousies and not of their duties and the good of those they serve. Yes, our good Dean but above all dear Doctor McLeod would have been a help and a comfort. He has such a heart, and such sympathy and love. Good Doctor Stanley is so cold,—and, to me, as if he were of no sex—though he is so good and clever and writes and preaches so beautifully.

You speak of sympathy and its power of soothing. There is one person whose sympathy has done me—and does me— more good than almost anyone's and that is good, honest Brown. You know him only as the active, careful, devoted and useful servant, but you do not know what a heart and head, what true, simple faith and sound sense and judgement there is in him. He has, when I have been very sad and lonely—often and often—with his strong, kind, simple words—so true, and so wise and so courageous done me an immensity of good—and so he would to anyone in sorrow and distress. I mentioned this to our good, warm and (under that rough exterior) kindhearted Dean and he says in a letter in answer to various things, which I asked him and wrote to him about, and alluding to my regretting almost that my grief was less poignant, less intensely violent—"It ought to be no matter of self-reproach that the first acute grief has given way to a settled, mournful resignation which is even a more lasting proof of the depth of affection. Nay it would itself be a state of mind intolerable to bear, especially when we are still obliged to perform our parts in life, did not one mode of God's help to us consist in throwing across our path some comforters who next to his own unseen help prove from their congenial natures and peculiar powers of sympathy most providential." To you, dearest child, who have a husband and who have many relations your own age (I have none or only those who are useless) this feeling of dreadful loneliness can never arise as it does with me, who see even my own children one after the other have divided interests which make me no longer the chief object of their existence; therefore to have one faithful friend near me— whose whole object I am—and who can feel so deeply for me and understand my suffering—is soothing and cheering to my poor heart. Oh! may you never, never know what it is to be so alone in heart, and to feel so desolate. No doubt you have been much separated but while you can still communicate your thoughts and feelings to one another and can get an answer—there is no real separation. But when all is still— no sign, no word, no power of communication, then it is that words and looks of sympathy do such good—even if they make your tears flow.

13th. Only this morning can I finish this long letter, for the blots and corrections in which I must beg pardon—but I have so little time to write undisturbedly that I have had to write *à plusieurs reprises*. I saw Sir A. and Wally Paget here on Friday. I thought him cross and wanting in tact in telling me as the only observation he made about the great events of the day "the Danes ought to be in good spirits now, as they will probably get back the Danish part of the Duchies; but the King has never given up the hope of having the Duchies back." Considering my known feelings and that our daughter has just married the brother of the lawful Duke it was a stupid, tactless thing to say. Wally was too frightfully dressed, with a gown far too much cut out, and a great leaf on the top of her head, but very sensible and amiable and very unhappy about Alix's going on—or at least going out so much in society, and people being so familiar with her in society. She wishes someone could tell them the truth.

I am sorry too for Bertie; I don't think she makes his home comfortable; she is never ready for breakfast—not being out of her room till 11 often, and poor Bertie breakfasts alone and then she alone. I think it gets much worse instead of better; it makes me unhappy and anxious.

From the Crown Princess

You are so fond of Tokay—and I have found some here by chance which is so very good—that I have got six bottles for you. If you will accept them, please telegraph to me so that I can send them without having to pay heavy duty.

I cannot tell you how heart-rending the sight of those poor men in the hospitals is! One died yesterday morning. I saw him, the night before, in his last agony—so sad to behold; I never shall forget the colour the poor creature was. He had a ball through the lung. There are three in the same ward who will follow him soon I fear—one of twenty-two and one of thirty. Poor victims they are so patient—some cheerful, some much depressed and shedding tears! Very few of the Austrians speak German—they are almost all Italians, Rumanians, Hungarians, Poles or Bohemians, small thin and dejected-looking—quite enjoying being taken care of. One or two Hungarians are very handsome. One of the hospitals here is very clean and nice but the other you must spare the description of. I can stand a great deal, out of philanthropy and patriotism, but two small wards I went into beat everything I have seen in the shape of disgustingness. Fritz says it was charming and tidy in comparison with what he was accustomed to in the little towns during the campaign! As excuse I must say the place is a coach-house—and not intended for such things.

You ask how Willy's tutor gets on? He is a good, excellent, trustworthy man, very good-natured, very methodical and not very bright, as matter-of-fact as possible. He eats with his knife and with his elbows on the table—this is not a crime—but I would rather Willy did not imitate it.[2] I hope before long to have a second tutor under him for the lessons, who will be more clever and enlightened and then, I fancy, we shall do very well. Nothing could be more honest and straightforward than

---

[1] Near the Bohemian Frontier.

[2] George Hintzpeter, who was appointed on the advice of Sir Robert Morier.

Willy's governor Monsieur de Schrotter, and that is a great thing.

From the Crown Princess

ERDMANNSDORF, AUGUST 27, 1866

You know the King and Queen never allow one to appear at Court on great occasions in black which I think so cruel. We can wear no mourning for my darling. It is foolish of me to care about such things—but I own it is a point on which I am easily wounded.

From the Queen   BALMORAL, AUGUST 28, 1866

Your descriptions of the poor wounded are very touching, and such sights are very useful and good for one. Anything that brings us closer to those beneath us—and makes us feel we are brothers and sisters—does one real good, and softens one's nature—besides teaching one lessons which do more good than anything else can do! But Oh! to think of the broken hearts as well as suffering! One great privilege is ours in our high positions, which I have often felt;—it is the happiness and the comfort, our kindness (be it ever so small) and sympathy give to the poor sufferers. To me there is nothing so affecting as to see a strong man in sorrow or in suffering! Far more so than to see a woman thus. We poor women are born to suffer, and bear it more easily, but a strong man laid low or in grief quite overcomes me.

From the Crown Princess

ERDMANNSDORF, SEPTEMBER 3, 1866

What you say about the comfort of a strong man's sympathy I understand quite well, particularly in your case; mine is so different. I think a woman's heart can better enter into my sorrow than a man's. A little child is more the object of a woman's tenderness than a man's; most of them can neither imagine nor understand it. But to comfort a widow in her great grief can be a man's vocation just as well as a woman's—and I can imagine that it is an element necessary for you.

From the Queen   BALMORAL, SEPTEMBER 4, 1866

In great confidence, for the letter was only written to me, I send you the copy of Uncle Alphonse's letter, thinking it might interest you to see a letter written by the other side.[1] Please return it. He seems to have suffered much.

Then as regards the King of H. do only try to get him a sufficient income to live upon abroad, for the Cambridges want *coûte que coûte* to establish him here—which would be perfect misery to me. That would make a most mischievous political clique. Affie (whom I am not at all pleased or happy about) is, I see, anxious about this, and would immediately try to marry the daughter—which would set him in enmity with Uncle Ernest—and I can't tell you what I should suffer! Affie makes me very unhappy; he hardly ever comes near me, is reserved, touchy, vague and wilful and I distrust him completely. All the good derived from his stay in Germany has disappeared. He is quite a stranger to me. Bertie, on the other hand, is really very amiable.

From the Crown Princess

ERDMANNSDORF, SEPTEMBER 11, 1866

Thanking for the letter from Count Mensdorff the Crown Princess writes:

On the subject of the letter I beg leave to make a few remarks. I have never dilated on the misdeeds of the Austrian soldiers or the conduct of their officers as I did not think it generous, and have no feeling of animosity towards them. But when I hear our officers and men thus spoken of, I must quote a few facts in return. First of all it is not true that the Austrians fought like lions. Fritz says it was a pitiful sight to see how they let themselves be caught at Königgrätz. Then their flight was not, as Uncle A. says, in rain and fog. Fritz says it was a splendid, clear night. They regularly ran away—panic had spread amongst them and, instead of retiring in order, it was an awful

---

[1] Alphonse Mensdorff-Pouilly—first cousin to Queen Victoria and the Prince Consort. He lived in Austria.

flight and that was one of the reasons why so many of them were drowned in the Elbe. They were unchivalrous enough to take prisoner one of our clergymen, two doctors and twelve women who came with provisions. We never would have thought of such a thing. The Prussian army is a body of well-trained, well-educated and thoroughly disciplined men, the Austrians are the very reverse—all sorts of different, half-barbarous nationalities jumbled together. That many of our men and some of our officers may have forgot themselves I do not doubt; they cannot all be angels and one cannot be answerable for all. But this is a fact that our army is (because composed of better elements) superior in behaviour and kindness and humanity to any other. Ask whom you like who has had an opportunity of seeing warfare in different countries.

The fate of Bohemia is terribly sad but people of the country hate their own soldiers worse than they do ours; ours pay for every trifle as long as they have anything left, theirs do not. The smallest theft found out committed by any of our soldiers is most severely punished. The account the Bohemians and Moravians gave Fritz of the behaviour of the Austrian officers is such that I cannot repeat it—the stories I know are too disgraceful. That the King's household expenses were not paid is a new Austrian lie, but as they spread so many and such gross ones it does not astonish me. They said it before so that the inn-keeper at Prague was obliged to contradict it in the newspapers.

It is true the King did not wish for war; his clique of bad advisers pushed him to it. The Emperor of Austria is blessed with a counterpart of this clique who push him and have pushed him to incur so many dangers and into so many disasters. But as the Austrian state is corrupt, and ours, in spite of bad government, benighted sovereigns and mischievous ministers, is not—it gained the victory; that is the explanation of the whole thing. The Austrians have long been going downhill, but have with a wonderful talent and subtlety succeeded in blinding the world at large and particularly the small German states to this fact; in the eyes of the governments of the small states, Austria kept its own prestige and has plunged its allies into all its own straits. I doubt not Austria will recover enough from this shock to keep, by exerting all its powers of intrigue and falsehood, its influence on the neighbouring states in the south of Germany—until some new facts convince these of their mistake in hoping for any good from that quarter.

You know I am not prejudiced. I am so partial to the Austrians I know, like their manners and dialect so much, and am so fond of our relations among them. I assure you I do not exaggerate. I will quote some more figures. We had forty-eight thousand Austrian prisoners alone, five hundred, unsurrendered officers. The Austrians had four officers and three hundred men of ours, counting the wounded too, two doctors, one clergyman and some camp-followers—not one trophy not one cannon. We had seventeen colour-standards, two hundred and fifty or more guns! With one single *corps d'armée* of Fritz's army (commanded by General Steinitz and most of the men Poles) we beat on three successive days three entire fresh Austrian corps—the elite of their troops commanded by their best generals. The Austrian wounded prayed and begged to be treated by our doctors as theirs were so rough and cruel. Many of the prisoners and wounded we have here are very sorry to go home. Anything to be compared to the organised system of spreading lies which they practice I never heard of—it beats the French and the Russians. For example all battles and engagements between the two armies before Koniggrätz were telegraphed to Vienna as Austrian victories!—so that the royal family of Saxony were profoundly astonished at receiving the following telegram from the Crown Prince after Koniggrätz—"terrible, bloody battle, totally beaten, lost beyond recovery. . . ." It is true that the Hanoverians fought very bravely but they were twenty-two thousand well-drilled and organised field-troops—against our six thousand men, who had only been in uniform a week—cavalry and artillery—only gathered together for the occasion out of the fortresses.

I must now end this long letter, returning Uncle Alphonse's with many thanks—none but Fritz having seen it. When you write to him say how I feel for him and Uncle Alexander please, and that I take great care of his countrymen in the hospitals. I have all their favourite dishes cooked in our kitchen for them—goulash for the Hungarians, and polenta and macaroni for the Italians. Only to show how kind Fritz is—he has equipped three young Austrian officer prisoners here from head to foot because their clothes were so worn. I lend them my newspapers and books, give them nosegays almost every day and mountains of cigars.

I quite agree with you about poor King George. I hope you will not have him. The Princesses and Queen are said to have become very fast, and it would be a misfortune if Alfred was to marry one of them. Their society is not desirable for Bertie and Alix.

From the Crown Princess

NEUES PALAIS, SEPTEMBER 22, 1866

With what feelings I returned here and to Berlin you can imagine, and how many bitter tears I shed. But the universal enthusiasm was cheering, as it was so spontaneous and I shared it with all my heart.[1] It must have been a great satisfaction to the King, and he made the best speech I ever heard from him at dinner, he really touched me; his manner had something so calm, and he seemed in the right frame of mind, also the Queen who was very kind again to me. Uncle Ernest at the head of his battalion was a fine sight and very gratifying; I am not accustomed to hearing so much praise of Coburg here, and I am very glad it is so and thankful for Affie's sake he is not among the crushed and beaten foe.[2] It is sad enough as it is to see so many of one's friends suffer from the effects of their miscalculation. The sight of Prince Hohenzollern and Leopold was very affecting to me. Altogether yesterday and the day before

---

[1] The Prussian Army, led by the King on horseback, entered Berlin in triumph on 20 September.
[2] Prince Alfred was the heir to the Duke of Saxe-Coburg; when the Crown Princess writes "he" she is referring to Uncle Ernest.

can only have served to strengthen the bonds between sovereign, royal family, army and people—and I am thankful for that as alas! so much is done to rend those bonds asunder. The beaming faces of our noble soldiers was touching to behold. The expressions of their faces I shall never forget, but what I miss on all great occasions over here in the throng is the hearty British cheer. In former days when you were the happiest sovereign on earth, how that cheer used to ring! The recollection of it echoes in my English heart and rings again and will do so until that heart has ceased to beat. The tones of "God Save the Queen"—give it whatever other name they choose will never convey another meaning to me than the heartfelt invocation of Heaven's blessing on your precious head and our dear English home beyond the sea—That is *plus fort que moi* and does not take away from my enthusiasm for this country.

From the Queen   BALMORAL, SEPTEMBER 24, 1866
     Though I only wrote to you a letter today, I must write again to ask you to tell Fritz that the long letter I write him is for him to show the King. It is written in consequence of Lord Augustus Loftus having written to say that there was some disposition to treat the unhappy King of H. kindly and generously—if he would take the initiative; but this is clearly absolutely impossible, as everyone here says, after the treatment he has met with. I have therefore written the long letter which goes by this messenger. If I can do anything to facilitate this painful negotiation I am ready to do it for I (nor you) cannot forget that the poor King represents, in the male line, our family, and the feeling here would be greatly roused against the King of P. if poor King George and his family, after being despoiled of their own lawful possessions, were left in poverty and in a position not befitting to their rank and near relationship to our family. The King of P. used to be kind hearted and generous, and ought to be the more so now when everything is in his power.

P.S. *25th September.*

It must have been a grand and touching sight that entry of your troops to Berlin. But mingled with sadness too—to think how many had suffered so cruelly. Now is the time when there should be magnanimity and generosity, for one can be kind and generous to a fallen foe! The King ought to feel this—if he has chivalry left in his nature.

How I understand your feelings about an English cheer. Now even the sound of it (though I have not been in any crowd since my misfortune) touches me to tears, and I always felt a lump in my throat when darling Papa and I were cheered, and warmly and heartily received as we always were.

From the Crown Princess

NEUES PALAIS, SEPTEMBER 28, 1866

May I request a favour? I am sending a young cook to England in the hopes you will let him have an opportunity of learning different things in your kitchen, and in the baking and confectionery department. Will you allow him to come to Windsor? He is called Carl Gödecke and is the fiancé of Mrs. Catt. The latter is going on leave of absence as she is not well. But I am sorry to say I am not at all satisfied with her in many respects—but please keep this to yourself. I have been really much distressed by the goings on in the house lately and I am sorry to say all owing to her habit of ruling everybody and everything and making no end to mischief.

Now about the King of Hanover. I cannot help thinking you have been misinformed; the King has treated him with every possible magnanimity and generosity personally. He has never taken any of his property away. His country has been conquered and is by right of conquest no longer his; my father-in-law cannot reinstate him. It is very sad that this has happened but it is a *fait accompli* and cannot be changed. I am certain that whatever can be done to make him comfortable—that is to say secure his immense fortune to him—the King will do but I hope you do not expect him to be replaced on his throne as it is an impossibility.

I hear he has bought or is going to buy a place near Vienna and said he did not wish to go to England and did not like England. Will you not make special enquiries as to how he has been treated? I think you will find that the King cannot be unchivalrous to a fallen foe.

The Crown Princess goes on to argue that the King of Prussia tried to persuade the King of Hanover to remain neutral:

but he was very difficult and tiresome and now that there is a chance of being rid of so bad a neighbour one should avail oneself of it. When once the sword is drawn other counsels vanish.

I cannot say how mortifying it is to one's feelings to think that all this should happen to one of our family. Poor, misguided man he brought this upon himself. You cannot know how great a feeling there is against the Hanoverian government in this country—much stronger than even the King's.

From the Crown Princess

NEUES PALAIS, OCTOBER 3, 1866

I am sorry to say that too many Englishwomen in the house together here do not do—they make themselves so hated by being so grand etc. (which they do not dream of as long as they are in England.) Thus the peace is impossible to be kept. Poor Mrs. Hobbs—in spite of her violence and her temper which she cannot help—usually ends by being reasonable, but the others are not only disobedient but get up a perfect clique of opposition to all that is ordered, and I could not allow them to go on particularly as I am left so much alone, Fritz's business engrossing him more and more and the household affairs falling more to my share. They did nothing but gossip, and quarrel and fight to spite one another and deceive me. Now I trust a new leaf is turned over and it will be all right.

From the Crown Princess

I took the opportunity of asking my father-in-law what he was going to arrange with the King of H., about his fortune, as you were anxious to see this arrangement comfortably made. His answer was "I have no idea of what the King of Hanover's expectation or wishes are he has not made any communication to the government and we cannot get any information out of him." Now as I understand you and General Grey, you think (as the King of H.'s letter during the war was returned unopened) it is our government that ought to invite the King of H. to come to terms and propose generous ones to him.

But as the sending of the letter was a totally irregular proceeding according to the rules of war, the King could not accept it. Moreover the King of H. will not abdicate, considers the Prussian incorporation of his kingdom as *non avenu*. How is the first step to be taken from here? Both with the Elector of Hesse and the Duke of Nassau the case stands quite differently. Fritz sends you this note of explanation in lieu of letter as he has not shown the King your letter. Fritz will write to you as soon as he knows something positive on the subject; he too wishes much that the King of Hanover may be treated with every possible generosity and *égarde* as to fortune and position, more especially as a member of your family, and feels certain his father can have no other intention towards him.

From the Queen   BALMORAL, OCTOBER 9, 1866

You speak of English maids not being grand in England. I assure you they are so—to an extent that is unbearable and that that is the bane of the present day. Pride, vulgar, unchristian pride in high and low.

From the Queen   BALMORAL, OCTOBER 14, 1866

After comparing her shattered life with the sorrow of her daughter:

All will still be very bright for you. I dislike to think I can live on, and yet I must and ought—and it is God's mercy to enable me to do. The dear old Baron's words I remember so well though I then thought they never could become true "you will get more accustomed to it—but you will never get over it".

Bertie is not going to St. Petersburg.[1] That odious, mischievous Queen Louise is coming to England!

From the Crown Princess

NEUES PALAIS, OCTOBER 16, 1866

We are so much disturbed and distressed at hearing reports, official and non-official, from all sides that dearest Charlotte is out of her mind. Of course I cannot believe such a thing unless I hear it from an authentic source, and I am sure if it was so you would know it and you would tell me, knowing how much I love her. Can you not give me any direct news by which I can contradict these reports? The King firmly believes them and everybody else here. The Prussian Minister at Rome has written all details and the Prussian Consul at Trieste. I find it in all the newspapers. Can she be seriously ill or what can have given rise to all this? It is said she is afraid of being poisoned, that she went unannounced to the Pope and ate her dinner dipping her bread into his soup plate, that she insisted on sleeping in the Vatican. That at Miramar[2] she ran furiously up and down the garden, that men keepers had to be fetched out of a lunatic asylum to take care of her, that the best doctors from these places have been summoned and that Philippe had been telegraphed for to take charge of her. The reasons for all this are alleged to be the unkindness of Leopold and Marie who are said to have refused to receive her at Brussels, and the Emperor N.'s refusals to all wishes she expressed about Mexico! The state of Mexico is said to be very sad. I do not think any of this is true but, as I tell you, everyone here believes it. I had two letters at Erdmanns-dorf from her—so kind and tender—saying that she hoped

---

[1] For the wedding of his sister-in-law with the Czarevitch.
[2] Miramar Castle near Trieste—the home of the Archduke Maximilian before he became Emperor of Mexico.

to see me somewhere or other before she went back. What has M. van de Weyer heard! What did Mr. Odo Russell[1] write about her stay at Rome? I think it all very strange and mysterious.

From the Queen   BALMORAL, OCTOBER 20, 1866
I told Lenchen to write to you about poor dear Charlotte whose state is too sad and dreadful, and grieves us deeply. So young, so handsome, and so clever! It is all that wretched folly of going to Mexico, which dearest Papa was so against that I think he would have prevented it, which has deranged her poor mind. She urged it, and she urged Max to go when he began to waver. And no doubt this and the failure of her attempts to procure assistance from France and elsewhere is the cause of this—added to fatigue and over-excitement.

From the Queen   BALMORAL, OCTOBER 22, 1866
I have nothing new to tell you of poor Charlotte, but I hope soon to hear again. It is dreadfully sad. And for poor Max it is really quite awful—for he is extremely fond of her. To my astonishment Bertie wishes to go to St. Petersburg, and the Government wish him to go as the Emperor of R. is so very desirous of it. Besides which poor Dagmar herself is so very anxious for it. So of course I did not object! Though I would have preferred his remaining quiet at home.

From the Crown Princess
                              OBERSCHLESIEN, OCTOBER 23, 1866
Only a few words today from this charming place of the Duke of Ratibor's[2] to say that I can hardly think of anything else than poor dear unfortunate Charlotte since your

---

[1] Odo Russell 1829–84. First Lord Ampthill. Representative of the British Government at Rome for many years.
[2] The Duke of Ratibor belonged to the Hohenlohe-Schillingsfürst family. He was brother to Prince Hohenlohe, the future Imperial Chancellor of Germany, and was one of the Crown Prince's circle of private friends. The Crown Princess was staying in Upper Silesia.

letter arrived last night in which you tell Fritz that all those dreadful reports are true! Oh how much better to be quiet at rest in one's grave than to live on deprived of one's reason—a torment to oneself and to others. Let us hope and trust that so dreadful a lot may not be hers. Fatigue and overwork may have excited her nerves to a great degree—and quiet can restore that I should think? She who was so quiet and self-possessed, so calm and serious and yet of cheerful disposition I cannot understand how such a thing could happen. I love her so much. I cannot tell you how grieved and shocked I am! I should not have been astonished if my brain had turned during the war and after my little one's death; often in the night I thought I should lose my senses, but you know what a sensitive, nervous, excitable, lively being I am with an imagination which is a burden to me at all times, but dear Charlotte whom I have never seen agitated, who indeed at times often appeared phlegmatic and inanimate, whose reason and caution was always above her years, what must she have suffered, what she must have gone through to come to that! Do pray give me some details. I would write to Philippe, but I think he would perhaps not like it, nor Leopold or Marie either—but if you think I might do so, please tell me. What would dearest Uncle have said—or the poor dear Queen? Thank God they are spared this greatest of sorrows!

From the Queen   BALMORAL, OCTOBER 28, 1866

I know nothing new about poor dear Charlotte except that Leopold hoped she was a little better. You are so exactly her own age and were such friends that I was sure you would be terribly distressed at this awful visitation. To me, like to you, it is incredible that this should happen to her! It is the greatest mercy that dearest Uncle has not lived to see this—as well as the poor dear Queen! I send you Leopold's last letter in case you would like to see just what he says. My imagination is also lively and, above all, I can conjure up alarms and worries and fancies about things at night and in the middle of the night, which in the morning vanish like smoke!

From the Crown Princess

The eternal Mecklenburg-Schwerins are here. One gets tired of those visits at last. The King is very kind to Fritz; he is quite changed since the war—his old kind nature has come out again; he is never cross or irritable. One can talk to him as one could years ago; it is a great comfort. Also with the Queen he seems to get on very well; he writes a great deal to her and talks most kindly of her. I wonder whether it is Bismarck's absence? I rather fancy so.

From the Queen   WINDSOR CASTLE, NOVEMBER 3, 1866

I am quite sick of George V and Uncle George teases me without end about it—I mean to leave it alone now.

From the Queen   WINDSOR CASTLE, NOVEMBER 12, 1866

I have just had a most affectionate and nice letter from dear Bertie from St. Petersburg in which he speaks so affectionately of you and all. Indeed I felt so differently on the 9th[1] to what I have done before and I thank God for it. He does send comfort where you often least expect it.

From the Queen   WINDSOR CASTLE, NOVEMBER 14, 1866

Dear Alix arrived here yesterday evening with her tiny little boys. She is dear and good and gentle but looking very thin and pale; but I think a little larger than last time. I was sometime alone with her yesterday evening and I shall take her out alone this afternoon. I have always longed to be able to do this but I never could.

What you tell me of Princess M. of Altenburg makes me quite shudder.[2] Of the three young people thought of for Affie we must thank God for the escape we had of two! The one, who looked fresh and blooming three years ago is dead![3] And the other turned out everything most

---

[1] The Prince of Wales's birthday.
[2] This letter has not survived, but the sense of what the Crown Princess had to say is tolerably clear. Princess Marie of Saxe-Altenburg married in 1869.
[3] Princess Anna of Hesse-Darmstadt, sister of Prince Louis.

undesirable. How often we see clearly that God knows, what is for our best—far better than we do ourselves. And now there is only Elizabeth Wied—as a Hanoverian is out of the question—left of those who have grown up, and I don't know if Affie has ever thought seriously of her! Unfortunately he is violently in love with Constance Grosvenor[1] —11 or 12 years older than himself—and this will keep him I fear from thinking of marrying which, however, is so very desirable. You mentioned to me some little while ago, the young Princess of Sweden, and I said I wished for no more northern princesses. Still, with the great difficulty there is to find anyone and with Affie's pride, we must not entirely exclude her—particularly as the Duchess of Roxburghe who saw her at Stockholm says she is not plain, promises to be nice looking and is very well brought up. Can't you enquire further about her?[2]

From the Crown Princess

NEUES PALAIS, NOVEMBER 16, 1866

I have just received your very dear letter of the 14th for which a thousand thanks. All you say about dear Alix gives me the greatest pleasure. I know she is not brilliant in mind or conversation, but I respect her and look to her as she is so thoroughly good, straightforward and unaffected, so equal in temper, so pure in mind. She hides under a little, stiff manner the kindest heart. I know how she deserves your love and how she values it, and I see with untold pleasure how Bertie and she are animated by the desire to do their duty to you and be agreeable to you. It is a thing so all important for all us children, for our beloved nation that the relations between you and them should be as affectionate as possible that I thank God with all my soul when I see that you are satisfied in that respect, and that their feelings are all they should be. All the wisdom

---

[1] Daughter of the Queen's friend, the Duchess of Sutherland, and wife of the first Duke of Westminster.
[2] Princess Louise (1851–1926) only child of Charles XV of Sweden and later wife of King Frederick VIII of Denmark.

and wit in the world is nothing compared to goodness; the older I get the more conscious of it I am. She will be more at home with Christian, I am sure, when she sees more of him, and sees what a good creature he is, and that, instead of his eclipsing Bertie and her in your affection, his presence and Lenchen's happiness only tend to make the family peace and unity increase.

You do not know how wicked people's tongues are. There is not a horror in Germany that is not told of Bertie, and how he and Alix are represented as a wretched couple and you as a most unhappy mother. Bertie is supposed to be much disliked in England. This is so much believed in society that it is quite tiresome. How glad I should be if you could, on some occasion when you write to my mother-in-law, drop a little word of your being pleased with Bertie and Alix. She has a great dislike of them and it often wounds me to hear the *mépris* with which she speaks of them. I fear Edward Weimar[1] and the Duchess of Hamilton[2] who live on retailing gossip of every kind do no good.

I will send you Fritz's description of the wedding[3] as soon as it is returned to me from the King. I fear the English and Prussian gentlemen have not scraped on together as well as possible; our dear people, who I am sure I love, do not understand English ways and manners, and when they are very civil expect the same in return, and when an Englishman means to be very civil—the Prussian does not take it in and is touchy and offended. It is too stupid. Of course in Germany I always take the part of the English-man—and in England I try to stick up for the German. But both are at present ungrateful offices.

---

[1] Prince Edward of Saxe-Weimar (1823–1902) nephew of Queen Adelaide and cousin to the Queen of Prussia. He was a naturalised Englishman and had a distinguished career in the British Army. He married Lady Augusta Gordon-Lennox.
[2] Marie (1817–88) daughter of the Grand Duke of Baden, cousin to Napoleon III, married 11th Duke of Hamilton.
[3] The Czarevitch, afterwards Alexander III, married the Princess of Wales's sister, Princess Dagmar, on 9 November.

From the Crown Princess

Prince Henry of Prussia was going on a visit to his grandmother at
Windsor.

I am sure you will like the poor child; he cannot help
being so ugly, and he is really not stupid and can be very
amusing. Lady Caroline must be kind enough to prevent
Bennett or Mrs. Catt from coming continually to see Henry
and sitting, for ever, gossiping with Georgina. Please forgive my bothering you with all these details which are in
fact not worth coming to your ears.[1]

I have not yet had an opportunity of mentioning a
great wish of mine to you viz. that you honour Monsieur
Geffcken the Minister of the Hanse towns with a conversation.[2] He is a friend of ours, a most excellent man—
clever and distinguished; he is a friend of the Baron's, of
Monsieur de Normann; he was at Bonn at the same time
as Fritz. If you want to be *au courant* of German politics
no one is better able to keep you well informed. He is the
object of the special spite of Bismarck—who persecuted him
until he was obliged to leave but the real motive of B.'s
dislike was that he was a friend of Fritz's. It is of great importance that he should get thoroughly acquainted with

---

[1] On this visit the boy said to one of the tutors to the English princes
"are you a soldier?" When the tutor replied "no", the child answered
"then you are a Regent Street swell". This phrase, which he picked
up from his nurse, was thought vulgar by his mother. No doubt he also
picked up chatter about Brown from the servants which explains this
passage in a letter from the Queen (8 December 1866)

> "I have never seen him cry but twice. First the evening he arrived
> when he was tired and then two days ago to my utter astonishment—
> when Brown came into my room, who was so pleased to see him and
> so kind and tender to children; I told Henry to shake hands with him
> which he did and then he made a face and began to cry!! He said I
> should not tell his Mama but I do, because I want just to know if he
> often does such a thing."

[2] Frederick Heinrich Geffcken (1830–96). He was at this time diplomatic representative of Hamburg in Berlin. He drafted the letter to
Bismarck when the Crown Prince came to the throne. He was subsequently charged by Bismarck with high treason for publishing part of
the Crown Prince's diary.

The Queen with Princess Louise and Princess Beatrice, October 1866, outside Balmoral.

The triumphal arch of coal erected at the Railway Station, Wolverhampton, in honour of the Queen's visit, December 1866.

England as at some future date I suppose Fritz will want his services. We shall miss him much at Berlin.

From the Crown Princess
I did not answer about the Princess of Sweden—you should not quite give up the idea should you? I hear she is growing up a nice girl and I can easily enquire more about her. Mrs. Grey[1] is sure to be able to tell Lady Caroline what she hears and sees of her, but I am afraid that Freddie thinks of marrying her.

A nice wife for Arthur would be Fritz Carl's eldest daughter;[2] she is such a good child with a gentle, amiable disposition and so reasonable, quite a mother to her little sisters and brother; she will have a very fine figure. Her hair is splendid which makes up for the head being somewhat turnipy in shape—which most German children's are. Elizabeth Wied is no doubt a most superior girl—but I am so afraid of the health of the family; the more I hear she seems to be the only healthy one. They have every species of disease in the family—only ask Christian. Heaven avert Alfred's taking one of the Princesses of Hanover. I thought they were so nice and alas! am quite *desillusionée*. They are grown very pretty I believe.

From the Queen   WINDSOR CASTLE, DECEMBER 1, 1866
The Queen is describing her visit to Wolverhampton to unveil a statue of the Prince Consort.[3]
Yesterday was a very gratifying day—although most trying and painful to go as formerly and yet with all changed. The immense loyalty displayed, the touching affection and admiration for beloved Papa in inscriptions and in the addresses, upheld me. I never saw greater

---

[1] William George Grey, youngest brother of General Grey and of Lady Caroline Barrington, had married the only daughter of the Inspector General of Cavalry in Sweden.
[2] In fact he was to marry the youngest daughter.
[3] This was the occasion when the citizens of Wolverhampton, in honour of the visit, erected an arch of coal ornamented with picks and shovels.

unanimity and we passed through some wretchedly poor parts—where the lowest, poorest people were assembled but all were the same! The population is 75,000 and I am sure near 100,000 must have been out—as the neighbouring towns all sent numbers.

From the Crown Princess   BERLIN, DECEMBER 4, 1866
Bertie's visit was so nice. He was so kind and dear; I was very very sorry to part with him. The King was extremely civil to him and I think all the others were so too. I shall be quite glad when he gets home as I think it is very trying for his health to spend so many nights in the railways in the cold, have such different eating and times of meals and be stuffed into overheated rooms. He has rather a sore throat and a heavy cold. Poor Lord Hamilton[1] looked wretched and the others tired out too. I think dear Bertie's face wears an expression of quiet and content which is so pleasing to look at—nothing fidgety or irritable—his manner is so kind that it must strike everyone, and I am sure he is a most kind brother, and seems anxious to please you as much as he can.

From the Queen   WINDSOR CASTLE DECEMBER 5, 1866
Have you ever read two pretty, simple but very pleasantly written novels called "A Noble Life" by the authoress of "J. Halifax" and "Janet's Home"? They have both been read to me of an evening and I liked them so much. Not sensation novels but pretty, simple stories full of truth and good feeling. Another old—but excellent Scotch one, which I am reading to myself is "Merkland". I believe also by a lady.[2]

---

[1] Afterwards 2nd Duke of Abercorn (1838–1913).
[2] *A Noble Life* by Mrs. Craik (1826–87) was published in 1866. *Janet's Home* by Anne Keary (1825–79) was an uneventful story of family life which centres round the marriage of the poor tutor to the well-born girl. *Merkland*, a story of Scottish life, was written by Mrs. Oliphant and published in 1851; it was one of her most successful novels.

From the Crown Princess
I know a "A Noble Life" quite well—it is so touching
and charming. Lady Caroline read it to me after Vicky's
birth; the other I have not read—newspapers, pamphlets
and reviews swallow up all my reading time when I am
at Berlin.

As you are so very kind to me I almost feel courage
enough to venture to say something to you—knowing you
will not be angry and never betray me. I know Alix has
the greatest wish to be now and then alone with you—
she says she is not amusing she knows, and she fears she
bores you. But she loves you so much, and it seems to me
a little ambition of hers to be allowed to be alone with you
sometimes. It was Bertie that told me this and it quite
touched me, as I saw it sprang from their love to you. He
has not an idea that I attached any importance to this
remark—or that I would ever say it to you. But I thought
I should tell you, thinking that while he was away it would
please them both so much if you took her once for a drive
or a walk alone with you. You cannot be astonished that it
should be a pleasure coveted by them.

Master Willy said to me this morning in French "when
I am grown up you will be dead. Is that not so?" Very
civil was it not? He is continually occupied with when I
shall die, and who will be his Mama.

From the Crown Princess
It interests me much to hear the remarks you make
about my children's characters. I think they coincide
much with my own observations; they are my constant
study and I fancy I appreciate them tolerably justly.
Children's faults often proceed from the people about
them—the damage done by an injudicious person, be they
ever so well-meaning, is not to be told. Therefore I feel
so grateful when I find persons of sense, tact and intelligence as I have the benefit of possessing in Dr. Hintzpeter and Mlle. Darcourt. I am so ready to follow their
advice about the children as I see how well they understand them. A mother is (as I feel) too apt to be too quick

and impulsive, because the children's faults aggravate her much more than other people; she is more ambitious for them and feels responsible for their dispositions—is it not so? How I can feel for you having had to put up with such a detestable child as I was, and yet I loved you so much and the thought that I could grieve you used to give me so much pain! I think you would find me much more gentle and sensible with the children than I was—more patient and forbearing. I have no need of acting the policeman now. I know there are two people about them who watch them and counteract their defects better than I can, as they have the experience of lives devoted to that most difficult of tasks—education; therefore I do not feel called upon to scold. Not one person in the house has as quick a perception of all the little failings that ought to be prevented from increasing, and my fear of their never being corrected made me perhaps see them in a stronger light than necessary, as my lively imagination dwelt on the consequences which might arise from them. Willy is a dear, interesting, charming boy—clever, amusing, engaging—it is impossible not to spoil him a little. He is growing so handsome and his large eyes have now and then a pensive dreamy expression and then again they sparkle with fun and delight. He too has his failings; he is inclined to be selfish, domineering and proud, but I must say they too are not his own fault as they had been hitherto more encouraged than checked. I do not believe that phrenology pushed to an extreme is to be relied upon—but I am convinced that the rudiments of it seldom go wrong, and I constantly find them confirmed.

From the Crown Princess   BERLIN, DECEMBER 22, 1866

Mrs. Hobbs and May[1] always use that silly expression to Henry in fun, when his hair was brushed and he had smart clothes on—"You look like a Regent Street swell".

---

[1] The Under-nurse.

From the Crown Princess   BERLIN, DECEMBER 28, 1866

I found yesterday in a shop a very good picture of dear Papa's grandfather Herzog August of Gotha and I thought you might like to buy it for Windsor as it is a family picture.[1] I take the liberty of sending it by today's messenger; it cost thirty thalers which is four pounds ten. If you do not want it please send it me back.

---

[1] The last Duke of Saxe-Gotha-Altenburg who died in 1822.

1867

From the Queen   OSBORNE, JANUARY 5, 1867

We have had deep snow lying for 3 days with sharp frost, and have been out sledging all about the country which was very pleasant and the only way of getting about. Dear little Henry is very well and a great darling and everyone admires him. But we don't spoil him.

From the Queen   OSBORNE, JANUARY 9, 1867

I am sorry to see all the trouble and anxiety you have about Charlotte,[1] which reminds me of Louise a little. She (Louise) is in some things very clever—and certainly she has great taste and great talent for art which dear Lenchen has not, but she is very odd; dreadfully contradictory, very indiscreet and, from that, making mischief very frequently.

How well I can understand you disliking to go to the Play and yet, at your age and with so much to make life happy and bright, it would never do to give that up.

I hope you will find dear Aunt Alexandrine well. She is so good and kind to all of you and has ever been a real sister to me. Do tell her all this.

From the Queen   OSBORNE, JANUARY 15, 1867

I this morning received your dear, loving, affectionate letter of the 11th and 12th and hasten to answer it—but first of all to say how greatly annoyed and vexed and distressed for your sake and for Alice's I am at the mistake about the letter, which is shocking and—to me—unaccountable as I am very particular about putting them up.[2] But I think—as it is—no harm is done, but good will

---

[1] The Crown Princess described her as "so very dull and backward".
[2] On 5 January the Queen wrote to the Crown Princess reiterating her complaints against Princess Alice and in particular her behaviour to Princess Helena. She tells the Crown Princess that she has written in strong terms to Princess Alice and then unfortunately (and most uncharacteristically) put the letters in the wrong envelopes so that Princess

come out of it. Tell dear Alice that now she properly and lovingly owns she is much grieved at what she did and said (I will truly believe out of hastiness and imprudence) that I will forgive and forget and receive her with open arms—and am indeed looking forward to seeing her for, I hope, two good months in the middle of June with dear Louis and the darling children. But she is quite wrong in thinking I heard tales told. First of all I never listen to anything of that kind (though I fear many do)—but no one ever said a word against her, but she injured herself by the way in which she spoke to many people about Lenchen and her remaining in England—and made great mischief with Louise, and both her brothers. Then, after originally at Darmstadt recommending Christian as so amiable and likely to do, she abused him and spoke in a very improper way of one who bears a very high character and has high principles and is one of the kindest and best people I know. Then she very rarely spoke kindly of poor Lenchen in her letters to me—and when she wrote, wrote bitterly to her. In short poor Alice was jealous—not because she wished to come here because that is quite natural and right, but about many things. I know people can't help that, and Alice is irritable and sharp. I think she is not strong and those large children so quick one after another have tried her very much. I only dreaded fresh mischief in the house and, rather than have that—which my health and nerves could not bear, for they require great quiet—I said I could not have Alice. But if she will be loving and affectionate to all, and not speak to Louise (who unfortunately is most indiscreet and then that makes great mischief very often) about Lenchen I shall only be too happy to have her with me, for my love is ever the same—God knows. I subscribe to every word you say

Alice received the letter of 5 January, intended for the Crown Princess, and setting out very bluntly the reasons for the Queen's vexation with her. The Crown Princess's letter of January 12, referring to the Queen's indignation with Princess Alice has not survived and was probably destroyed by the Crown Princess when she borrowed the correspondence from the Queen at the end of her life.

about life being so short that there ought to be nothing but love and affection. It was never written to Alice that I wished the one and not the other to be with me—and that the two sisters were not to meet. I will write again. We are all busy but bless you for being the peace-maker.

From the Crown Princess　　　GOTHA, JANUARY 15, 1867
We are spending a very pleasant time here. Dearest Aunt is so truly kind—really her goodness is too touching and, I am happy to say, I find her in better spirits than I have known her for a long time! Uncle has given her dozens of smart gowns—and she appears in a new one every day and is in very good looks. Fritz's visit to Carlsruhe and Alice and Louis' visit to Berlin will do a great deal towards smoothing down matters between the governments and princes and I rejoice at both. If all can be good friends in earnest, and understanding can be come to, I have no doubt a war with France (the thing of all I dread) will be rendered next to impossible; and therefore I am so anxious for the reconciliations to take place.

From the Queen　　　OSBORNE, JANUARY 19, 1867
Our severe frost continues but with such bright sun and blue sky that it is very pleasant. The skating (it is quite safe here—for one can't be too careful after the frightful catastrophe in London) I cannot look at.[1] It brings back too fearfully the absence of that one noble, splendid figure that used to sail about so beautifully. Affie came on Thursday and leaves on Wednesday. Alas! I am anxious about him! He seems to undertake this great responsibility with such reluctance and suspicion.[2]

From the Crown Princess　　　BERLIN, JANUARY 20, 1867
It is no merit of mine that matters with Alice are straight again; I only sincerely rejoice that I could be of

[1] On 15 January, 40 people were drowned in the ornamental water in Regent's Park due to the ice giving way.
[2] He was about to command the *Galatea* on a cruise to Australia.

any use to you, to her and to Lenchen. I am sure when she goes to England again she will behave quite differently. She sees what harm she did herself—by working herself up into such a state of mind and speaking so harshly and rashly, and I know it is her sincere wish to do away with the impression she made. And I am sure she will be as gentle and amiable as possible. She is so to me.

In May the Crown Princess and Crown Prince were planning to go to Paris for the Exposition Universelle, and the Crown Princess wrote that they would love to go to England either on their way or on the journey back

Should we disturb you at first, it would be possible perhaps to go to Bertie for a week—or we might make a little stay in London if we can have a room or two at Buckingham Palace? There are so many things and people I want to see in London. Perhaps we could be present at the christening of a small Wales, a little Schleswig-Holstein and a little Teck? If these charming fêtes happen to take place at that time please will you think this over and tell me what you wish. You know, dearest Mama, it is not at every time of the year we can get away, but we would not for the world be in the way—I know visits are agitating to you when they are *mal tombé*.

From the Queen   OSBORNE, JANUARY 22, 1867
I grieve to say that your plans do not suit me, for that it is quite impossible for me to receive you in April on account of Lenchen's confinement.
I wish to say a few more words in confidence about Alice, but which I would beg you to make use of. I told you in my last letter that she had, from the time when she married and came back here, not been liked in the house from her ordering and commanding and from want of tact and discretion. I felt this less then, for I was still so crushed that I lived as in a dream. But I did—the last two times. As time has worn on and my life has become alas! a sad reality I have naturally tried to make that sad life as

bearable as I can, and I think all those who truly love me are anxious that I should be kept as quiet as possible, and able as much as possible to do what I have found suit and and comfort me. Well, when Alice came the last two times she grumbled about everything—and Louis also sometimes—the rooms, the hours, wanting to make me do this and that and preventing my being read to of an evening as Louis would come and he always fell asleep. Of course this is not kind or right and if Alice wishes to come, she should accommodate herself to my habits. God knows if my misfortune had not changed everything, all would be different, but as my life is made up of work, I must live as I find I best can to get through that work. Mine is a weary, weary life—a hard struggle which it requires much courage, patience, resignation and faith in God's love and wisdom to go through. I therefore require to shape my own life and ways, and I think Alice does not see this. I know dearest child that with your loving heart and wise head you will see and understand this and will be able to talk all this over with Alice.

I know not really what to send dear Willy. I will send him a whip but it can't go tomorrow. He wished for an English uniform but I really know not how to fulfil that wish.

From the Queen   OSBORNE, JANUARY 25, 1867
Morier comes tomorrow for 3 nights.[1] Unlike you I hate politics, and nothing but the strongest sense of duty makes me talk about them.

From the Queen   OSBORNE, JANUARY 30, 1867
Morier was here 3 nights and told us a great deal that was very interesting. He was in great form but is enormous.

---

[1] Sir RobertMorier (1826–93) diplomatist. He had held appointments at various German states since the early 1850s, and the Crown Princess had much wanted him to be given the Berlin Embassy. In later life he described his work as "the political and heart union of England and Germany."

From the Crown Princess   BERLIN, FEBRUARY 2, 1867

You are quite mistaken if you think I like politics. I should prefer never to hear a single word about them. But I feel a deep interest in the cause of liberty and of progress— on each and every ground, and in all things; and wherever they are concerned I feel my zeal and my interest kindle, and can get very excited. I know no greater pleasure than to discover a like feeling in others, to hear and to have discussion on this subject and to relieve my feelings by giving vent to my enthusiasm for this cause. The course of daily, political events or rather diplomatical, small-talk— I think the greatest bore in the world. I love Germany. I glory in national feeling, and I am ambitious for her greatness, unity and happiness. I am anxious that Fritz's endeavours to promote this end may some day be crowned with success, and that dear England may sometime or other look upon us as fit to share her position in the world—not only by the force of our arms, and the military talents of our nation but by the development of our freedom and our progress in civilisation. I do not know whether this is being fond of politics. It is more a feeling of the heart than of the head, and consequently a woman's *point de vue*. All interests me that can lead to this result—every branch of science, art and industry, and I should like to help to push on and give all I possess to make the conditions of my fellow creatures (more especially my countrymen) better in every way, to raise them each individually. You see with me the desire is not to meddle with or to direct things which are not my business—I am far too lazy for that—but to try and add my little might to all great and good purposes gives me pleasure, and not for the effect it may produce for myself but for the inward satisfaction it causes. I think this is a part all women may take in politics and the one they are most fit for. Besides which I enjoy hearing clever talk and conversing with them—and I know you like it too.

From the Queen   OSBORNE, FEBRUARY 3, 1867

I send you here—which I meant to do some days ago— a heart-broken letter from poor Uncle Alphonse whose misfortunes have begun again. He has lost his eldest child of his second family, a lively little thing, and I think you will feel for him. I am sure a few words from you would do him good. He lost, you know, two children by his first wife—and that wife, whom he adored. This second one seems an excellent person and has the greatest *culte* for the memory of poor Reny (the first). Alphonse himself always says that happy as he is with this one, the real love and passion was for the first and that that could never be extinguished. I am sure that must always be so! That can only be once in a life.

From the Queen   WINDSOR CASTLE, FEBRUARY 5, 1867
Yesterday was a wretched day, and altogether I regret I went—for that stupid Reform agitation has excited and irritated people, and there was a good deal of hissing, some groans and calls for Reform, which I—in my present forlorn position—ought not to be exposed to. There were many, nasty faces—and I felt it painfully. At such times the Sovereign should not be there. Then the weather being very bad—the other people could not remain to drown all the bad signs. Of course it was only the bad people.[1]

From the Queen   OSBORNE, FEBRUARY 9, 1867
I did not tell Alice so—but I think those photos of Louis with his beard not favourable. Fritz looks so well with his beard.
Affie will start shortly—and I hope the responsibility and the separation from his London flatterers will do him good. He sadly needs it. I am very unhappy about him. On the other hand Bertie is so dear and affectionate and has improved—but I do not think him well, and looking very far from so.

---

[1] This was the second time that the Queen had opened Parliament in person since the death of the Prince Consort. The weather prevented many of the public from lining the route, but it was noticed that both sides of Parliament Street were "densely packed". The Queen means that it was only the "bad" people who hissed.

From the Crown Princess   BERLIN, FEBRUARY 10, 1867

May I ask a favour? I am going to arrange a bazaar
here in our house and the money is to be for our "invalids"
for the widows and orphans and wounded. I mean to sell
the things myself in a stall—and I should be so glad if you
could send me some things from England—not things of
value but trifles—which are not to be had here and which
are sure to sell well. Photos of you and the brothers and
sisters, of Windsor, Osborne or Balmoral, book-markers,
almanacs, little baskets etc. Would you kindly contribute
something for me?

From the Queen   OSBORNE, FEBRUARY 13, 1867

I rejoice to think that you had her (Alice) with you so
much longer than you originally expected. But I am sorry
to hear she was so much made of by the King and so much
admired, for it is that that has done Alice so much harm;
she is vain and conceited and then, when she comes here
and is not made such a fuss with, which she cannot (and
ought not to) be, she is dissatisfied and disagreeable. This
is the truth and I grieve for it—for her own good. With
you who are much more humble-minded this is so different.

What you say about the poor Queen, I think you must
exaggerate a little, dear. She always writes most kindly
about your children, but you know many people do not
care about little ones, and very few worship babies as you do;
for my part I can't understand it at all.

My gratitude for what was, my love and adoration for—
and devotion to—adored Papa are as great, and are part of
myself. But with the easing of that violent grief, those
paroxysms of despair and yearning and longing and of
daily, nightly longing to die which for the first three years
never left me, and which were a rending asunder of heart
and body and soul—the power of realising that married
life seems gone. I look on adored Papa, who is ever mingled
with every event, every pleasure, every pain as an Angel—
no longer an earthly being.

But there is great bitterness in the constant depression
and listlessness, and total saltlessness of my life. A heavy

cloud weighs down body and spirit—and I long often to cry bitterly. You will hardly understand this, and no one can who has not gone through all I have. But God in mercy willed it so! I was to live—and therefore I was to accept helps and comforts to help me on, and not to live solely in the past. And He will help me on further and further and turn the present sufferings and trials into a state for me to go to and join Papa hereafter for ever. He has never forsaken me, and I have felt his love and power and strength as none can but those who seek Him in the hour of agony and desolation.

From the Crown Princess   BERLIN, FEBRUARY 13, 1867

May I trouble you again about my bazaar? If it were possible that you could send me an Indian shawl, I would set an enormous price on it and I am sure it would be bought.

Yesterday our elections took place—and I am happy to say the liberals have the majority. And they will see here that the Prussians are not quite so dead to the sense of liberty, and blinded by the victories of last year as they are represented and as Bismarck tries to make them. The King is not nearly so amiably disposed as when Alice was here— he thinks me ugly and a bore and therefore I have not the same influence with him as she has. I think he would do anything to please her.[1] Last night we were at the Queen's. Tonight Mrs. Key Blunt the American reader will give a reading here in our house—and the Queen will come. Mrs. Blunt has a horrid accent but she has so much dramatic taste and feeling—and it is a pleasure to hear her in spite of her disagreeable English.[2]

---

[1] The King had an eye for feminine attractions, and his admiration for Princess Alice's beauty particularly incensed Queen Victoria.
[2] Ellen Key Blunt (1821–84). Her father was the author of *The Star Spangled Banner*. Earlier she had occupied the time of the American Minister in London by her efforts to be presented at Court. No lecturer or theatrical character, was, by the custom of America, entitled to this distinction. See *Journal of Benjamin Moran*, edited by S. A. Wallace and F. E. Gillespie, 1949.

From the Queen

Princess Alice had annoyed the Queen by asking for pearls for her children.

Pearls of any good size cost nearly £30 to £40 a piece now, and two of them to each child each year would be far more than I could give to all her children. I have not been able to give Louise and Beatrice pearls regularly to go on with, or only one at a time, and I wish to give all my grandchildren something and divide it fairly. Alice and Louis get money from me for their birthdays and Xmas to help them in furnishing their house—and always more and more is asked for.

Is Philippe's marriage really going to be as soon as May? I hope not in May, for it is so unlucky. In Scotland nobody would marry in May and you know Uncle Leopold and Princess Charlotte were married in May, Grandmama and my poor Father, the Duke of Orleans and Helene and Pedro and Stephanie. I never would let one of our children marry in that month. I have quite a feeling about it.

I can't understand the King's passion for Alice in preference to you, and I think it a great shame. The photo of you two is not favourable and I was shocked to see poor Alice looking so thin and old. Her poor Baby has got the whooping-cough—a nasty thing for little children and if poor, dear fat Ella was to get it, I should really be alarmed, for she chokes so easily.

Affie gives me a great deal of trouble about his ships—wanting to come home for the Season which did him so much harm last year. But I and the Admiralty will be firm and do only what is for his good and the good of the Service.

From the Crown Princess

Writing of the Queen of Prussia's lack of interest in her grandchildren the Crown Princess says:

She hardly ever sees them and seldom enquires after them though I believe she is at heart fond of the elder ones. It is her way and I must get accustomed to it—indeed I am so already—but the coldness towards the one I loved best and lost will ever possess me. She was just the same towards her daughter's children at first, and it used to grieve Louise. Whereas you are as a grandmama like the fairy godmamas in the story books—and I look upon you as the children's real grandmama; but please keep this to yourself. I do not say that here.

From the Crown Princess   BERLIN, FEBRUARY 22, 1867
But now how am I to thank you for your splendid contributions to my bazaar! The shawls, the photos, the other things all in such abundance. I cannot say how grateful I am—but you may be assured that I shall make the most of your generous gifts, and it will please your kind heart to think that it will be the means of relieving many a sad and suffering heart.

From the Queen   WINDSOR CASTLE, MARCH 6, 1867
You may imagine that this really great indignity about the King of Hanover's letter has again encouraged his friends.[1] But I say all these acts do Prussia immense harm. Why not treat the King and Queen as they ought—with all possible personal respect? Another thing I wished to ask you viz. could you not, in confidence from me, tell Lord A. Loftus to do anything he can to discourage the King of Hanover and family coming here? I told Lord Bloomfield[2] so, who entirely agrees and will do all he can; for he knows the poor blind King with all his illusions would be utterly miserable here—besides being a great nuisance. You could easily explain this in strict confidence to Lord Augustus.

During these days the Queen's letters are largely concerned with the very serious illness of the Princess of Wales.

---

[1] This is presumably the letter which the King of Hanover sent to the King of Prussia during the war. The letter was returned unopened, and the news about this was probably circulated now.
[2] Lord Bloomfield (1802–79) was British Ambassador to Austria, where the King was living in exile.

Prince and Princess Louis of Hesse with their children, July 1867.

A wedding photograph of
Princess Helena and Prince
Christian, July 1866.

Prince Alfred, Duke of
Edinburgh, September
1867.

From the Queen   WINDSOR CASTLE, MARCH 13, 1867

I am so glad to hear young Lorne is so much liked![1] For I always rejoice first to see good parents have good children and then rising up to high positions who promise to be of use to their country both socially and publicly.

Were you not grieved to hear of the death of our greatest painter—Phillip? His pictures were so beautiful and darling Papa had such an admiration for him. He was only two years older than me.

From the Queen   WINDSOR CASTLE, MARCH 16, 1867

Referring to the death of Princess Helena's mother-in-law.

For me and dear Papa it was so far worse; for he heard quite suddenly of his father's death, and his despair at being away from him—in a strange country with no one but me, who did not know his home (although I knew and dearly loved his father) near him—was dreadful![2] I shall never forget it. It was then he said to me he could not understand how anyone could think the loss of a child equal to that of a parent to whom you owe all. And God knows he was right.

From the Crown Princess   BERLIN, MARCH 16, 1867

Commenting on some photographs which she has sent to the Queen the Crown Princess alludes to herself as looking stout. But she goes on:

. . . that is not the truth and "I am quite slight—all my gowns are too large". I shall never be ethereal, slim and graceful like Alice, but I am for my build quite thin at present except my unhappy face which is like a platter! If all the worry, sorrows and tears of last year have taken

---

[1] Lord Lorne, afterwards 9th Duke of Argyll (1845–1914). He married Princess Louise in 1871.
[2] The Duke of Saxe-Coburg died in 1844. Writing to Stockmar the Prince Consort said "Here we sit together, poor Mama, (the Duchess of Kent), Victoria and myself, and weep with a great, cold public around us, insensible as stone". Martin, *Life of the Prince Consort*, Vol. I, page 202.

no effect on my face I don't suppose anything ever will. I hear nothing but politics from morning till night and of course people are much excited.[1] One does not grow fat on that. My spirits often flag and are very low at times— but *"mon bon gros rire"* (as poor dear Charlotte used to say) I have not lost.

From the Queen WINDSOR CASTLE, MARCH 20, 1867

The Queen of Denmark arrived on Thursday and the King arrives today. I saw the Queen yesterday and found her very sensible. She says (as I did) that she foresaw an illness from the reckless life of fatigue and excitement her poor child has been subject to—and chiefly to please Bertie! She is greatly distressed about it and we must all combine to bring about a great change of system, but God knows it will be months before any activity can be thought of even.

The christening of the Maharajah's baby (now eight months old) took place this morning.[2] A lovelier child I never beheld. You, with your mania for babies, would have gone wild with it. But the dear little Shahgadah Victor Albert is indeed most beautiful. And the dear young parents are much delighted with him. I never saw such eyes—except the Maharajah's own.

---

[1] The Crown Princess is probably referring to two things in particular. First the opening of the North German Confederation, the Reichstag, under the Presidency of the King of Prussia in Berlin at the end of February, and secondly the attempts of France to annex Luxemburg, at this time under the sovereignty of the King of Holland.

[2] Maharajah Dhuleep Singh (1833–93). Deposed as ruler of the Punjab in 1849 when he came to England and was converted to Christianity. His wife was a young lady whom he admired when giving away the prizes at a school in Alexandria. The Shahgadah married a daughter of Lord Coventry, and died in 1918. When the Maharajah married, the Queen wrote to the Crown Princess on 20 August 1864: "The Maharajah's marriage I hope will be a happy one. But the Maharanee is of no birth, half an Eastern—only 15, brought up at a Missionary School at Cairo, where he saw her and at once decided to marry her. She is the natural daughter of a German missionary by a Copt slave. But she is very pious, gentle and pretty though no beauty and very small." Her name was Miss Bamba Müller.

From the Crown Princess   BERLIN, MARCH 26, 1867

I have been in the Reichstag today and heard some very good speeches but which I fear will not please the Government as they showed very plainly that people will not only keep their love of constitutional rights and liberty but care to express it, and will not accept this new, sham constitution without making their objections. Of course no true patriot considers present arrangements anything else than quite provisory but hope, by not opposing them too violently, to prevent a *coup d'état* which Bismarck is always inclined to, and hope for better laws in the future—in which I earnestly believe they will not be disappointed.

From the Crown Princess   BERLIN, APRIL 2, 1867

People are in a wonderful state of excitement about Luxemburg, and I must say I think anything preferable than giving France a bit of Germany—as a sort of compensation for our unity.[1] France has no right to interfere in our internal affairs—and if she sees that she can so easily succeed in frightening us into giving her a bit of our country she will soon ask for the Rhine. Should there be a war against France—which would be a dreadful calamity on the one side—the unity of Germany would be effected at once. Neither the King or Bismarck or the Emperor Napoleon want war I think—but as matters stand I do not suppose all danger of it is over.

From the Crown Princess   BERLIN, APRIL 8, 1867

Many thanks for saying you will buy fifteen pounds' worth of things. I will choose them for you. Drawings of mine there are none. I have not done any since Heaven knows when. The last I did was a screen for the Queen Dowager; that was in November before we left Potsdam and since we are here I do not recollect having one evening

---

[1] The Crown Princess means that the Grand Duchy, although the King of Holland was sovereign, was a member of the German Confederation. In the result, Luxemburg was made independent and its fortress dismantled and the sovereignty was vested in a collateral branch of the Dutch Royal House.

to myself. I have always been out or had guests to attend to. I have quite lost the habit I had of scribbling on bits of paper for amusement. I paint a large, oil picture now and then when I can give all my attention to it—and do that in a studio which is lent me—and when I get home I have too much to do ever to make me feel inclined to draw.

My bazaar is answering pretty well, though the debates of today in the Reichstag, and the panic at the Exchange and the pouring rain have kept many purchasers away. An account of all shall be sent to you.

From the Queen   WINDSOR CASTLE, APRIL 10, 1867
The King of Denmark is coming to take leave today, and will meet Christian but please don't mention this to anyone. I will add a line after he has left. . . . The meeting has gone off quite pleasantly—the poor King was kind and civil, and they shook hands. I think this is a great thing. You may tell Fritz but no one else; for I believe it is the King's own subjects who are his difficulty in this affair.

From the Crown Princess   BERLIN, APRIL 11, 1867
I have just sold your shawls at the bazaar to W. Gerson—a rich merchant from whom we so often buy our things. There was such a crush of people that no one could move backwards or forwards. I thought that the tables would have been upset upon us! Of course there was very little sold in consequence, as people had to stay just where they were, and could not get at the stalls. However I think we may consider the bazaar a success. I have bought for you a drawing Louise of Baden made, a case of photographs of ourselves, and today I could not resist buying a watercolour I believe done by one of our very first artists—Richter—representing me selling your shawls. I thought it would please you but I am afraid it will cost you five pounds. I hope you will not be angry with me for overstepping the already so liberal a sum of fifteen pounds.

From the Queen   WINDSOR CASTLE, APRIL 17, 1867
I will tell General Grey to write to you about Luxem-

burg. I fear there is great dishonesty on the part of Bismarck
—who makes a proposal to one person and another to
another. Still I hope and pray that so dire a calamity as a
war between France and Prussia may be averted.

From the Queen   WINDSOR CASTLE, APRIL 20, 1867
    I can't by post write about politics but this I can say
viz: that France (the E.N.) is most anxious for peace and
if he is met in a conciliatory spirit at B. war will be avoided.
He wants no territory. This I have from Paris.[1]

From the Crown Princess   BERLIN, APRIL 20, 1867
    What you say of Bismarck may be true but I do not
think he is in the wrong for once in his life. The aggression comes from France—and it is there they wish for the
war and not here. For my part, if the peace cannot be
maintained I think it better the war should be now than
later—horrible as it is. A war with France will be a very
different thing from a war with Austria but if our honour
is at stake—for the sake of Germany we must not hang
back. That is my feeling and Fritz's and most people's
here—not the Queen's; she fancies that anything is better
than war now or war at all. I think the great united empire
of Germany will never consolidate itself in peace—before
France is not[2] reduced to a second power on the Continent.
I consider that as desirable for England as it is for us
Germans. But please do not betray me to anyone—this is
my own individual opinion and may be worth nothing. I
trust and hope that England will not be against us and
with France, and assist in dismembering Germany. I dare
not think of such a possibility.

From the Crown Princess   BERLIN, APRIL 23, 1867
    You ask how much we realised at the bazaar? Nearly

---

[1] From the King of the Belgians who had just been in Paris.
[2] So written—but the Crown Princess clearly means "until France is
reduced. . . ."

forty thousand thalers—it would take me too long to do the sum and turn it into pounds (I am ashamed to say).

From the Queen   WINDSOR CASTLE, APRIL 24, 1867

With respect to what you say regarding the present critical state of affairs, I must say I am surprised at it! The Queen is quite right in wishing for no war, and that is what every woman should do. She should not only wish for it, but should do everything to prevent it. In the present instance it is not France or the Emperor who wish for war— quite the contrary; and I repeat it again—it is Bismarck who has for the last eight months encouraged the Emperor to believe he could get Luxemburg without difficulty.

I can really also not understand how you can say that that proud old state, which has ever belonged to the Great Powers, which Prussia has only done within the last century, should be made a second-rate Power! She, who stands on a par—or at least next to us—in the advancement of civilisation! I am sorry you should say such a thing. I am afraid the time may come, when Europe will wish France to be strong to keep the ambition of Germany in check.

Those who lightly encourage war, will have to answer in another world for the souls of many innocent lives who have been sacrificed.

From the Crown Princess   BERLIN, APRIL 27, 1867

In these days of bustle, such as I never remember having seen before, I could not find a minute's time to write to you before today, and now I am so fatigued, worn out, and the excitement of other people's nerves is so catching that I fear I shall write nothing but nonsense so please be indulgent.

We have just accompanied the dear young couple with the Hohenzollern family to the station, and had the satisfaction of seeing perfect happiness written unmistakeably on the beaming faces of dear good Philippe and his dear young wife. The marriage ceremony was very splendid. I will send you a better account of it than I can give you myself through one of the ladies. Dear Marie looked very pretty though I thought the dress heavy, tasteless and unbecoming —her pretty manner and expression quite made one forget that. The church is one of the ugliest I ever beheld. Fancy an orangery or a riding-school embellished with cobwebs, dirt, pasteboard images of saints and covered for the occasion with curtains and carpets from the Schloss. It made me quite sad when I thought of sweet Stephanie whom I saw standing before the same altar looking like an angel! Marie has not that sweet touching expression; she is much livelier and has rather a roughness in her manner—which I thought much gone off now. She is a dear girl. Her features are much more regular than Stephanie's—her profile is faultless—but she has not the charm of her sister nor the lovely eyes and skin. She was delighted with your present—and told me to tell you so again and again.

Philippe also sends you his respectful love—as do Leopold and Antoinette, who is in the greatest beauty and invariably admired.

Leopold of Belgium is so amiable and sensible; his visit really has been of great benefit, and I think he has had great success politically and has shown great tact, and he seems to give himself so much trouble to do his duty in his position in every way he can, and has won respect and confidence by his conduct. We are very glad he came.

Now as to politics I see that what I wrote to you last time I ought to have explained more and better as, by your dear letter received yesterday, I perceive that I have given you a false impression of my opinions. When first the steps Holland had taken and France had so rashly acceded to were made known here; —viz. that France demanded of Germany to withdraw Prussian troops from the garrisons of Luxemburg, it appeared to the Germans merely in the light of an aggression and an insult to German honour, and created a powerful feeling which neither Bismarck nor the Emperor Napoleon were prepared for—as they both had made blunders (I suppose). The notion that the first act of the North German Confederation should be the abandonment of a fortress, considered in a military point of view highly important to Germany, raised a strong national feeling of independence. Our liberals thought it was an unheard of pretension on the part of France and thought that if Prussia showed herself inclined to give way then the Emperor, pushed by his nation so greedy of "gloire" and so dissatisfied with him for his failure in Mexico and for his moderation in not asking for more for himself at the time of the peace of Nicolsburg,[1] would be led to ask for Mayence or the left bank of the Rhine. Prussia's language towards France in the Luxemburg question was decisive for Bismarck's position in Germany. This was the spirit that animated the interpolations of Monsieur de Bennigsen,[2] and Bismarck's answer satisfied the Diet; and that was one of the reasons why the constitution was adopted so quickly unsatisfactory as it was in its details and hard for many a one to accede to. All united in coming to a conclusion so as not to put fresh difficulties in the way of the Government in case of a war with France. This feeling was a respectable one and that is why I shared it with all my heart. And there it was that I did not understand the Queen—that her fear of a war with France should make her nearly overlook the —in my eyes—far greater danger of our losing ground in Germany by a semblance of timidity and undue weakness (the fault which for years had so cruelly damaged our interests). But every day changes our situation—people are satisfied on the score of our not being too hot-headed and the danger of a war approaching makes us see its awful chances. Do not for a moment think I am blind to this side. I know we may lose all by such a war and gain little. We cannot admit the maxim that France has a right to compensation if Germany becomes united; if France maintains this maxim we have nothing left but to go to war. But if the Luxemburg question is not a mere pretext on the side of France which, when arranged, will quickly be followed by

---

[1] Here were signed the preliminaries of peace after the Austro-Prussian war.
[2] Rudolf von Bennigsen (1824–1902). He was the founder of the National Liberal Party—patriotic in foreign affairs but liberal in home affairs. He persuaded Bismarck to agree to reforms of the North German Confederation.

another, I think it would be folly not to try to come to an honourable and amicable settlement. I have done all in my power to further this (in my small way).

I asked the King yesterday whether he had any message for you; he answered I was to thank you for your letter and he would answer as soon as he could, but he regretted you were under the false impression that he was the aggressor.[1] I said I thought people in England had a notion Bismarck had encouraged the Emperor to think he could have Luxemburg upon which the King replied; "That is not true; Bismarck, Goltz and I have always said if a proposal could be made to us for an arrangement by which we could honourably withdraw our troops from the garrison we should have no objection to treat on the subject with France; it is the French who made propositions to us we cannot accept." I give you the King's words. I then spoke to Bismarck—which I never have done before on politics as he is such a dangerous person. I said he knew I was no blind admirer of his, that my admiration for him would be greatly increased if he found a means of honourably preserving peace. He said it did not depend on us; if the French armaments had reached a certain extent, we must re-arm also. I said "cannot you stop the French armaments by making some arrangements for treating with the French?" He gave me no decided answer so that I do not know on which side are his wishes and intentions; but from all I hear he is not much inclined to war. But one never can know what he really means.

The King wishes for peace, so does Fritz, so does the Minister for War. The army I believe thinks if peace cannot be honourably preserved, a war is better now than later. Uncle Ernest thinks the reverse. And the opinion which prevails among many that if time is left to consolidate ourselves and get into order in Germany, a war is more unlikely because we shall be a more powerful enemy, had doubtless much in its favour. If I am to sum up all our impressions, I should say that peace seems more likely than

---

[1] On 22 April the Queen wrote to the King urging him to be conciliatory.

it did a few days ago and that all depends upon the French showing they are sincere in wishing to come to an agreement by not proceeding further in their armaments whilst negotiations are being carried on. We have not armed—but of course must do so if the French go on and then as we know by experience it wants but the smallest spark to set the whole train of gunpowder in a blaze.

Fritz, Leopold of Belgium and Uncle Ernest have all done what they can, also the Queen and I: I was out of the way civil to Benedetti and asked whether we were soon expected at Paris etc.[1] Now I have told you all I know, dearest Mama. I hope it is not too confused. Please burn this letter and my last.[2]

From the Crown Princess   NEUES PALAIS, MAY 3, 1867
Indeed we feel a little more reassured about peace. It is very difficult for us to judge of what the real feeling in France with regard to war is. On the one hand all we hear through England and Belgium is most conciliatory—the demonstration of the French liberals, the visit of Monsieur Garnier Pagès to Berlin and the way in which he and his friends were received proves how many people in both countries there are who desire peace and goodwill to reign reciprocally, also the address of the German residents at Paris. On the other hand the opinion prevails amongst our most enlightened military men that the Emperor is bent upon war, and is only deceiving us and lulling us to sleep by his peaceful language, that he wants the conference to give him time to complete his armaments and that as soon as it suits him he has a thousand pretexts in his pocket with which to bring on the war. Pray read the articles in the *Libertè* of the 28th, 29th and 30th April and you will see that the provocatory language is not on our side. Still I think if one sums up what is said and written in France and here, the majority of voices are in favour of peace and that

---

[1] Count Vincent Benedetti (1817–1900) French Ambassador at Berlin. The Crown Prince and Princess were going to Paris for the Exhibition.
[2] The Queen evidently thought these letters too informative to be burned.

is a great thing. I who live in the midst of all this pleasant embroglio can perceive a great difference with last year. Austria was worried into imprudent steps which were then seized upon as a *casus belli* by Bismarck. It is well for Germany that it has turned out as it is, but those who know the *"dessous des cartes"*, as we do, can never respect or admire Bismarck; his good luck may be of use to us, also his energy, but as long as he is at the head of affairs I shall always feel that we have a sword hanging over our heads.

From the Crown Princess　　NEUES PALAIS, MAY 9, 1867
I have seldom found the King so sensible, quiet and moderate. Fritz says the same of Bismarck. The immense armaments which increase from day to day have frightened people very much, and I do not think that our generals, Moltke and Roon, could take the responsibility on themselves of not advising the King to take steps for arming ourselves, and I am sure you will agree with me that they cannot do otherwise. The more I think of this war, the more evident it is that we gain nothing, that we risk all and that, in the best case, the devastation, loss of life and damage we shall have to shoulder will crush poor Germany for many years to come and change the aspect of Fritz's future immensely—so you can imagine that we are very anxious.

From the Queen　　OSBORNE, MAY 11, 1867
Referring to the christening of the daughter of the Prince and Princess of Wales:

I really don't know why they had such hosts of sponsors. The child ought to be called "Victoria".[1] But upon those subjects Bertie and Alix do not understand the right thing. Just as your children were called after the Prussian Royal Family, Bertie's ought to be after the English Family.

---

[1] The child was christened Louise Victoria Alexandra Dagmar. The Queen of course means that Victoria should have been the first name.

From the Crown Princess   NEUES PALAIS, MAY 11, 1867

I cannot help thinking the French nation at large will be grateful to the Emperor for not having gone to war and that, as years go on, they may see that Germany's welfare is no detriment to theirs. When our commerce, our arts and all have improved—as they no doubt will if they are given time—we may hope to be on equal terms of friendship and of the greatest use to one another, and that then France may no longer consider us Germans as dangerous rivals to be kept down at any price.

I must end my scribble here I fear—but first let me ask why should Dr. Mcleod's book be too simple for me? And why should you think so? In literature simplicity is of all beauties the one I admire the most. That is why I am so fond of Platt Deutsch. The highest art is that which comes nearest to nature, and I don't know why you should suppose I think the reverse.[1]

From the Crown Princess   NEUES PALAIS, MAY 13, 1867

I send you a bad photo of my little Vicky—she has on the little garden hat and jacket her little brother wore so much last year; they are the things he had on when he was taken ill!

From the Queen   OSBORNE, MAY 15, 1867

Thank God this senseless war has been averted. The Emperor is quite delighted at this result, for he from the first was against it. I repeat this again as a positive fact. You always seemed to doubt it—and that is what makes me always believe that Bismarck exaggerated all the reports from France in order to bring on the war.

You are shocked at my thinking Dr. Mcleod's book too

---

[1] In her letter of 8 May the Queen complained that the Crown Princess had never commented on "Dr. Mcleod's pretty book. I fear it is too simple for your grand head." The book was *The Highland Parish*. Platt Deutsch is the North German dialect spoken by educated people in the 18th and 19th centuries. Fritz Reuter (1810–74), humorous writer and poet, writing in Platt Deutsch, was much in vogue at this time.

simple for you. I may have expressed myself wrongly—for I know you admire simple and touching poetry, but I meant that you are so fond of political and scientific writings that such little things you would hardly find time to read. I must however send you two Scotch novels, which are quite charming, by Mrs. Oliphant which the Duchess of Atholl read to us.

From the Queen   OSBORNE, MAY 18, 1867
Let me thank you for your dear letter of the 13th. But, dearest child, that photograph of little Vicky in those clothes distressed me. It is not right, really dearest, to do that and I own I think it almost tempting providence to dwell so much on all that you cannot get back on earth, and on all the material past. Your Darling—God took to himself and he is safe and happy! You will see him again there —where there is no sorrow or pain or parting and if you would but dwell on that (as I do) and have that faith and trust you would not have that sad and agonising repining— surrounded as you are too by so many blooming children, and above all—and worth 20 children—by your dear, good husband. I should have almost a superstitious feeling about putting another living child into the clothes which had been worn by one who is dead. I say all this in love and affection and in perfect sympathy with your loss, dearest child, but from a loving, sorrowing (heart)* which has suffered more than anyone almost and which trembles to see such a constant dwelling on what can not be altered.

From the Crown Princess
               THE PRUSSIAN EMBASSY, PARIS[1], JUNE 5, 1867
The King arrived today. We went quite early this

---

* One of the rare occasions where the Queen leaves out a word.
[1] The Crown Prince and Princess were visiting Paris for the Exhibition. "Parisians of all shades of opinion were proud to see, laid out in the heart of their city, the fruits of the inventive genius of mankind, achieved by the toil of every race, creed, and social order and offered to the critical appreciation of the whole world They were proud to be hosts to the world". *The Empress Eugénie* by Harold Kurtz, Hamish Hamilton, 1963.

morning to see the beautifully restored, splendid old castle of Pierrefonds[1] and then met the King at Compiègne. The King's reception at Paris was very fine and gratified him; he was much better received than the Emperor[2] who heard hisses and cries of "Vive la Pologne". It is so nice to have dear Alice here—she is looking so pretty and seems to enjoy seeing Paris; we see very little of each other I am sorry to say as we go about in different directions. Winterhalter has a great wish—which would I am sure be in your power to grant and make him very happy—which is to have those prints or lithographs of his works (or rather photographs) which appear in the publication called "The Royal Collections" of Windsor, Osborne and Buckingham Palace (of which you once gave me a number) in which were Landseer's picture of Däckel and Dandie.[3] Can he get them? He has done heads of Fritz and me which are very good I think. I have seen many interesting men here at Paris—amongst others Augusta Stanley's friend Monsieur de Mohl.

From the Queen   BALMORAL, JUNE 10, 1867
    Sir Ed: Landseer has been here ever since the 5th—doing some beautiful things, and I never saw him more amiable or more *en train* and amenable to observation.

After describing in detail the illness of John Brown's sister the Queen says: "and I feel it much as Brown is so devoted to me and has shown and does show me such sympathy and devoted attention."

From the Crown Princess   BADEN, JUNE 10, 1867
    I am very thankful to be out of the noise and whirl of Paris—especially those dreadful late hours and suffocating ballrooms—for I began to get quite knocked up. Still I enjoyed my stay so much. I saw so many interesting things

---

[1] A ruin being restored by Viollet-le-Duc near Compiègne.
[2] of Russia.
[3] The Queen's dogs.

and people, and the real kindness of the Emperor and Empress, the charming way in which they do the honours and the trouble they give themselves to see all their guests, left a most pleasing impression on me. They spoke so often and with such real attachment of you and dear Papa—and asked so much after you. The Emperor said of dear Papa— *"C'était bien l'homme le plus distingué et le plus remarkable que j'ai jamais vu."*

Our King seemed so happy at Paris, everyone was very civil to him, and he was in the highest good humour, and enjoying himself like a schoolboy on a holiday. The day of the "attentat"[1] you would have pitied the Emperor and Empress. I never saw anything like their consternation. The Empress cried all the evening and would not be comforted, and the Emperor was as white as a sheet. Both of them said in one breath they regretted the Emperor Napoleon had not been touched, and they wished to make it appear as if he had been shot at and not the Emperor Alexander—but there was no doubt that it was the latter. Our carriage was close behind—but we saw nothing of it all—except the horse covered with blood and we thought it had met with an accident. The Emperor Alexander looks much aged and not well—almost older than my father-in-law who is as fresh and active as a young man. The young Grand Dukes grumble at everything, keep talking Russian to one another and won't admire anything at Paris. They are so *blasé*. I think their manners are very bad but the eldest has something good natured about him, and I cannot help liking his face as I do the Emperor's, who really is such a kind-hearted man.

I think I have not yet told you about the little Prince Imperial. What a darling he is! I think he is the prettiest, most interesting child I ever saw. With very regular features, a beautiful complexion, most sweet expression

---

[1] On 6 June a Pole fired two pistol shots at the Czar as he was driving with the Emperor in the Bois de Boulogne. The first shot hit the horse of one of the French Emperor's Equerries, and the second, being overcharged, burst the barrel.

and fine large blue eyes with a fringe of black eyelashes and black hair—the same graceful manner as his mama—he seems very forward and intelligent. He seems quite recovered, and did not walk lame—the parents seem quite wrapped up in him, which is very natural with such a charming child.

From the Crown Princess   NEUES PALAIS, JUNE 16, 1867
I am so glad the Reform Bill is going on so well. I saw Monsieur Geffcken at Paris and asked him much about it. The poor man is in very bad health, and I fear that makes him dislike England which does so provoke me! When I hear of anyone who does not sufficiently appreciate the enormous privilege of living there I feel a desire to shake them or to quarrel with them. When one is obliged always to live elsewhere one becomes daily and hourly alive to the immense superiority of England in a thousand things, which often escape one when one is there.

From the Queen   FROGMORE GARDENS, JUNE 22, 1867
I went to visit Mary Teck and found her pale and not thinner—with the exception of her face—and very happy and the baby (in Mrs. Innocent's arms) a very fine child, with quantities of hair—brushed up into a curl on the top of its head!—and very pretty features and a dark skin.[1] It was very strange to me to go to my poor, dear, old home again—after 30 years! (It was 30 years yesterday that I first drove away from that door with an escort as Queen to my Proclamation!)
The Sultan's visit is no satisfaction and I wish he were not coming. It is also, politically speaking, a bad moment. He can't moreover speak a word of anything but Turkish. I shall see him at Osborne for luncheon and (weather permitting) take him to the Review at Spithead.

---

[1] The future Queen Mary. Her parents were living in the apartments formerly used by the Duchess of Kent, where Queen Victoria was brought up.

From the Queen   FROGMORE GARDENS, JUNE 26, 1867
After explaining that Prince Leopold's tutor is leaving.

But he will not have a stranger, for Mr. Duckworth, his instructor, and a really most talented and charming person, will become his tutor or governor. The only objection I have to him is that he is a clergyman. However he is enlightened and so free from the usual prejudices of his profession that I feel I must get over my dislike to that. Mr. Duckworth is an excellent preacher and good-looking besides.

From the Queen   WINDSOR CASTLE, JULY 3, 1867
Here people are half-mad about the Sultan and altogether in a state of feverish excitement about everything; and most absurd and unreasonable. It makes me quite ill, to feel I can't do things, and they want to force me to do it. However that will pass off, and what I can do I will.

Now comes the horrible news of poor, unhappy Max's execution which I fear must be true; and as the Emperor Napoleon has put off everything—naturally I must do the same, as Max is the husband of my first cousin. It is I fear true and a dreadful outrage.[1]

From the Queen   WINDSOR CASTLE, JULY 6, 1867
Oh that horrible murder of poor Max has indeed given me the same feelings as it has given you. Awful, too awful! Everything was done, and messages and representations were sent—but all in vain. Marie of Belgium is to start tonight for Vienna and Miramar and hopes to bring poor, dear, and most unhappy Charlotte back to Belgium. May God in mercy support her—Uncle Leopold's and dearest Aunt Louise's dear child. It does seem too dreadful.

---

[1] This official notice was issued to the people of Mexico: "Ferdinand Maximilian von Habsburg, a Grand-Duke of Austria and an ally of Napoleon III came to Mexico to rob the country of its independence. . . . The usurper having been captured, he was sentenced to death by a military court-martial, with the concurrence of the nation, and was shot for his crimes on the 19th of June. . . . Peace be to his ashes".

From the Queen   FROGMORE GARDENS, JULY 10, 1867

Alice has written to tell you all about the Turks and Egyptians of which we have a perfect inundation—and how worried and bustled about it we are. I shall not add much having just written a long letter to Leopold about our poor dear Charlotte and about this fearful tragedy in Mexico which haunts me. And how dreadful that we can do nothing to avenge his horrible murder—and that the days of chivalry have passed away. I am sitting in this dear lovely garden—where all is peace and quiet, and you only have the hum of the bees, the singing of the birds, the occasional crowing and cackling from the poultry-yard. It does my poor excited and worried nerves good.

From the Queen   FROGMORE GARDENS, JULY 13, 1867

I have breakfasted here with Louise and Beatrice in order to be quiet before this tremendous affair of the Sultan's visit. It will be in great state like when the Emperor and Empress came—only the State Entrance being in process of alteration I must receive him at the usual entrance. Arthur and Louis go to the station—the others will be with me at the door. At 4¼ we go to dear Osborne —there to be quiet till Wednesday, when the Naval Review takes place.

Alice is very amiable but she and Louis are no comfort. They are not quiet. Alice is very fond of amusing herself and of fine society and I think they do everyone harm. They ruined Affie.[1]

Later.   Everything went off remarkably well, and the sight was really very fine. The Sultan drove through the town from the station and up the front road lined with the Scots Fusilier Guards and Life Guards on foot—the full Captain's Escort of Life Guards accompanying him. The Sultan sat in an open carriage with Arthur, Louis and Fuad Pasha[2] (who always interprets for him and is a clever,

---

[1] By "they" the Queen means society people.
[2] Fuad Pasha (1814–69) a celebrated and enlightened Turkish Foreign Minister.

agreeable man). I received him at the door and gave him my hand which he shook. He offered me his arm, and we went upstairs and on to the White Room—the corridor being lined with Yeomen of the Guard. Here he presented his dear little boy[1] (who is nine years old and led Beatrice and sat near her at luncheon) and his two nephews—one of whom is his heir.[2] None speak French. Then we sat down for a few minutes, after which the Sultan presented his whole enormous suite including his Aumonier (his Priest) a good-looking man, in a green robe with a white turban, two or three Syrians in a very picturesque dress and two Albanians. Then we went to luncheon to the Oak Room (we were 18) and I sat between the Sultan and the little boy; Fuad Pasha sitting next the Sultan and interpreting extremely well. The two nephews, ourselves (to the number of seven) Musurus[3] and three other Pashas, Lord Tanker-ville (Lord Steward) and the Duchess of Wellington. The Sultan is a handsome man, broad and fat rather, but with the true, splendid, soft, brown oriental eyes—a fine nose and a pleasant expression. He wears the usual, present Turkish dress—richly embroidered, with a low, broad fez, a good deal out from his face. He never touched wine. Luncheon over they all left, and I took him down as before.

All the pages served in State Dress—Brown and his brother and Ross[4] in full Highland dress—Cowley[5] in his full uniform. Quantities of gold plate on the table. The band played in the quadrangle (for the first time these 6 sad

---

[1] The Queen and Princess Beatrice kissed him. (See Annual Register.)
[2] The Sultan was Abdoul Aziz (1830–76). The succession in Turkey was not necessarily from father to son. One of the two nephews was the Sultan's successor Mourad V and the other was almost certainly the future Sultan—Abdul-Hamid familiar to Gladstonian Liberals as Abdul the Damned.
[3] The Turkish Ambassador in London.
[4] The Queen's pipe-major.
[5] Edward Spencer Dickin Cowley. Before entering royal service he was in the Royal Horse Guards. Before this he had fought as a volunteer against Dom Miguel in Portugal. He served the Royal Family from 1847–82.

years) and the six pipers of the S. Fusilier Guards played alternatively with them. The whole was over in an hour.

From the Queen   OSBORNE, JULY 16, 1867
After referring to her prostration after the Sultan's visit.

I often wonder how I shall ever be able to go on. Everything upsets me. Talking especially tries me. Reading in the open air quietly is what does me the most good. Sitting and reading and writing, working and drawing soothes me.

I reopen my letter to add the copy of one from Marie of B. to Leopold, relative to poor Charlotte which he has sent to me. It is after all true that one of her dressers hung herself![1]

From the Crown Princess   MISDROI,[2] JULY 16, 1867
A thousand thanks for your dear letter of the 13th with the interesting description of the Sultan's visit. It must have been very trying for you but I am glad you received him so, because, after all the splendours with which his eyes have been dazzled at Paris, it is a good thing that he should be able to form an idea of what the English Court is—and nobody knows so well how to do the honours as you do. I have now seen so many courts and crowned heads and that has always been what I have observed. The Empress Eugénie with her exceeding gracefulness, has a shade of diffidence which—when she appears in public—is more than her station permits but which in her peculiar position only adds a charm to her sweetness of manner. The Empress of Austria, with her surpassing loveliness, is too silent and stiff. My Mama-in-law has too much "phrase" on these occasions and is not natural, though she feels at her ease. And in all the other minor queens that I know there is a something wanting to make up the ideal of a queen. But

---

[1] The Empress of Mexico (Charlotte) had been out of her mind for several months. By the time of this letter she had improved, and the King of the Belgians was arranging for her move to Belgium from Miramar. She was not told of her husband's execution.
[2] On the Baltic in the Pomeranian Bay.

it is not strange that I should not find one to compare to my own dear Mama. Prince Humbert of Italy told me that you were the only person living *qui a imposé à mon père.* And I fully believe it.

If Alice, as you say, is fond of amusement and fine society it is because there is none at Darmstadt—the same reason why I like quiet and retirement and liberty because I cannot get it at Berlin. Allowances must be made for us both.

From the Queen   OSBORNE, JULY 20, 1867

You write so warmly and affectionately about your poor old Mama that I am greatly touched by it. I have been now 30 years in harness—and therefore ought to know what should be—but I am terribly shy and nervous and always was so. The dear Queen has a very fine presence I always thin, but perhaps it is a little put on. Our Naval Review was a very fine sight in spite of the most awful weather—and really it was an act of great *devouement* to my Oriental Brother to go out in it and to have to go in and out of boats in a horrid swell which always frightens me so. We were from half past ten to half past five doing nothing but standing and sitting about, and being blown about;—the whole ship swarming with Turks! The poor Sultan was not comfortable and had to lie down a good deal below. I fastened the garter round him myself—and he smiled and laughed and coloured and was very much pleased. I wish you had seen it darling. He is so sorry to miss you at Coblentz and I like his fine, soft eyes—and his pleasant smile (reminding one of the Maharajah) would have pleased you.

From the Queen   OSBORNE, JULY 24, 1867

The dear Empress, who is really very much what she was ten years ago—tho' a little aged—was very, very kind and amiable. She came quite incognito with only the Duchesse de Bassano and the Comte de Brissac (a funny, little, civil man—very ugly) and without attendants, and by some extraordinary mischance—while we were all looking out, watching, and waiting she arrived and came into the house!!! You may imagine our horror from highest to lowest.[1]

It rained that evening so we could not drive out but I went and sat with her for some little time and she was most kind, and spoke very kindly of you. I gave your message. We dined *en famille,* and the Ladies and Gentlemen came in after dinner. But it was all too much. Yesterday morning after breakfast (with a very bad headache, which lasted all day as it had done the day before, and disgust for food) I took a drive round the grounds with the Empress— and showed her the little church with which she was much pleased. And then in the afternoon I and the sisters took tea with her at the Swiss Cottage and then drove round by Newport. In the evening the Empress's people and the Duchess of Roxburghe and Lord Alfred[2] dined. Ross played at luncheon and dinner and walked round the table, as the Empress is so fond of it and everything Scotch. This morning before 10 she embarked at our pier to which we took her, and steamed off to Brest.

From the Crown Princess   MISDROI, JULY 30, 1867
The photograph of you and the Queen is charming— that is to say I have hardly seen her with so pleasant an expression and I never saw you with so black a one—you are really not flattered, dear Mama. But how could you persuade the Queen to sit because she never will?[3]

From the Queen   OSBORNE, AUGUST 7, 1867
Dear Bertie came here yesterday evening till tomorrow, very kind and amiable—but I think he wants change of air and scene. Poor Boy, it is very sad to think of his whole existence changed and altered and *derangé* by this lamentable illness. Please God that poor Alix may recover her

---

[1] Being the wife of a reigning sovereign she should have been met at the front door by the Queen.
[2] Lord Alfred Paget (1816–88) chief Equerry to the Queen.
[3] This is almost certainly the photograph reproduced in *Queen Victoria* by Helmut and Alison Gernsheim, page 182.

health, but I own I fear very much she will never be what she was.

I now wish to ask your opinion upon a subject which Bertie has been talking to me about, which Alice also did and which I understand from her you also had been thinking of. It is about Affie's future marriage prospects. Everyone feels anxious that he should settle when he returns, and the object is one of such importance for himself and for us all that if he can only find a Princess likely to suit and please him I would not mind who she was. The choice is becoming so narrow that I think we must get over the difficulties concerning religion—that is to say as regards the Greek religion—and I believe it could be got over easily if there was a person likely to suit. I had thought and hoped at one time for dear little Olga who is now to marry King George.[1] That is gone now. But there is a person who Bertie and Alice think would be the right person for Affie —and that is Maroussy's sister Eugénie.[2] And I understand from Alice that you thought the same? They say she is so good, so steady, very honest, clever and very German in her feelings and that Affie liked her. The mother is of course a terrible drawback, but hardly so bad—certainly not even so dangerous—as Queen Louise for active mischief. And then she has no home, and it would be entirely new blood which is an absolute necessity. You must look at all the sides of the question and especially on the great importance of the individual herself. Hanover and Altenburg won't do, poor Tina Oldenburg is dead, and I fear Elizabeth Wied (whom I should so much have liked) won't do—as he don't care for her. So, here we are *planté*, and I cannot tell you how anxious I do feel about Affie and how all important it will be to secure for him a person he liked and could look up to.[3]

---

[1] Of the Hellenes.
[2] Daughter of the Grand Duchess Marie, sister of the Czar, and grand-daughter of Eugene Beauharnais. She married Prince Alexander of Oldenburg a few months later.
[3] Some six years later Prince Alfred married the Czar's only daughter— the Grand Duchess Marie. She, of course, belonged to the Greek church

From the Queen   OSBORNE, AUGUST 14, 1867

Leopold B. was here for one night, having come the whole way across from Ostend to see me. He told me much about Charlotte who is improving since she came to Tervueren.[1] She has more liberty, goes out driving in the morning, and the great object is to let her be reassured that she will not be shut up—or force used—which I fear has been the case at Miramar. The doctor there seems, with the best intentions, not to have been judicious, and the servants not good or responsible. Leopold says that her cries of *déraisonnement* (for she is never violent and is quite aware of her condition) are the exceptions, and for the greatest part of the day she is perfectly sane. The eating is the great difficulty, she speaks but little of Max and Mexico. She suspects things are not prospering but they have not told her the truth as yet.

From the Crown Princess   NEUES PALAIS, AUGUST 17, 1867

You ask how Fritz Carl's boy is getting on.[2] He is made a tremendous fuss with by everybody such as we never made or allowed to be made with Willy. On all occasions when the family is assembled Fritz Carl's boy is the principal attraction and Willy is not at all noticed (which I am very glad of as it would do him a great deal of harm) but still it is strange. Other members of the family look upon him half with pity and half with dislike. Their pity he does not want, thank God, and he will have to do without their love—as his family have. *Il s'en consolera* as we do. The said boy of Fritz Carl is a heavy lump of unintelligence with pretty features, lovely hair, a big head—and an inanimate expression. In height he is the same as my funny little Vicki; he moreover always wears a military cap—and the Papa

and Dean Stanley pointed out to the Queen that, although the Greek church held many of the superstitions and erroneous views of the Roman Catholics, they did not as the Roman Catholics did, refuse to acknowledge any other church but their own. *Later Letters of Lady Augusta Stanley*, edited by Hector Bolitho.

[1] A royal castle south-east of Brussels.

[2] Prince Frederick Leopold: he was not quite two.

Queen Victoria with her dog, Balmoral 1867.

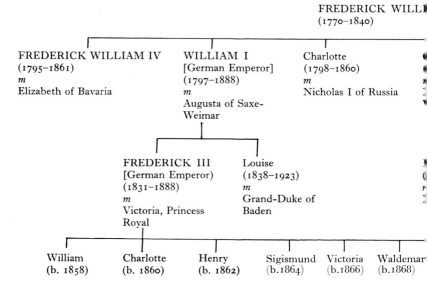

FREDERICK WILLI
(1770–1840)

FREDERICK WILLIAM IV
(1795–1861)
m
Elizabeth of Bavaria

WILLIAM I
[German Emperor]
(1797–1888)
m
Augusta of Saxe-
Weimar

Charlotte
(1798–1860)
m
Nicholas I of Russia

FREDERICK III
[German Emperor)
(1831–1888)
m
Victoria, Princess
Royal

Louise
(1838–1923)
m
Grand-Duke of
Baden

William
(b. 1858)

Charlotte
(b. 1860)

Henry
(b. 1862)

Sigismund
(b.1864)

Victoria
(b.1866)

Waldemar
(b.1868)

THE ROYAL HOUSE OF HOHENZOLLERN

se of Mecklenburg-Strelitz
       (1776–1810)

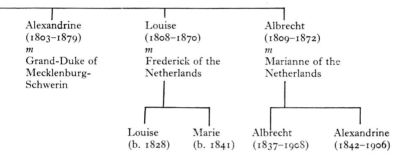

Alexandrine
(1803–1879)
m
Grand-Duke of
Mecklenburg-
Schwerin

Louise
(1808–1870)
m
Frederick of the
Netherlands

Albrecht
(1809–1872)
m
Marianne of the
Netherlands

Louise
(b. 1828)

Marie
(b. 1841)

Albrecht
(1837–1908)

Alexandrine
(1842–1906)

nhalt

garet
872)

The investiture of the Turkish Sultan, Abdoul Aziz, with the Order of the Garter on board the *Victoria and Albert*, 1867. From the painting by G. H. Thomas in the Royal Collection.

who never took up his little girls or seemed to take the slightest notice of them, torments the nurses about every single thing the boy puts on, has him on his lap all dinner time, and carries him about afterwards. Prince and Princess Charles are in a state of adoration—the latter talks of nothing but *"notre garçon"* and the Queen Dowager is wrapped up in the child as if he were her own, and thinks our children very plain and wrongly brought up, though she is kind to all children. They say the Duke of Brunswick (bosom friend of Fritz Carl's) has left all his fortune and his fine place at Silesia to Fritz Carl's son. The Duke is god-father to Ditta, but he has never made her the smallest present. Our children are invariably pitied for having the great misfortune of having me for their Mama. It is supposed they cannot possibly turn out well; this I am so accustomed to hear that I have got quite used to it, and do not care a straw for all their bosh. I trust my children may grow up like my Fritz, like Papa, like you and as unlike the rest of the Prussian royal family as possible; then they can be good patriots and useful to their country—call it Prussia or call it Germany.

From the Queen   BALMORAL, AUGUST 31, 1867
Staying with the Duke and Duchess of Roxburghe at Floors, the Queen had visited Abbotsford.

I saw at Abbotsford all Sir Walter's relics, and his only surviving descendant, a pretty girl of eleven—daughter to Mr. Hope Scott whose first wife was W. Scott's only grand-daughter Miss Lockhart. This Mr. H. Scott became a Catholic and forced his poor wife to become one. She died —a good deal from this—and then the marriage with his present wife, Lady Victoria, sister to the young Duke of Norfolk was arranged by the Catholics and hurried on, she never having seen anyone else.[1]

---

[1] He was actually guardian to Lady Victoria. Side by side with what the Queen says a somewhat different picture of Hope-Scott can be set. He was one of the finest products of the Tractarian Movement, a man of great ability and generosity. He left the Church of England with Manning at the time of the Gorham Judgement.

From the Crown Princess   NEUES PALAIS, AUGUST 31, 1867

I think I told you that we were about to take one of the Crown farms into our own hands; it will be a great comfort and amusement and a very interesting occupation to us both.[1] Did I also tell you that G. von Putlitz our great friend was going to be our Master of the Household? We rejoice very much at it. We are going to take him to England and I am sure you will like him he is so charming.[2]

From the Queen   BALMORAL, SEPTEMBER 3, 1867

I have had much to try and worry me this year—and I feel broken down in body and spirits. The beauties of nature I enjoy more and more but the wickedness of mankind shocks me more and more—and makes me long to go and bury myself quite away from the world.

From the Crown Princess

NEUES PALAIS, SEPTEMBER 11, 1867

We have had great difficulties about Willy's governor— quite unexpectedly. For, after the King had given his consent, he was suddenly about to withdraw it; the intriguing mischievous Head of the *Cabinet Militaire*, M. de Tresckow, having persuaded the King our choice was not judicious and the person was too young. T. went on (with an impertinence trying to bear) to suggest four persons to the King as the right ones—these four—creatures of his own and Bismarck's, in every way most undesirable and not possessing one quality needful for the position. We luckily carried the point and Lieutenant O'Danne will be appointed but I think this interference in our concerns too bad. You have no idea what trouble the reigning party take to put their spies about our court—nor to what a degree they hate us. I can tell you much more about it when we meet.

What you say about Lord Stanley's readiness to appoint

---

[1] Two miles north-east of Potsdam.
[2] Gustav zu Putlitz (1821–90). Playwright. Director of the Court Theatre at Schwerin and Karlsruhe. Married Elizabeth von Konigsmark. Chamberlain to the Crown Prince.

Morier—when the place is vacant—rejoices me exceedingly, but may I say a little word which it would be perhaps good for Lord Stanley to know?[1] Lord A. Loftus and Morier are great friends, but Lord A. is—and has of late—become a very great admirer of Bismarck with whom he is on a friendly footing. Bismarck hates M. because he knows that you are partial to him and that Fritz and I like him, and also for political reasons; if he hears that he is likely to come he will tell Lord A. Loftus to prevent it and I am afraid Lord A. may give way if it is put amiably to him. There is an Attaché of the English Embassy a Mr. Sandford[2] a great "snob" who is always in Bismarck's house, and goes to him in the country; they now say he is going to marry Bismarck's daughter. I fear you will think all this gossip.

From the Crown Princess

NEUES PALAIS, SEPTEMBER 21, 1867

Do you remember a Mr. Bancroft who was in London in '48 as American Minister and who is here now in the same capacity? Such a pleasant, interesting man. He is the author of an American history, and is acquainted with all our distinguished men of science and letters in England and also in Germany. He says dear Papa was very kind to him.

We have closed the accounts of my Bazaar which has brought a sum of 85,000 thalers, exclusive of the expense which was considerable. I am very proud of the result—nothing approaching to it was ever known in this country.

Another plan of mine—at which I have been working very hard for the last three years seems at last to be ripening —that is the erection of a museum and school of art and industry on the same principle as Kensington. Most of the difficulties and opposition the plan met with seem to have subsided and the first small beginning will open in January. My Society for the Employment of Women and the school

---

[1] William Lowther (1821–1912), father of the Speaker, was about to resign as Secretary of the Legation at Berlin.
[2] Probably W. G. Sandford (1834–84).

belonging to it makes but slow and small progress—but the shop or bazaar for women's work is getting on very well. How kind you would be if you could once send them a little order, it would help them so much—anything in the way of linen, drapery, or embroidery, or knitting—which you might wish to give away. I only ask for a small order because I do not think it fair to your subjects to ask for money for a foreign charity though it will be my own special undertaking. My plan for a hospital is quite at a standstill—the next years I must spend in collecting. I hope to be able to see Miss Nightingale when we are in London and show her the plan. I fear I bore you with my descriptions of things in a country indifferent to you, and which you will perhaps never see—but they absorb much of my time and are of deep interest to me so that you must excuse my mentioning them. M. de Normann is my right hand in all these things and has a capital head for them. If you care to hear more I can tell you a great deal about them when we meet.

From the Crown Princess

NEUES PALAIS, SEPTEMBER 28, 1867

M. de Holzmann[1] is here again about the Hanoverian business—and Uncle George wrote to me expressing several wishes which Fritz kindly laid before Bismarck but that is all we can do—as Bismarck has already accused me to different people of intriguing for my Hanoverian relations against the interests of Prussia which I certainly have not done.

From the Queen   BALMORAL, OCTOBER 1, 1867

I can't tell you how shocked I am at Alix's refusal of seeing the King for which there is no good reason. Alice dreaded this. Bertie merely says "I went to Frankfort last Wednesday to see the King of P. He had proposed coming here to see Alix—but owing to her mourning" (which did

---

[1] Afterwards Sir Maurice Holzmann (1835–1909). German secretary to the Prince of Wales, and an enlightened continental Liberal.

not prevent her going to the public gardens to hear the band!!!) "and not feeling quite up to seeing him—begged to be excused". I have written strongly to Bertie about it. The Queen is with right much hurt. Alix did not make a favourable impression on her when she was in England, which I am not surprised at.[1]

From the Crown Princess

NEUES PALAIS, OCTOBER 2, 1867

The Cesarewitch and Dagmar were here. She was not well so I went to Berlin and spent the day with them. She certainly is a very attractive, charming and interesting little person. I never thought she would become so pretty. She seems quite happy and contented with her fat, good-natured husband who seems far more attentive and kind to her than one would have thought. I was pleased to see that she has not become grand—and does not give herself airs as all the Russian Grand-Duchesses do. She has remained simple and unaffected; she has only been a short while in Russia since her marriage—but it does not seem as if the splendours of the Russian Court would dazzle her, and turn her head nor the servile flattery, which is the tone there, could spoil her. She seems so little occupied with herself.

From the Crown Princess

NEUES PALAIS, OCTOBER 4, 1867

The Crown Princess is referring to the vacancy in the Berlin Embassy; she writes:

Those you have named viz—Odo Russell and Julian Fane[2] are certainly the fittest for the post after Morier, for none knows the terrain as he does. I am sure Germany ought to be thankful to you for your unwearying endeavours

---

[1] On 12 October the Queen writes: "I am so glad that matters have been set right and Alix has seen the King. Bertie telegraphed to me that the visit went off very well."
[2] Julian Fane (1827–70) son of 11th Earl of Westmorland.

to befriend her, whenever you can—and most certainly Fritz and I are.[1]

From the Queen   BALMORAL, OCTOBER 5, 1867
I am glad you were pleased with Dagmar and think her so unspoilt and simple. That is the case also with Alix. If only she understood her duties better. That makes me terribly anxious. If only I had the comfort to feel that if I closed my eyes, things would go well—but alas! I feel just the contrary, and see it more and more every day. I feel how necessary my poor life is—and yet how uncertain is anyone's life!

From the Crown Princess
                          NEUES PALAIS, OCTOBER 11, 1867
Many thanks for the copy of Lord Derby's letter—and Lord Stanley's, also of the answer you had written. I see that it is impossible that Morier can come now, which I am very sorry for, but I comfort myself with the hope that he may come at some future and not too distant period. At any rate I cannot say how grateful I am for the trouble you have given yourself about the business. I now hope we may have Mr. J. Fane as I think Mr. Odo Russell will hardly be able to be spared from his post, which is at present so interesting and important and which he fills so well; the next best after him would be Mr. Lytton[2] I suppose.

From the Crown Princess
                          NEUES PALAIS, OCTOBER 15, 1867
The Queen Dowager is very angry that the King of Bavaria's engagement is broken off. It is a funny proceeding, and an awkward position for the young lady but the country did not like the marriage as they thought it was arranged

---

[1] In her letter of 1 October the Queen wrote: "I send you the copy of what I have written to Lord Derby on the subject—that you may see how I try to fight it—or at any rate to get a fit one for the post".
[2] Edward Robert Bulwer Lytton (1831–91) afterwards 1st Earl of Lytton. At this time Secretary of Legation at Lisbon.

by the Ultramontane Party, and the King was caught against his will, in an intrigue of the old Archduchess Sophie and her sisters, so that one can be a little thankful that they will see the truth of the motto "there is many a slip 'twixt the cup and the lip". Still it is an unpleasant business for the whole family.[1]

The Crown Princess was expecting a child, and was on her way to England. But she was unable to continue her journey, and is at this time staying at Cassel.

From the Queen   BALMORAL, OCTOBER 25, 1867

I cannot say how grieved and distressed I am at this terrible contretemps! But, dearest child, why did you not tell me, your own mother, when you first began being in that way—for I could have understood your difficulties and tried everything to arrange them? To attempt a journey and voyage in a very advanced state (for so Alice calls it— who I suppose knew all when your poor Mama did not) unless you intended to come for the event is I think hardly wise; at any rate very fatiguing. But what can we do? Let us hope and pray we may make some arrangement to meet ere long—for I know that you feel the want of seeing old Mama and your dear home, and I long to see our own, dear, first born, who darling Papa so watched over! He would be much grieved at so long a separation. Nearly two years— indeed two years all but six weeks! I can't think what can have caused this indisposition. So many people are able to travel till quite the last. But you have never told me when you expected the event. I have just a week longer here— and then I must go to that dungeon Windsor, where your dear presence would have cheered me so much.

---

[1] The young lady to whom the King of Bavaria was briefly engaged was Sophie, afterwards Duchess of Alençon and a sister of the Empress of Austria. The Queen Dowager and the Archduchess Sophie were her aunts.

From the Queen   BALMORAL, OCTOBER 28, 1867

I yesterday evening received your sad and distressed letter and send this by messenger with a proposal which I do hope you will consider and accept. You are more than half way on your road. Six hours more—divided into two easy days—would take you to Antwerp and you could remain quietly on board till the sea was perfectly smooth, and then come over. You would wait at B. Palace till you felt perfectly rested and could then come on to Windsor, and you could perfectly remain there or at least in England for the event, if the homeward voyage would be too much —as I gather from you and Alice that the event is not so very distant. I could desire Gream[1] to be on board and come over with you. You will have sixteen hours rail back to Berlin, which would be very fatiguing and I am sure the rest and quiet with me will do you good. I write at the same time to the Queen to tell the King of this plan begging him to allow it. Fritz could naturally go back between. To be longer than two years without seeing you and with the uncertainty of when you could come again is really too dreadful. The trouble to me is nothing—quite the contrary —the pleasure to have you for some time longer would be so great and would I am sure do you good. Kanné[2] is to take this and wait for an answer. I do hope it may be managed.

From the Crown Princess   CASSEL, OCTOBER 31, 1867

I do not see how I could possibly go to England for such an event—it would be so ill-taken by the country. You know how unkind public opinion is already towards me, and how unpopular I am, how jealous the Prussians are of my making any show of my being English—which I am constantly accused of on every occasion. I would not willingly do anything to hurt their feelings—and this really would.

---

[1] J. T. Gream (1812–88) Physician accoucheur to the Princess of Wales.
[2] Joseph Julius Kanné, the Queen's courier, and described as director of Continental journeys.

Then you cannot judge how impossible it is for me to leave my house—children etc.

You know that in my position here in Germany I dare not consider my wishes alone and it is a difficult position; my only desire is to fill it, and discharge the duties belonging to it as your and dear Papa's daughter should, and I am sure you would not wish me to do anything which exposes me to fresh malevolence and ill nature. I shall say nothing about politics today though I am very anxious to know what you think about Italy, and what Mr. Odo Russell says and thinks.[1] I am all for Italian unity and for poor, ill-used though often benighted Garibaldi. Of course our Government is not—the cause of national liberty and unity is one all the world over and as such I sympathise with every demonstration of it—where it is real and spontaneous, (at the same time cordially hating Mexicans, Poles and Fenians).

From the Queen   WINDSOR CASTLE, NOVEMBER 6, 1867
For fear of forgetting what I have forgotten three times already let me begin at once by asking you if Mr. West was ever an *attaché* at Berlin, and if so whether you liked him as there is a question of sending him as Secretary of Embassy there?[2] The other person named is a Mr. Herries,[3] said to be a quiet, sensible man. Mr. Lytton was too low down to take unless very far superior to the others, and Mr. Stuart[4]—perhaps the best of all—declined the post which would have been the same with Mr. Fane and Mr. Odo Russell. Now would you telegraph back to me—"Should like W."—or in the other case "Have no

---

[1] Three days before the Crown Princess wrote French troops occupied Rome to save the city from Garibaldi.
[2] Lionel Sackville-West (1827–1908) afterwards Lord Sackville. He was attaché at Berlin 1853–58. He lived with—but did not marry—a Spanish lady, Pepita.
[3] At this time Chargè d'Affaires in Florence.
[4] William Stuart (1824–96) son of Lord Blantyre; at this time at St. Petersburg.

choice between H. and W.". I should be thankful as time passes.[1]

Alice's two eldest girls are indeed quite lovely and Victoria most engaging. Irene is very plain. She is not at all well.[2]

Have you read the Duke of Argyll's book "The Reign of Law?"[3] Skerrett[4] was delighted with it—and I am now reading it and am much interested with it. It requires careful and slow reading.

From the Queen   WINDSOR CASTLE, NOVEMBER 9, 1867

Bertie and Alix are here since the 6th, and most amiable and kind, and everything quite pleasant between Christian and them, which is a great comfort. Really Bertie is so full of good and amiable qualities that it makes one forget and overlook much that one would wish different. Dearest Alix walks about, and up and down stairs—everywhere with the help of one or two sticks—but of course very slowly. She even gets in and out of a carriage, but is a sad sight to see her thus and to those who did not see her so ill as we did, when one really did not dare to hope she would get better, it is sad and touching to see. She is very thin and looks very frail but very pretty, and is so good and patient under this heavy trial. The poor leg is completely stiff and it remains to be seen whether it will ever get quite right again. I much fear not.

From the Crown Princess

NEUES PALAIS, NOVEMBER 9, 1867

I am quite as active again as I was before I left, and take my two daily walks without their tiring me, and as much exercise indoors as possible—which is called for when I look after the children in their different apartments upstairs and

---

[1] The Princess knew neither man. Herries was appointed, and declined so that West was the man chosen.
[2] Princess Alice.
[3] 8th Duke of Argyll (1823–1900). The book, which had just been published, was written to reconcile the claims of science and religion.
[4] The Queen's dresser.

downstairs. You are very kind to say you will take Henry again for this winter, but luckily it is not necessary for his health, and for educational reasons we do not wish to send him away. We have settled all for the winter; the new military governor comes, when we return to Berlin, and Henry is to leave the nursery and be made over to the schoolroom, begin lessons by degrees and get into regular habits which is very necessary for him.

We are going to have a little amateur theatrical entertainment on my birthday which M. de Putlitz is arranging.

I had collected a basket of fruit, grown in our little garden, as specimens of what it produces which I meant to bring to you. I sent it off to you last week. I hope that it arrived safe and that you tried the fruit as my gardener will be broken-hearted. I fear it is finer to look at than to taste; it is grown on the French system of Lepère of dwarf trees.[1]

From the Crown Princess

NEUES PALAIS, POTSDAM,[2] NOVEMBER 12, 1867

The King has got it in his head that on your return from Scotland you had to have an immense military and police escort; this is not true is it?[3] What you say about Italy is no doubt most true; in many things there has been a great want of faith, the King and his Ministers[4] and the French and all of them together have not behaved honourably. But I have a great sympathy for the nations that have suffered so much and been misgoverned so long. There is a deal of ardent and patient patriotism amongst the Italians—which one cannot but admire and sympathise with. And I do hope that the temporal power of the Pope may be at an end, and that under the next Pope, whoever he may be, there may be reforms of the terrible abuses of Papal government,

---

[1] Thanking, the Queen wrote: "We greatly admire the pears and the apples but they do not taste as fine as they look."
[2] The address of the Neues Palais was Potsdam, and the Crown Princess from now on uses either in her letter-heading.
[3] On account of the Fenians.
[4] The Crown Princess means by this that the Italian Government was carrying on clandestine intrigues with Garibaldi while outwardly opposing him.

which could only be a boon for the whole of the Christian world. People will have it here that the Catholic religion is making rapid progress in England, that the aristocracy are all going over to the Church of Rome—and that there are new conversions every day. I consider this a very great exaggeration, and always maintain it is not true and that in spite of the noise the Catholics and High Church people make—and the nonsensical extravagances committed by certain Sectarians which have been so much talked about in the press—England as a nation is as Protestant as ever. I wish you would kindly ask General Grey to write to me on the subject once and also on that of the Fenians—which latter often make me uncomfortable, so as I may have something to answer when the King says all this.

From the Queen   WINDSOR CASTLE, NOVEMBER 13, 1867
          (Anniversary of dear Uncle Charles's death.)
    I send you today some new and very successful photos taken at Balmoral. My likeness in the wagonette is thought particularly good.[1]
    I find Henny[2] very gentle and amiable—but I could forgive anyone for being violent in the cruel position in which her family have been so shamefully placed—the Power swallowing them up who fought for their rights!!
    Dear sweet Alix (who really is so good and so patient) has been out driving with me every day and we understand each other's feelings (her own country and Mama excepted whom we do not talk of) extremely well.

From the Queen   WINDSOR CASTLE, NOVEMBER 16, 1867
    I can only write you a very hasty letter as I am going today to Knole to see poor old Lady Delaware[3] who is very ill, and I shall be away seven hours.

---

[1] This is reproduced on page 184 of *Queen Victoria* by Helmut and Alison Gernsheim.
[2] Henriette, sister of Prince Christian. The Queen's allusion to Prussia is sharp.
[3] Elizabeth, wife of the 5th Lord De La Warr and heiress of the Duke of Dorset. She was married in 1813, and died in 1870.

The state of the Church is very serious—and I am sure there will have to be a new Reformation. I am very nearly a Dissenter—or rather more a Presbyterian—in my feelings, so very Catholic do I feel we are.[1]

From the Queen   WINDSOR CASTLE, NOVEMBER 19, 1867
I have just returned from a drive with dear Marie F.[2] and think her very dear and nice, something so frank and open about her, and very pretty. What a lovely little mouth and nose, such sweet eyes and eyebrows, and the forehead and shape of face—all very pretty. I can't judge of the figure in her out-going dress, and have not yet seen her without her bonnet. She likes England very much. He is very deaf.

From the Crown Princess
                NEUES PALAIS, POTSDAM, NOVEMBER 19, 1867
They are very busy in the house preparing the theatricals—and George[3] is very nervous for fear his piece should not be a success. You must read it, as I am sure you will like the fine language; it is meant to be a sequel to Goethe's "Iphigenia". Professor Eggers has written a very pretty prologue and von Putlitz has managed the whole so I hope it may succeed. Instead of an overture a very fine march of Abbat's composition will be played.

From the Crown Princess
                NEUES PALAIS, POTSDAM, NOVEMBER 29, 1867
Your visit to Claremont must have been sentimental for

---

[1] This year the Government appointed a Royal Commission to enquire into the growth of Ritualistic practices, including the wearing of vestments, in the Church of England. This no doubt explains the Queen's remark.
[2] Flanders.
[3] This is probably Prince George of Prussia whose father was first cousin to the King. He was born in 1826 and died unmarried in 1902. Several of his plays were performed at the National Theatre. He wrote under the pseudonym George Conrad.

many reasons. I can still recall your birthday there so well![1]
The verses Meyer made for us to repeat, the cowslip balls
old Mrs. Duke[2] made, Mr. Mallison's[3] cottage, and Sir
Robert Gardiner's house, my fright at having to run down
that slippery bank. I remember dear Papa ironing a lot of
letters on the floor in your sitting-room with one of your
maids.[4] I remember Uncle Charles and the Mensdorffs and
the Duke of Nassau paying you a visit there and Lenchen
as a little baby crying and screaming so much, and your
coming downstairs when I was in my bath and poor
Charrier[5] and Mlle Gruner[6] were there! That all seems
such a long time ago to me; I dare say you will have forgotten many of the unimportant little incidents which I
remember. I remember your drawing at the window of
your sitting-room, and Papa carrying Affie about—who
was such a beautiful child!

From the Queen   WINDSOR CASTLE, NOVEMBER 30, 1867
    I fear I can only write a very stupid letter as I am so
tired and knocked up—merely by having visitors for two
days. And having to talk more, and losing my little bits of
time for rest—or rather more for work—which then gets
all hurried and scrambled—have made me feel as though
my head were of china and thoroughly exhausted body and
nerves. I shun in consequence talking to people for

---

[1] Claremont, near Esher, where Princess Charlotte died, was the property
of King Leopold, remaining in his possession after he went to Belgium.
Part of the early married life of the Queen was spent there, and in 1848
it became the home in exile of King Louis Philippe and his family. The
Crown Princess is remembering the events of the early summer of
1846.
[2] Probably King Leopold's housekeeper at Claremont.
[3] The gardener at Claremont.
[4] The stoutness of writing-paper in those days made it difficult to fold
letters neatly.
[5] Aimée Charrier, nursery governess to the Crown Princess. She came
from Geneva, and had lately died.
[6] Charlotte Gruner who was German governess to the Royal children.
She married Pastor Brecht in 1850, and died in 1876.

long, more than I can say, as it causes such positive suffering.[1]

From the Crown Princess

Since M. de Putlitz is Master of the Household Count Eulenburg has undertaken to manage the whole of the stables retaining his place as Fritz's aide de camp; and we send him to England to buy carriages for us. We shall be very grateful if you will kindly grant him the favour of a few minutes' audience. I can now tell you what it was that I hinted at as having been an unpleasant occurrence in our household. Countess Pourtales has resigned. On the whole I am not sorry as she was not qualified for her post though a very good and estimable person. I was never the least intimate with her and we had always remained on a formal footing. Last year she wished to resign and I begged her to stay on until I had found someone fitting. What brought the business to a crisis was that she did not return from Switzerland in time to do the honours on the evening of my birthday—although we had expressly begged her to do so.[2] I now think of Mme. de Putlitz in her place who has long been a friend and whom I love very much—but I have not yet mentioned it to the King and Queen. I have been very busy these last few days at the farm arranging a new dairy and trying to organise an evening sewing-school for the village girls—also visiting the school and distributing prizes to the children. May I again trouble you with the same eternal question? Have you seen Mr. Hadwyn Wheelright's pictures? Can you not induce the Kensington Museum to buy the collection? I think it is unequalled.[3]

---

[1] The Queen would have agreed with a question asked by Charles Lamb, "Whither can I take wing from the oppression of human faces?"

[2] The departure of Countess Pourtales was a misfortune. She was born Bethmann-Hollweg, and her family was very influential.

[3] A water-colour painter; much of his work was after the Italian masters. He exhibited in London in the 1830s and 1840s.

From the Queen   WINDSOR CASTLE, DECEMBER 7, 1867

Mary and Francy Teck have been here for two nights with their little baby—a dear, sprightly, little thing, but not a fine or remarkably handsome child, but I am sure she will be pretty. It is a real pleasure to see dear Mary now, she is so bright and happy and all her fine qualities come out to such advantage now that she is happy. But her size is fearful! It is really a misfortune.

I admire Elizabeth[1] very much and I like the sentiment that true love and noble hearts can unite high and low in friendship and affection! As time goes on, whatever people may say and do to prevent it, the fences which hedge in rank, will not be possible to be maintained unless they are justified by character and merit.

I must not forget to say that I was immensely pleased on Thursday with Foley's proposed statue of darling Papa for Cambridge, which is simple and dignified—and with his small model for one of the great groups for the Memorial. His monument to poor General Bruce is also so fine. He is a man of great genius and talent, and dearest Papa admired him so much. He had also two of the figures of the group in life-size.[2] Poor Noble, on the other hand, is devoid of all real genius and has a horrid, colossal statue of me for India which Louise is going to try and greatly alter.

From the Queen   WINDSOR CASTLE, DECEMBER 11, 1867
Writing of the Crown Princess's ladies the Queen says:

I am glad for you that Countess Pourtales resigned. She was not *sympathique* to you, and I hope you may be able to get Madame de Putlitz who seems such an amiable person.

I know too well—how dreadful it is to have people (they may be the very best) who are unsympathetic. No one feels this more than I do, in my sad and isolated position, and no

---

[1] It is difficult to say who this is, but it is almost certainly Miss Pulleine, an heiress and a niece of the Queen's banker, Edward Marjoribanks. She married John Cowell, Master of the Household, an officer in the Royal Engineers, on 5 February 1868.
[2] Groups round the base of the Albert Memorial.

one has this instinct so strongly. There are people—low as well as high—to whom I am drawn from the very first, enormously as by a magnet, and others who repel me! The dear old Baron said I was always right and I must say— with but very few exceptions—I have been. But I am very careful not to let myself be carried away by it. I hope your new governess will be a success. Only don't teach dear Henry too much. Nothing is gained by it—and it weakens their brains. We found this, and taught the younger ones all later.

From the Queen   OSBORNE, DECEMBER 18, 1867

I wished to answer what you said about the bar between high and low. What you say about it is most true but alas! that is the great danger in England now, and one which alarms all right-minded and thinking people.[1]

The higher classes—especially the aristocracy (with of course exceptions and honourable ones)—are so frivolous, pleasure-seeking, heartless, selfish, immoral and gambling that it makes one think (just as the Dean of Windsor said to me the other evening) of the days before the French Revolution. The young men are so ignorant, luxurious and self-indulgent—and the young women so fast, frivolous and imprudent that the danger really is very great, and they ought to be warned. The lower classes are becoming so well-informed, are so intelligent and earn their bread and riches so deservedly—that they cannot and ought not to be kept back—to be abused by the wretched, ignorant, high-born beings who live only to kill time. They must be

---

[1] The Crown Princess had agreed entirely with her mother, while suggesting that "the lower classes must rise to the upper—and not vice versa—or the consequences are dreadful, as the first French Revolution has proved". Although Ruskin was not a writer whom the Queen would have been likely to read she was echoing some powerful words of his written a few years earlier:

"No agitators, no clubs, no epidemical errors, ever were or will be fatal to social order in any nation. Nothing but the guilt of the upper classes, wanton, accumulated, reckless and merciless, ever overthrows them. Of such guilt they have now much to answer for—let them look to it in time." *The Two Paths*, Lecture III.

warned and frightened or some dreadful crash will take place. What I can, I do and will do—but Bertie ought to set a good example in these respects by not countenancing even any of these horrid people.

From the Queen   OSBORNE, DECEMBER 21, 1867
After alluding to Balmoral the Queen writes:

It makes me think of my little book which you know I gave you a private copy of. Well, it was so much liked that I was begged and asked to allow it to be published—the good Dean of Windsor amongst other wise and kind people saying it would, from its simplicity and the kindly feelings expressed to those below us, do so much good. I therefore consented—cutting out some of the more familiar descriptions and being subjected by Mr. Helps and others to a very severe scrutiny of style and grammar (the correspondence about which would have amused you very much) and adding our first journeys and visits to Scotland, yachting tours to the Channel Islands and visits to Ireland. I have likewise added a little allusion to your engagement to Fritz and what I wrote on the death of the Duke of Wellington. The whole is edited by Mr. Helps, who has written a very pretty preface to it. It has given a great deal of trouble for one had so carefully to exclude even the slightest observation which might hurt anyone's feelings. But it has been an interest and an occupation—for no-one can conceive the trouble of printing a book, and the mistakes, which are endless.[1]

---

[1] *Leaves from the Journal of our Life in the Highlands* (1848–1861) was published early in 1868.

1868

From the Queen   OSBORNE, JANUARY 4, 1868
    You will be dreadfully shocked to hear of the sudden
death of Marochetti. He will be a terrible loss here where
we have so little genius. Good General Grey does not see
this which provoked me not a little.[1]

From the Crown Princess   BERLIN, JANUARY 4, 1868
    I am so glad you liked Willy's photo; without being
pretty he has a charming countenance, and very pleasing
expression—particularly in his eyes. I think he would be
very good-looking someday, if it were not for the distressing
crookedness caused by his poor arm, which is very visible
in his face as his head is not straight and the whole left
side of neck and face much thinner and flatter than the
other. The arm gains in strength; he can use it more than
he did. But it seems to get stiffer and he cannot bend it or
turn around any better, and I think it even looks more dis-
figuring than it did—particularly when he runs. It is a
great distress to me still. He has begun Latin and a little
drawing for which he seems to have rather a turn.

From the Queen   OSBORNE, JANUARY 8, 1868
    All you tell me about dear Willy interests me very
much. That poor arm is a sad thing, but we must take it
as a cross sent us and must be thankful if he is so dear,
good and clever. But you begin too early with Latin. Our
boys only began at 10—and Willy is not 9. I hope the new
person in the nursery will suit but you should not call her
Nurse. Two nurses never will do. Dear Papa, the Baron

---

[1] Carlo Marochetti (1805–67) sculptor. General Grey, with possibly
somewhat insular taste, would have also disagreed with Ruskin who
described Marochetti's Coeur de Lion, outside the Houses of Parliament
as "the only really interesting piece of historical sculpture we have
hitherto given to our City populace." Ruskin, *Art of England*, Lecture
II.

and Sir James as well as Lady Caroline will tell you and can tell you that that never can answer. I mention them as I know that my experience and advice never goes for much with you, dear child.

From the Crown Princess   BERLIN, JANUARY 8, 1868
        The Fenian movement continues to cause great sensation and concern here; people think the government has not shown energy enough quelling it at the beginning, but from what I can gather from all I read on the subject it appears to me that all measures that can be taken to stop the outrageous proceedings of these disturbers of the peace have been taken, and I admire the calm and dignified way in which the thing is taken in England. If the like evil had been on foot here—the measures taken would be such as to make the whole country suffer, I am sure, and then *"le remède serait pire que le mal"*. The winter continues dreadfully severe and the distress is very great here at Berlin and also in the provinces. We have been very busy getting up a committee for the relief of the poor—collecting things and money and organising a system to give the poor people work in the districts where the famine is worst. The Queen is at the head of another committee, and going to have a bazaar in the Schloss. It is not a lucky idea as it comes too soon after mine, and people's pockets as well as their energies have not had time to rest from the exertions of the last bazaar. So I fear it will not be a success. We are not in London or Paris—the means here are very small compared with there.
        Pray thank Lenchen for the charming photographs of her little boy. What a nice, dear, little thing he seems—but who is he like?[1] Neither Lenchen nor Christian I should think by the photograph. And he has got one of those German things around his neck "—a dribbling-bib". I am sure someone from Germany has made Lenchen a present of it. It belongs to the swaddling clothes and baby-binder

[1] Prince Christian Victor. He died on active service in the Boer War on 29 October 1900.

and the rest of the antediluvian apparatus the poor little Germans are stuffed into, shortly after their appearance into this vale of tears, which always shocks my English principles!!

From the Queen OSBORNE, JANUARY 11, 1868

I am sorry I could not send you my book before it was published, but I could not, as they only came to hand on the Thursday night. By Wednesday's messenger you, Fritz and the two Queens shall receive copies. It has been most affectionately, warmly received by the public and you will be gratified and touched by the articles in *The Times* and *Daily Telegraph*. Good Mr. Helps says "It is a new bond of union" between me and my people; that I was "immensely loved before" but "will be still more so now". And many other true friends express the same feeling. There is much about you as a dear little girl which I am sure will recall former happy days to you.

Do not be alarmed about the Fenians. There has been a great deal of nonsense and foolish panic, and numberless stories which have proved sheer inventions!! One, most absurd one, frightened people so much that they took endless, useless precautions here.[1] However Mr. Hardy[2] is the right man in the right place, besides being a most delightful person, he is so calm and quiet—though harassed from morning till night with rumours—false and possibly some true. But the country was never more loyal or sound. I would throw myself amongst my English and dear Scotch subjects alone (London excepted as it is so enormous and full of Irish) and I should be as safe as in my room.

From the Crown Princess BERLIN, JANUARY 14, 1868

Indeed I do think both Count Furstenstein and Wally

---

[1] It was rumoured that the Fenians intended to capture the Queen when she was at Osborne. The Queen complained to the Prime Minister "such are the precautions taken here—the Queen will be little better than a State prisoner".

[2] Gathorne Gathorne-Hardy, afterwards Earl of Cranbrook (1814–1906), Home Secretary at this time.

Paget would be much touched and gratified by your sending them a copy of your book as you kindly offered to do so—and I am sure dear Marie Goltz would too.

We hear that poor, unhappy Charlotte has been informed of Max's death. How sad one feels for her! How difficult it must be for Leopold and Marie to weigh every word they say to her, though it must have been running a great risk to tell her the dreadful truth. I can see it was impossible to keep up fiction any longer—as she might have found it out by chance, and then one could never have persuaded her to believe anyone again—and she would be more difficult to treat than ever before. But how melancholy it all is.

From the Queen   OSBORNE, JANUARY 15, 1868

Regarding Willy's learning Latin and the tutors deciding it—I never now do these things without consulting the physicians as I think all tutors and masters are inclined to expect too much and too soon.

We have poor Mr. Martin laid up here with a bad knee from a fall on the ice on Friday. But we are too glad to keep him, and Mrs. Martin a very charming person (who was an actress) is here also taking care of him.[1]

From the Crown Princess   BERLIN, JANUARY 17, 1868

A thousand affectionate thanks for your very kind and dear letter of the 15th by messenger—and for your book. The newspaper extracts are written in a kindly and sympathising tone. I have collected what I have found on the subject in the German papers and send them off to you tomorrow. It will be a sentimental pleasure to me to read over recollections of the happy, old times—of which my memory retains so vivid and grateful a picture! I send you a note from the Queen Dowager which will show you how pleased and gratified she is that you thought of her.

---

[1] The Queen was making preparation for the official biography of the Prince Consort on which Theodore Martin (1816–1909) was engaged. He had married Helen Faucit, the Shakespearean actress.

The other copy I sent my mama-in-law this morning. Fritz sends his warmest thanks for your book and the kind words you have written in it which gave him great pleasure.

From the Queen   OSBORNE, JANUARY 18, 1868
    I told the Queen to give you the copy of a letter from Leopold B. about poor Charlotte. It was absolutely necessary to tell her the truth—now that poor Max's funeral takes place.[1] It is today.
    I send you again several newspaper articles about the book, the effect produced by which is wonderful, and will I know gladden your heart from the extreme loyalty it displays. From all and every side, high and low, the feeling is the same the letters flow in, saying how much more than ever I shall be loved, now that I am known and understood, and clamouring for the cheap edition for the poor—which will be ordered at once. 18,000 copies were sold in a week. It is very gratifying to see how people appreciate what is simple and right and how especially my truest friends—the people —feel it. They have (as a body) the truest feeling for family life.

From the Crown Princess   BERLIN, JANUARY 21, 1868
    I had a few lines from poor, dear Charlotte herself which were very touching but very calm! How dreadful is her lot! For her, poor thing, the sun has set; she has nothing more to hope or look forward to in life, no interest and no one object to devote her energies to. If she was of a less active mind I should not wonder if she went into a convent—it is one of the only instances in which I could understand taking such a resolution.
    You have heard no doubt of the foolish marriage Elischen is going to make—to a very cracked and absurd little Prince Salm, who has not a penny, and whose vocation is distributing tracts and trying to cure people of drinking, which is very commendable but he is the most ridiculous, affected creature you ever saw. He would put

[1] In Vienna.

you into fits of laughter. I for my part could not consent to be present at his presentation to you—for fear of being seized in the way I was once upon a time when you went to see the Italian artist copying dear Grandmama's picture at Osborne downstairs, and as I was on the memorable occasion when Gruner[1] wanted to explain a drawing to you in the audience room at Windsor. That only happens to me now when the Grand Duke of Weimar or Roggenbach talk English—that is more than any human gravity can stand!

From the Queen   OSBORNE, JANUARY 22, 1868

Newspapers shower in—the poorest, simplest full of the most touching and affectionate expressions. The kind and proper feeling towards the poor and the servants will I hope do good for it is very much needed in England among the higher classes. The cheap edition for the poor is to be published as soon as possible. A second edition like the first is coming out immediately.

I send you several of Mrs. Oliphant's charming Scotch novels, which I have mentioned to you before and which I am sure will amuse you.

As for the "bib", which horrified you so, you are quite old-fashioned in thinking it antediluvian for, for the last six to seven years, every English child wears one, and Mrs. Mason and Mrs. Bland make them always—as much as any other things.[2]

From the Crown Princess   BERLIN, JANUARY 25, 1868

The cold is so intense that I cannot venture out of the house today, as I have still the least little remnant of my stupid cold. Inflammation of the lungs and throat are raging here—and many poor little children are being carried off by these horrid diseases, and the distress among the poor is very great. We have not had such a hard winter for some years; the men are thrown out of work and their families starve from the cold—wood and coal being so dear—

---

[1] Ludwig Gruner, an authority on Italian fresco painting.
[2] These ladies were presumably needlewomen in Royal service.

and from the bad harvest the price of bread has risen so much. We are obliged to give extra sugar to all our married servants.

Our gentlemen that have returned from Vienna[1] say that nothing can be kinder or more cordial and civil than the reception they met with—as well in society as at Court—which I am glad of, as I wish a good feeling to be re-established between us and Austria, and then with France and England—so that these four powers may join in preventing Russia from making further progress in the East. This seems to me clearly the duty of civilised nations, and in uniting for this purpose the chances for a war between France and us seems to me to diminish considerably. They are still the *cauchemars* which keep tormenting me—whenever a French or German newspaper article touches on any subject of difference between the two countries.

From the Queen   OSBORNE, JANUARY 29, 1868[2]

I have such quantities of beautiful and touching letters from people whom I don't know, or have ever heard of—all about my little book, but I send you none, and indeed have been doubtful of sending you the *Quarterly* with a review by the Bishop of Oxford, as you seem to take so little interest in it and only mentioned it once. Here everyone is so full of gratitude and loyal affection, saying it is not to be told the good it will do the Throne, and as an example to people in the higher classes.

From the Crown Princess   BERLIN, FEBRUARY 1, 1868

I do not know why you should think I am indifferent about the appearance of your book and what is said about it in the press—whatever concerns you and our home is of vital importance and greatest interest not of indifference. The article in the *Edinburgh Review* (which I always take

---

[1] From the funeral of the Emperor of Mexico.
[2] The Queen had been obliged to postpone going to Windsor because Prince Leopold had a serious attack of internal bleeding. She wrote: "he has been fearfully ill."

in and read regularly) I thought very kind and well
worded.

I have begun to read one of the Scotch novels—"Lily's
Leaf" which I think is very pretty—simple and true to
nature.

They say the season here is very gay—at any rate there
is an immense deal going on and the streets are very noisy
at night, with all the carriages to and from the balls and
parties.

From the Queen   OSBORNE, FEBRUARY 22, 1868
Bertie has been here for one night—very kind and
amiable, looking well, but getting bald!

From the Queen   OSBORNE, FEBRUARY 26, 1868
Poor Lord Derby was so alarmingly ill and the attacks
of gout from which he suffers are so serious that he has been
obliged to resign and Mr. Disraeli is Prime Minister! A
proud thing for a man "risen from the people" to have
obtained! And I must say—really most legally; it is his
real talent, his good temper and the way in which he
managed the Reform Bill last year which have brought this
about.

From the Queen   OSBORNE, FEBRUARY 29, 1868
My letter of Wednesday and General Grey's yesterday
will have answered that part of yours about the change of
Government which yours spoke about. I will however add
that I think the present man will do well, and will be
particularly loyal and anxious to please me in every way.
He is very peculiar, but very clever and sensible and very
conciliatory.[1]

---

[1] The Crown Princess had written on 26 February:
"I hear Lord Derby has resigned and Mr. Disraeli is in his place. I
fear that will not be exactly what will suit you and I feel very sorry
that there is no one else to fill that place at present." Unfortunately
General Grey's letter explaining to the Crown Princess about Disraeli
has not survived.

From the Crown Princess   BERLIN, FEBRUARY 29, 1868

I hope Mr. Disraeli will fill his important place well, and that you think him up to it. He is vain and ambitious is he not? He must feel very proud of having risen to his present position which he owes to his talents, and to the dearth of clever men in the Tory party I suppose? But I speak quite without *connaissance de cause* as it so long since I knew the rights about English affairs—and from the newspapers one cannot tell all the ins and outs, and whenever I ask Lord Augustus, he seems to know very little about what is going on at home. In fact it is not to be wondered that a sober diplomatist should find watching and trying to understand Bismarck's dodges is work enough for any man's brain, and leaves him no time for other thoughts. The artificial, complicated and unnatural state of things here sets one's judgement, reason and imagination so much to work that even the shortest conversation on German politics is a mental effort, which I feel to be positively exhausting. And this is an unwholesome state of affairs, for everybody gets into a state of excitement which is often hurtful to their commonsense and completely upsets their temper (especially irritable ones such as crowned heads and Bismarck possess).

Many thanks for the charming flowers "sweet harbingers of Spring"; when I catch a glimpse of my window it is to see the dreary streets and people wrapped in their furs —all looking so bleak and winter-like and melancholy. I quite pine for a little fresh, country air but for the next eight or ten weeks we cannot go to Potsdam!

From the Crown Princess   BERLIN, MARCH 3, 1868

I have this moment received General Grey's letter of the 28th which interests me immensely. Will you kindly thank him for it for me. It is absurd to have an aristocratic prejudice against Mr. Disraeli—on account of his being a Jew and an adventurer. A person that rises to a high place by his abilities has surely as good a right as anyone to be your Prime Minister. My fear was that his other qualities were not such as to enable him to fill the place well.

From the Queen

I write to you from this dreary old place, a sad contrast in air and everything to dear, bright Osborne, to thank you for your dear letter of the 29th. I am truly grieved to see you still feel anxious about dear little Vicky. Alas! that is our portion in this world—always to tremble for those we love. That cruel uncertainty poisons every happiness! No doubt it is to show us our Home is not here!

I have had much less than ever to do with the change of Government. Mr. Disraeli will, I think, make a good Minister and certainly a loyal one to me, for he has always behaved extremely well to me, and has all the right feelings for a Minister towards the Sovereign. I enclose you a copy of his first letter to me which may interest you. He is full of poetry, romance and chivalry. When he knelt down to kiss my hand which he took in both of his he said "in loving loyalty and faith".

Lord Cairns is one of the best speakers and most distinguished men at the Bar. He is a few months younger than me, which makes me feel very old, as one generally thinks the Chancellor a venerable personage. Mr. W. Hunt is enormous—but has a pleasing, good-looking face. He weighs 22 stone and really must be above 6 ft. 4 inches and very broad and large.[1] What a mess the King of Hanover or rather more King George has been making. Uncle George is furious—for he ruins the future of his unfortunate son, who is a good young man I believe. German politics are most confusing.

From the Crown Princess

The names we have settled upon for baby were Frederick Joachim Ernest Waldemar and for him to be called by the last.[2] You expressed a wish that we should add Victor Albert on account of the dear 10th of February. We think six too

---

[1] George Ward Hunt (1825–77). Disraeli told the Queen "he has the sagacity of the elephant as well as the form". He was Chancellor of the Exchequer.
[2] Prince Waldemar was born on Queen Victoria's wedding day. He died on 27 March 1879. He did not carry the names Victor Albert.

many; now we are ready to give up Ernest (though we wished the name as none of our children have it) if you will say which you would like to have Victor or Albert. Willy has them both, and we thought it was a privilege we should reserve for the eldest. Fritz insists upon Joachim (which I cannot bear, and he kindly at last gave way to my entreaties not to call the child so—and as he is fond of the name Waldemar, which is historical in this country and family, I agreed to it gladly.) Frederick he also insists upon so you see we are in a fix, as he thinks six too many; and wishes for three or four at the utmost. Will you kindly answer soon whether you wish your name or dear Papa's instead of Ernest. It will always be in remembrance of the 10th of February.

From the Queen   WINDSOR CASTLE, MARCH 11, 1868
My first Drawing-room will be tomorrow. Last Friday was a Court by invitation. But on this occasion no more of my Ladies and Gentlemen will be present than at a Court, and only the heads of the Embassies and Missions—not to make the room hot, which always makes me feel faint. I can't stand well at all; my feet swell so.

From the Crown Princess   BERLIN, MARCH 11, 1868
I received your telegram yesterday and accordingly the names will be Joachim Frederick Ernest Waldemar— the latter to be the name he is to be called by. It will sound very bad in English I am afraid. How very sad it is that the poor King of Hanover either does—or rather is made to do by his evil genius Count Platen—such imprudent things—which forces the government to take measures against him. Between pity for him and his misfortunes, and annoyance at all his foolish acts—one really feels so distressed.

Please tell Bertie that poor Stockmar visits no one— already since two years; he is indeed often prevented from being "at home" even to his friends when they call; for weeks together sometimes even we cannot catch a glimpse of him, and at times he feels too unwell to answer even questions in writing. When he feels more unwell than usual he is so low spirited and wretched that he becomes quite indifferent to what goes on around, and at such times making acquaintances is very irksome to him and he shuns even the exertion of talking. He saw Holzmann once when H. called upon him but did not return his visit—so there it ended. On the whole I find Stockmar better in spirits (not in health) this winter than last. He wants someone to nurse him and take care of him, to cheer and humour him. His is a sad and lonely life—never to feel well is a hard trial; his mind and his heart are ever the same, to be compared to none except his father whom he grows more and more like in manner as he grows older. When he is pretty well he thoroughly enjoys a joke or a good story, and is as witty and mischievous himself as possible—but that is not often. Still we now and then have a good laugh together (usually about Meyer I am afraid) who is an incorrigible original—as in old times.

From the Queen   OSBORNE, MARCH 14, 1868
    The Drawing-room went off well; it was not longer than the Courts and therefore I could remain till the end, but I could not have stopped longer, as I was very tired. Going back to the station I had quite an ovation; I never saw such crowds on any other occasion going back to the station and there were numbers of carriages full of well-dressed people three rows deep in some places. It was very marked— especially as it was chiefly the so-called upper 10,000 who are not near so loyal as the people. My book, everyone says, has had such an extraordinary effect on the people. The cheap edition will be out on Thursday and the 20,000 copies are already bespoken, and 10,000 more have at once to be printed.
    I have just made the acquaintance of Mrs. Oliphant, who wrote those pretty books I sent you. She is very pleasant and clever looking.

From the Queen   WINDSOR CASTLE, MARCH 18, 1868
    Today is dear Louise's 20th birthday. She is (and who

would some years ago have thought it?) a clever, dear girl, with a fine strong character, and a very marked character—unselfish, affectionate, a good daughter and with a wonderful talent for art. She is now doing a bust of me, quite by herself, which will be extremely good.

From the Crown Princess   BERLIN, MARCH 18, 1868
Many thanks for your dear letter of the 14th. I am so glad your Drawing-room went off so well, and that the people crowded in their carriages to the railway station to see you. It reminds me of old times when we used to drive in the park, and I so often wondered at your memory, remembering all the names of the people we met. One used to see on many of their faces how pleased they were at your recognising them.

From the Queen   WINDSOR CASTLE, MARCH 21, 1868
My account of Louise crossed yours.[1] She is a distinguished girl, and very much liked and, with right, much admired—for she is very handsome. Such a beautiful figure and so quiet and graceful.

Poor good Hill, my messenger, 47 years in the service, father to 'pretty Sarah'—died quite suddenly in a cab coming back from the offices—on Thursday morning. He is universally regretted in the house. I went to see the poor widow and daughters yesterday and saw him in his last bed, looking peaceful with a smile on his face.

I am so glad you like Mrs. Oliphant's books. I think there is much knowledge of human nature in them—so much good and right feeling and observations of feelings which one has so often experienced and yet never seen written down. Her descriptions of nature are very sweet also. Which have you read?

---

[1] The Crown Princess had written: "Since she has grown up I have seen so little of her that I can say I scarcely know her."

From the Crown Princess   BERLIN, MARCH 24, 1868
A thousand thanks for your dear letter received yesterday—enclosing that sad letter from Harriet Phipps.[1] I am indeed grieved for poor Minnie![2] What can one do for her? Education is much cheaper abroad than in England. I would willingly pay for the schooling of one of the boys. There is a very good school at Bonn where there are hosts of English who go there for that reason. Shall I enquire? You would perhaps say nothing about it for the present and kindly find out for me whether any other help could be afforded by me. You know I unfortunately cannot give much as there are so many calls on my purse and what would be a considerable sum in some parts of Germany is next to nothing in England. But I should be so glad to be of service to the Phipps's in grateful recollection of Sir Charles's devotion to you and kindness to us children.

The christening went off very well, dear little Waldemar behaved very well on the whole and was much admired. The King was most kind and amiable, and really it is amazing to see how handsome and young he still looks—so erect with such a fresh complexion, his white hair and moustache do not make him look older and he is as gay and lively and does as much as a young man would.

From the Queen   WINDSOR CASTLE, MARCH 25, 1868
There is great excitement about this Irish Church question, and Mr. Gladstone has done immense mischief.[3] The old religious feuds will return with great fury and bitterness.

I send you one of the copies of the cheap edition of my book—which costs only 2/6d. It is nicely got up. 35,000 copies have been sold of it—and 15,000 more are printed since.

---

[1] Harriet Phipps (died 1922). Daughter of Sir Charles, Keeper of the Privy Purse.
[2] Eldest daughter of Sir Charles Phipps. Her husband, Captain Sayer, had died in Cairo.
[3] Disestablishment of the Irish Church. In the House of Commons Gladstone said that the Irish Church, "as a State Church, must cease to exist."

From the Queen   WINDSOR CASTLE, MARCH 28, 1868
I am glad Dagmar is going on well. She will be kept so quiet that there will be no danger of her being confined too soon, but I fear it will be a very small child.[1]

From the Queen   BUCKINGHAM PALACE, APRIL 1, 1868
Many thanks for your dear letter of the 28th with its confidential communication which I will burn as you wish it, though I think there is nothing private in it.[2] I see not the slightest objection to the proposal when Thyra will be old enough—but she is not 15, and not very strong and extremely plain. Those children's marriages are so very bad—and the children are never strong. There is Olga, only 16½ and will be confined before she is 17! That may do in southern climates, where people are grown up at 12— and old women at 28! But not in our northern climes. I know it is one of the things which physicians and psychologists (Combe for instance) most strongly deprecate. Otherwise I should think the parents in two years time, would not object. But really not now. I would honestly myself feel bound to persuade the parents and family against such a child's marriage. I was completely beat by the Drawing-room and though I only stayed 35 minutes I had to go away before the last 80 people—and was all in a tremble and quite exhausted. The noise of London, and driving in the streets tires my head and nerves very much.

From the Crown Princess   BERLIN, APRIL 1, 1868
The Duchess of Altenburg is here with Princess Marie, who is engaged to the Prince of Schwarzburg-Sonders-hausen (the greatest Ostrogoth you ever saw).[3] The Duchess's little girl is here also. The Grand Duke (Sacha)

---

[1] The future Czar Nicholas II was born on 18 May.
[2] This concerns the Princess of Wales's younger sister Thyra (1853–1933). She married King George of Hanover's only son in 1878. Queen Victoria evidently burned the Crown Princess's letter, and it is difficult to say who the possible bridegroom was—probably it was Abbat.
[3] The Crown Princess presumably means that his manner was rough. He belonged to one of the oldest royal families in Germany.

was here today on his way back to St. Petersburg. I like him very much — though I did not when I first saw him. He is awkward, shy and uncouth, from being so very big, but he is simple and unpretending not proud and capricious as most Russians are, and has something straightforward and good-natured about him which I like and I think you would also. All the reports I had at Paris of his being so unhappy with Minny—and she having only married him to please her mother—are not true. I think they are very domestic and happy and attached to each other, he makes a very good husband and can do Bertie no harm if they are ever thrown together again, although I think he is rather idle and lazy.[1]

The Queen's cold is not much better and she is in a very unfortunate state, satisfied with nothing and nobody, and so excited and irritable. It is very difficult to bear with the right patience. It has been with great difficulty that I have received leave to go to Gotha, and I fear neither the King or Queen will ever hear of my having a little change of air for my health this summer, and taking the children with me. The King has decided to set his face against the children ever leaving the country at all. I must say nothing now—but when the time comes—I must try again whether I cannot persuade him into letting us make a tour. He paid me a visit the day before yesterday, was very kind and amiable.

From the Queen   BUCKINGHAM PALACE, APRIL 4, 1868
Alluding to her dislike of London the Queen says:

The fearful noise in the streets, when I try to get any fresh air, the constant interruption from morning to night and the dreadful atmosphere (we have a dense yellow fog this morning) makes me quite ill, and affects my nerves very much.

I must now tell you about dear Papa's statue which I went to see on Tuesday morning which will alas! not do.

---

[1] The Cesarevitch. Minny was the family name for Dagmar.

The head alone might do—but the figure in this form with large high boots is bad and quite out of character. I wish if possible to retain the head and get another artist to make the figure.[1]

Mary T's baby is a dear, merry, healthy child, but not as handsome as she ought to be.[2]

From the Queen   WINDSOR CASTLE, APRIL 8, 1868

You will I know grieve deeply to hear that we are very anxious about dear old Sir James—the last of our old, confidential friends and who is really like a father to me and a grandfather to you all. He spent a week here from the 23rd to 28th and had been quite well—and not had a cold the whole winter. It seems he left with a bad cold after that Saturday which has completely prostrated him—which however I knew nothing of till we came back here on Saturday last (4th), and each day the reports are much the same. He is dreadfully weak—though he does take nourishment and is much distressed by a violent cough. He has great rallying power but at 80 one must feel very, very anxious. I am going over to see him with your sisters this afternoon. His loss would be irreparable, for he is such a wise, devoted friend in so many ways, who dear Papa consulted about many, many things—and I too. He was with me through the eventful years of my life, stood with me in those two chambers of death and woe in '61, and was so kind then! Add to this Sir William Jenner has been laid up for a fortnight and will be unable to leave, and Doctor Fairbank (our doctor here) has got the mumps which makes him quite useless! As dear old Mr. Brown's health does not admit to any dependence on his health—we have got Doctor Hoffmeister with us since last Monday 30th when we went to London.

What you say about the Cesarevitch quite confirms what dear Alix told me. He is most kind and attentive to

---

[1] This is presumably J. H. Foley's statue for the Albert Memorial.
[2] Queen Mary. The Queen means, we may suppose, that she should have been better looking with her handsome father and mother.

Minny, but still I know neither wished to marry the other. All those children of the King and Queen of Denmark make such good *ménages*. Alix is a pattern of self-denial.

From the Crown Princess   BERLIN, APRIL 10, 1868
    Fritz goes to Italy—for a fortnight to be at the wedding of Prince Umberto.[1] It is a very good thing politically speaking but the Queen does not think so and that is one of the reasons she is so excited. You know she has a great leaning towards the Roman Catholic religion—and much interested in the Pope's temporal power—and in having a 'nuncio' here—which I should look upon as a perfect disaster. These are the things which irritate her so excessively particularly as she sees that Fritz is not on her side.

From the Queen   WINDSOR CASTLE, APRIL 11, 1868
Referring to Prince Leopold, the Queen says:

    Thank God he is going on very well—and is very clever, taking interest in and understanding everything. He learns, besides French and German, Latin, Greek and Italian; is very fond of music and drawing, takes much interest in politics—in short in everything. His mind and head are far the most like of any of the boys to his dear Father. I think he is happier now because he sees where his course lies, and does not think of what he cannot have.

    I grieve much about the Queen.[2] I have not observed anything of this in her letters. But I should be sure to pour oil and not to let her think you have said anything. I always try to do that. I am sure it is her health and that when she has left Berlin she will be much better.

    We found dear Sir James quite himself and much better when we arrived on Wednesday afternoon.

---

[1] Prince of Piedmont (1844–1900) afterwards King Humbert of Italy. He married his cousin, daughter of the Duke of Genoa.
[2] The Crown Princess had written "she is very dis-satisfied with dear Fritz on politics and Catholic matters."

From the Queen   OSBORNE, APRIL 22, 1868

Bertie's and Alix's visit to Ireland has gone off well—
as ours always did—but like ours, it will be of no real use.

From the Crown Princess   GOTHA, APRIL 22, 1868

Alice and I pass very pleasant hours together. Indeed
you need not dread her visit. She is so gentle and amiable
and so delighted at the thought of going to England as she
looks forward to meeting you so much; I am sure you would
not wish to throw a chill or a damp on that feeling. You
will think her in great good looks; she is rather stouter; I
am always admiring her—she is so graceful and elegant,
dresses so well and with her lovely complexion is allowed
by all to be a charming personality. I am sure you like to
hear that.

From the Queen   OSBORNE, APRIL 25, 1868

My hand shakes as I have just heard (though still only
by telegram) a full account of this merciful escape of our
poor dear Affie! God has been very merciful in sparing
him—I trust for good. I send you a copy of the telegram
begging you to show it to dear Uncle and Aunt and to Alice.
I hope dear Affie's health will not suffer but he has not
a strong constitution. I grieve to say it was again a Fenian—
or an Irishman—though I hope an American Irishman.[1]

From the Queen   OSBORNE, APRIL 29, 1868

This dreadful attempt on poor dear Affie is very sad—
and this telegraphic message which I enclose shows only
too sadly the vile and atrocious purpose intended. How
easily Bertie might have been struck in Ireland! I fear the
wound must be a severe one, though please God it will leave
no permanent effect on his health.

---

[1] He was shot in the back while taking part in a public picnic near
Sydney in aid of the Sailors' Home at Clontarf. His assailant was an
Irishman, O'Farrell, who admitted being a sympathiser with the Fenians,
though he was not directly connected with them. The attempt took
place on 12 March. O'Farrell was executed on 21 April.

I think that frequent visits[1] (not State ones) of any of the Royal Family will be a good thing, but I cannot believe it will have any permanent, good effect.

From the Queen   OSBORNE, MAY 2, 1868
The Queen is referring to the fact that the Princess of Wales was expecting a child.

It is not for herself that I grieve but for the poor child! For they are such miserable, puny, little children (each weaker than the preceding one) that it is quite a misfortune. I can't tell you how these poor, frail, little fairies distress me for the honour of the family and the country. Darling Papa would have been in perfect despair.

From the Crown Princess
                            NEUES PALAIS, POTSDAM, MAY 5, 1868
Willy and Henry are much delighted with a model of a mast of a man-of-war with sails, rigging, flags, and all—complete for them to learn climbing up and down. It stands on the middle of the lawn.

From the Crown Princess
                            NEUES PALAIS, POTSDAM, MAY 9, 1868
Many most affectionate thanks for your dear and kind letter; your kind expressions went to my heart it is such a happiness to hear from your own lips, or rather in your own hand that it will be a pleasure to you to see me again after so long a separation.[2] What it will be to me to hear my own beloved Mama's voice again—which I have so often longed for, in moments when my heart was wrung with sorrow and heavy with anxiety! How many things there were which I should have wished to have said during

---

[1] To Ireland.
[2] The Queen had written on 6 May: "To think that you have two children whom I have never seen—seems incredible—and I think shocking. I hope to see all in the autumn—but above all my own dear darling first born—one of her precious father's greatest objects in life—and to fold her to my heart".

the past three years—the most serious and eventful ones of my life. 1866 has left its mark upon my heart! My spirits have recovered their elasticity—but the one sore spot is there and not a day passes but what I feel it's paid in one way or another! The King has told me you had written to him asking him to give me leave for the autumn and that he had granted it. But you will kindly let me know will you not at what time and for how long you expect me— because of our arrangements? I fear I cannot bring all the children. Willy's studies must not be interrupted and I cannot take Henry away from their tutor—nor Ditta from Mlle Darcourt. Their education—mental and physical—is so important and it has been so difficult to get perfect regularity and order into it all, that it would not be for their good if we were to take them on a long journey.

From the Crown Princess

NEUES PALAIS, POTSDAM, MAY 12, 1868

I do hope your visit to London will go off well and that the heat and the unwonted exertion will not be too much for you and give you one of your bad headaches. I am indeed distressed to hear that the blood so easily gets to your head and that your feet swell. I fear you are already approaching a stage in your health, which is said to be the most trying and unpleasant in a woman's life, and at which the strongest constitutions suffer as well as the most delicate. I shall feel anxious for you all the time, as I shall be fearing you will be in so much discomfort of body which must always affect the nerves and spirits and make the mind more sensitive and less up to much exertion. But when I look at my mother-in-law, and think how well and strong she is compared with what she was when we married, I cannot but hope it may be the same with you. The Queen can stand more fatigue, excitement and knock-ing about than any man I know; she has more physical power and stronger nerves than anybody. She wears everybody out who belongs to her household—gentlemen and ladies! She never sits down indoors; for fourteen or fifteen consecutive hours she is never without talking, loud and long on exciting topics to fifty dozens of different persons (not having a quiet chat). She walks, eats, dresses and writes in the most tremendous hurry. She has parties every night. She is never alone. She never takes up a book or a paper because she has no time. She reads the newspapers aloud at breakfast. She pays visits innumerable—she inspects all public establishments—she gives audiences unceasing—in fact the very thought of what she does all day long makes me quite giddy! And while she does all this, she complains of her health all day long. Anybody who could manage to do all this must be immensely strong, because although she was always unusually active and used to make even pleasure a toil, yet she could not do what she does now, in 1858. But this sort of existence is a bane; it has taken all peace away; it makes her excited and irritable. And being of a violent disposition by nature it works up her temper to a pitch which makes it very difficult for us who surround her, and yet it cannot satisfy or content, it leaves a *vide* behind it—which at times makes her feel very unhappy and deeply to be pitied because she fancies that this world she lives in is the discharge of her duties and she feels the result to be but unsatisfactory. I could sit down and cry when I think of it all. When she leaves Berlin there is hardly a person from first to last (even those who are most attached to her, ourselves not excepted) who has not a feeling of instant relief. As for the King he enjoys himself like a schoolboy during a holiday, doing all day long just what he pleases dining at the hour he likes—in short leading an easy life. The Queen herself is glad to get away! And yet this is her home. It is too sad—and yet all this need not be.

But to turn to a pleasanter subject I have been very busy at the farm all these days—furnishing and doing up the rooms in the little farmhouse—of course only very simply—with white paper on the walls and very plain furniture, but I think it will look, if not very pretty, yet fresh and neat and clean. I hope to surprise Fritz with it when he comes home. We can go and take our meals there whenever we like and put up a visitor or two. It amuses me very much.

Queen Victoria and Queen Augusta of Prussia at Frogmore, July 1867.

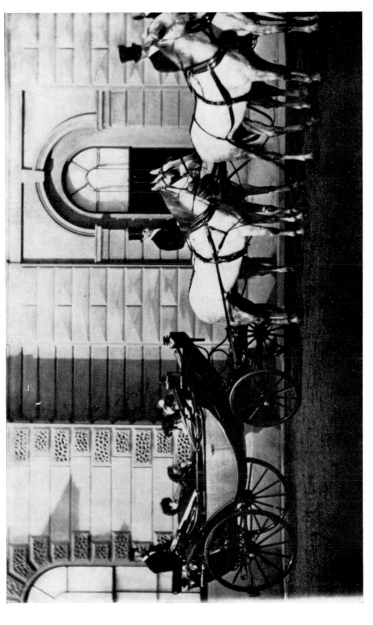

The Queen and the Empress Eugénie with Princess Louis of Hesse and Princess Louise, 1867.

Is it not strange that my nettle rash comes out again every day? From one o'clock in the middle of the day until after I go to bed, so that of an afternoon I am obliged to hide myself, I am such an awful object, and it is so uncomfortable. In the morning there is not a trace to be seen. Do what I will— go out or stay indoors—eat or not eat—try medicines etc., washes and salves, nothing is of the least use—and the weather hot or cold makes no difference whatever. It is too provoking.

From the Queen   BUCKINGHAM PALACE, MAY 13, 1868
    I have just returned from the ceremony of laying the first stone of St. Thomas's Hospital. There were an immense number of people out and the reception warm and hearty.
    You never told me how you liked dear baby's photograph or how you liked the cheap edition of my book of which I sent you six copies! I asked you several times. 80,000 copies were sold! I now want to mention to you that as baby no longer wants a nurse, Ann Pulman is going to leave and I am very anxious to recommend her as a nurse. She gets a pension, but not enough, she says, to live upon, and as she is a young person still, she is right to work on. There are so many people abroad who like to have English nurses that I mention her to you, for she really is a very good nurse—clean and tidy, and with good taste for dressing children. She was 10 years with us—having replaced May in '58. She had £40 here. In Germany and Russia English nurses are in great requisition and I thought, dear, you could help me.

From the Queen   OSBORNE, MAY 16, 1868
    Things are a good deal better in politics. Mr. Gladstone's conduct is recoiling upon himself—and many of his followers are greatly shocked at his conduct.[1] Mr. Disraeli received quite an ovation the other day on the occasion of the laying of the first stone! and was much cheered in the streets too!

---

[1] Over the Irish Church.

From the Crown Princess

NEUES PALAIS, POTSDAM, MAY 16, 1868
I thought I had thanked you for the six cheap editions of your book—I think they are so nicely got up. I gave them away here.

From the Crown Princess

NEUES PALAIS, POTSDAM, MAY 20, 1868
The appearance of your dear birthday again calls forth all the wishes, the blessings and the prayers of a tender and grateful heart, full of a daughter's reverent love! What can I say that will adequately render in words what I feel on a day so dear to the first nation in the world—and so dear to us! The dear old words of the dear old tune, which ever made one's voice tremble and the tears gather in one's eyes—"God Save the Queen" rise to my lips as to those of the rest of your loyal subjects, quickly followed by those I have so often heard in our beloved English home "And God bless her!" I wish indeed I could be with you to kiss your dear hand! As one grows older and lives through more trials and difficulties one's love to one's mother grows and deepens. When I feel how great is the love I give my children—I also feel how grateful I am for the same love that was bestowed on me—which a child cannot understand. Our present, a very humble one, consists in a bracelet which I trust you will like. We give a large dinner in honour of the day and a tea at the farm.

We had a great fright last night. A man (who was mad) broke in at the door and smashed the window pane, got into the nursery, flung some of the nursery-maid's clothes about, had a scuffle with one of the footmen who prevented his getting into Ditta's room. Vicky woke in a great fright at the noise—it was between twelve and one—and screamed at the top of her voice. Luckily I never found it out till the morning but I felt the fright after. It was a mercy nothing happened—the maids were frightened out of their senses but showed much presence of mind.

From Prince William of Prussia   POTSDAM, MAY 20, 1868
My Dear Grandmama,

I hope you will be quite well to enjoy your birthday.
I wish I were near you to congratulate you and to kiss your
hand. It is so long since I have seen you, dear Grandmama.
We have a large mast. It is the foremast of the Hela. I
went up three times on the foretop with Captain von
Dresky. The whole length and breadth of the ship is
marked out on the ground. We play in it, and about it and
enjoy ourselves famously. I am now learning Latin. I like
it and hope it will please you to hear this. I must end my
letter here because I have so much to do; I beg leave to
kiss your hand, remaining with all love and respect your
most dutiful, obedient and affectionate grandson William
of Prussia.

From the Crown Princess

NEUES PALAIS, POTSDAM, MAY 24, 1868

How glad I was to receive your telegram last night with
the good accounts of darling Affie! Heaven be praised that
he is, so far, well again! The day before yesterday I received Mr. Haig's[1] letter. I cannot tell you how it affected
me. I cried so much that I was quite ill, and I still feel
shaky and headachy from it. When I picture the whole
scene to myself and that dear, darling boy! But what a
merciful escape his life is spared—for good I hope and trust.
May he feel this and then out of this dreadful occurrence
a blessing may yet spring! The poor people of the colony,
I do pity them so much! I hope you will send them a kind
and cheering message; their loyalty is so touching! Dear
Affie's letter is very dear, and affected me very much. I
think he must have behaved very well throughout the
whole affair, and I am sure that is a comfort and pleasure
to you. Mr. Haig's letter is so nice that I thought it would
not be an indiscretion to have an extract translated for our

---

[1] Lt.-Colonel Arthur Haig of Bemersyde, 1840–1912, Equerry to
Prince Alfred 1864–80.

papers now, as there is so much interest taken in Affie and so unfeignedly expressed.[1] I hope you will not object. Mr. Haig is an excellent, charming, young man—it is a comfort to think he is about Affie. He is so steady and so gentlemanlike. In fact in all this sad business it is a satisfaction to see how everybody about Affie did their duty and what nice feeling they showed—I own it gives me great pleasure. But how the dear love must have suffered! And what a comfort it is that his health seems so sound, for his recovery seems wonderful! This makes me hope that he has been leading a more regular life of late—had he not, he would never have got well so fast. Indeed it is true—mankind ought to thank Miss Nightingale. What she has done for the suffering is hardly equalled by anyone living.[2]

From the Crown Princess

NEUES PALAIS, POTSDAM, MAY 28, 1868

It is as hot as at Paris last year, but the vegetable world is in the strangest state of confusion. It is like a Russian summer—violets, thorns, laburnums, lilies of the valley and roses all blooming together and all have done flowering in two days, so that one cannot even get a nosegay, and the sudden heat after the icy month of April makes the flowers weak and wretched, and the petals drop off as soon as the blossom opens, whereas the foliage is very magnificent and the gardens are very lovely.

From the Queen   BALMORAL, MAY 30, 1868

Poor Affie, may it be for his good and may he come back an altered being! His presence in my house during the last year was a source of no satisfaction or comfort. He only came for moments and, when he did, displeased high and low, and made mischief. In short he was quite a stranger

---

[1] As heir to the Duke of Coburg. He was always more popular in Germany than was the Prince of Wales.

[2] Rather a confusing sentence. "Indeed it is true" refers to Florence Nightingale not Prince Alfred's life.

to me, and I cannot deny that I feel very uneasy at his return—though I long to see him safe. You cannot think what a sad, sad feeling this is—to a poor widowed mother.[1] On the contrary Bertie is most kind and affectionate. I assure you children are more anxiety and sorrow than pleasure. When they grow up, their divided interests prevent them even understanding what a parent suffers and feels. When one's beloved husband is gone and one's children are married one feels that a friend, near your own age, and who can devote him or herself entirely to you is the one thing you do require to help you on—and to sympathise entirely with you. Not that you love your children less but you feel that, as they grow up and marry, you can be of so little use to them, and they to you (especially in the higher classes), and that they do what they like and how many break their parents hearts! You will say I paint a dreary picture, but I fear it is not untrue. As long as children are young all that is very different. There are exceptions to all this, of course, but they may come from peculiar circumstances.

From the Crown Princess

NEUES PALAIS, POTSDAM, JUNE 2, 1868

A thousand thanks for your dear letter of the 30th May —which seems like a conversation with you. I think I can understand your feelings—at least I think them natural. Children grow up and leave their home and go forth into the world and found homes of their own, give their love, time, attention and labour to their children until they in their turn are left alone. So it is in the whole creation; the part of a parent is one of abnegation, and it seems to me that the love of parents is the purest and most disinterested as it never can be fully requited, but if it be true, which I believe, that it is the love we give and not that which we receive that constitutes our happiness—how many thousand-fold times more blessed are those who have children than

---

[1] Not, naturally, that he was safe but that she should feel uneasy at his return.

those who have none! The latter are spared anxiety, trouble, fear and grief untold—but their life is not worth having. I can imagine how doubly hard it is for you to feel yourself alone without beloved Papa, when the house is fast becoming empty, and anxieties are growing and crowding upon you; you must indeed feel weary, and long for a heart your's entirely and for a helping arm, a wise friend and companion. I wish with all my heart you had one—such as the old Baron or Countess Blücher—always near you. It often makes me very sad and anxious when I think that you have not this one comfort. You say your tears have ceased. That too must surely be in the course of nature; like the calm after a storm when the force of a bitter grief is spent there comes an exhaustion, a reaction! It was in mercy so ordained. When I try to study the wonderful and beautiful laws which gave us this world—the moral and the material—how perfect is their harmony—I am always filled with admiration and gratitude, and would not wish to change anything even if I could—all the bitter sufferings, all the grief included—for that is a part of the rest and is as necessary, though we cannot see and comprehend it at the time we are stricken. This is a comforting thought, and very like Christian resignation though in other words! The source of my tears has not dried up. My life is a happy and busy one, but there are moments when I feel the whole sharpness of sorrow! In this month of June there is not a day when my tears do not flow. Never when I go to the little chapel—there all is peace—as becomes the resting place of an innocent little child, sweetly asleep, safe from the toils and the trials of the world he knew so little of. But many times in the course of the day, when suddenly there again my recollection of his last hours comes across me or when anything reminds me of him—for how I loved this little one I have no words to describe—then I feel bitter pangs; when my tears begin to flow I cannot stop their course. But enough of all my own feelings I am really afraid you will think me so selfish talking so much of them.

You will be surprised at receiving a book from Count

Munster.[1] I have seen him several times and ventured to say that I had heard you speak of his parents and mention his name, and he has consequently thought he might take the liberty of sending you his book. It will make him very happy if you will accept it and perhaps desire me to thank him in your name. The King tells me you are coming to Switzerland in August. Is that true? What does Sir William Jenner say of Leopold of Belgium's son—I fear the poor child has been very ill.

Ditta's governess is away for a holiday and I give her some of her lessons with the help of a Scotch lady, the sister of an Edinburgh painter called Archer. Ditta's hair is cropped down to her head like a boy's because it was so thin.

From the Queen   BALMORAL, JUNE 8, 1868
I am very much surprised about what the King told you about my plans. Of course for very long I was very uncertain as to what I could do—but Sir William Jenner was very anxious I should go to Switzerland, quite incognita and as it might do my nerves good. But I told no-one except those two or three on whose secrecy I can implicitly rely. I can receive no-one neither the children, relations or acquaintances for else it becomes what the Rosenau was each time—a great fatigue and excitement.

From the Crown Princess
                    NEUES PALAIS, POTSDAM, JUNE 10, 1868
Writing of Vicky the Crown Princess says:

She is the only one of our children who does not speak German; she will not say any German words. She would amuse you I am sure—she is so funny. I only wish she were less shy. It is hopeless to make her even look at a stranger much less to show off her accomplishments; she

[1] See page 243.

hides her face in my gown or Mrs. Hobbs's and roars at the top of her voice.

We paid a visit to Lord and Lady Brabazon yesterday; they are such nice people—it was quite a treat to me to see someone English, and to go into a house which, although foreign, showed unmistakeable signs of English comfort and civilisation having been carried into it. I have read attentively Dr. Stanley's able and excellent address on the Irish church, and even tried very hard to explain part of it to the King, who has been a great deal with us lately, which I always am glad of.[1] He is such a different person when we get him to ourselves, like his old former self—so amiable and kind and easy to get on with. Alas! as soon as he is with the Queen they both lose. How sad it is. If they could but both be well disposed at the same moment, our life would be very different. This I only say to you, dear Mama, and not as a complaint.

From the Crown Princess

NEUES PALAIS, POTSDAM, JUNE 15, 1868

I hear Mr. West is going to leave the Embassy here and, if that be true, might I mention the name of a Mr. Peter who was at Florence and who, from all I hear, would be fitted for this place? I have never spoken of him to Lord A. Loftus but the last time there was a move you asked me. The Windhams have gone to Brussels, would the Peters do in their place? And is there any better chance for Morier now? Pray do not name me to Lord Stanley. Lord and Lady Brabazon are only here for a year I believe. I think him charming. Pray do not think me too troublesome or meddling.

---

[1] The Crown Princess must be referring here to "Church and State" an address given by the Dean of Westminster at Sion College in February. This carried no specific references to the Irish Church but argued the pros and cons of cutting off "the nation at large from any control over the greatest and most sacred of all its interests".

From the Crown Princess   BORNSTAEDT, JUNE 19, 1868
Here at our little farm we are very busy. We have got
a great part of the hay in, and the wool is gone to Berlin
to the market—but unfortunately the price is very low
this year.

From the Crown Princess
                    NEUES PALAIS, POTSDAM, JUNE 24, 1868
I have just received your dear letter of the 20th. The
heat is also very great here, and I rather suffer from it
though I admire the sunlight and worship the blue sky,
and am very glad that we shall have ripe currants, rasp-
berries, and gooseberries which we have missed for three
summers. Fritz is gone to Worms, which makes me think of
the riddle why Luther was like a blackbird suffering from
indigestion—"Because the diet of Worms disagreed with
him", which fact cannot be denied. We had our last singing party yesterday and sang out of Romeo and Juliet by
Gounod. Please tell Alice that the chorus at the beginning
(instead of an overture) did beautifully and sounded very
well. The music is so fine!

From the Queen   WINDSOR CASTLE, JUNE 27, 1868
Alice is not strong—but most kind, amiable and discreet. I never saw her so amiable, gentle and sensible since
the summer of '63! Indeed it is a great blessing. There are
some things which I can wish different but I think they
come from the people she lives with. And all is most comfortable between her and Lenchen.

From the Crown Princess
                    NEUES PALAIS, POTSDAM, JUNE 30, 1868
What you say about dear Alice gives me the greatest
pleasure. I was so unhappy to think there should be a little
cloud between you. She is really so dear and good, and I
love her so tenderly that it made me quite sad to think her
visits were not quite so comfortable as they used to be. Her
life in Germany, though she enjoys more liberty than I,

and has her husband much more to herself, has its disadvantages and I have always admired the way she has taken them. Her mental development to use this phrase (so much loved by the family of Weimar) has made great progress these last few years—so much so that she is the only one of our brothers and sisters with whom I can talk as with an older person. Both for her and for me, the bitter loss of dear Papa makes itself more keenly felt from year to year. We have become more independent, and have seen more of the world. These last few years in Germany have been so hard, but perhaps a useful school, and how important would dear Papa's advice and sympathy have been now! My life is really very difficult at times, all is so complicated; one has to feel one's way, and often difficulties seem to spring up so fast that when one is got over, two others take its place! Alice knows all this. She has seen how little liberty we have at Berlin and how much is required of us by everyone!

From the Queen   FROGMORE GARDENS, JULY 1, 1868
    Affie was here again on Sunday—when he showed me his wound; it is very small—quite a little hole—and the merest scratch where the ball was cut out. He seems decidedly improved. I don't know at all yet what he means to do; his ship is to be the Guard Ship while I am at Osborne. He could not go abroad with me as I do not wish to increase the numbers—already necessarily so unfortunately large— for our journey, though I only take two Ladies, one Governess, Leopold's governor, two Gentlemen and the Doctor.

From the Crown Princess
                REINHARDTSBRUNN, JULY 4, 1868
    How sorry I am there is no hope about Morier! I cannot help thinking that the Foreign Office are altogether wrong and that in a place so important as Berlin now is, they ought to have the very best minister. Lord Augustus— the best-intentioned of men—was not gifted by Heaven with intellect; and in such times as these—and affairs so difficult to understand as our German politics—I should

surely think that about the only Englishman who thoroughly understands them must be in the right place. As for his being too German—or a partisan—that is surely only a *façon de parler*. The Foreign Office always were much prejudiced against Morier. Lord Russell was the one who did him justice, Lord Clarendon and Mr. Hammond never did. It would be a thousand pities if he left the service in disgust because he is never made use of, and at a small post such as Darmstadt there is really almost nothing to do for a man of his capacities.

I spent a very nice morning with the Queen before we left. When one has her to oneself you know she is quite different—she is so kind and quiet then, and so easy to get on with that it is quite a pleasure to be with her. Indeed it is my earnest wish and endeavour not only to bear with her but to be of use to her in soothing and calming her, and diverting her attention from those unhappy politics (which act like poison on her nerves) if she would but let me. You know I really love her dearly—and pity her from my heart as a most unhappy person with the best of intentions. I know well what we owe her—that Fritz never would have been what he is had she not so watched over him and done her duty by him. Not a day passes that I do not dwell on that theme. I really am so inexpressibly thankful for peace and goodwill, it is so painful to me when there are rows; I never begin them—indeed do my utmost to avoid them as they make me perfectly ill. When I left all was in the most perfect harmony, thank God. These last few days it has been so cold that even with fires lit, and with warm clothes on we could not keep ourselves comfortable. We have got Professor Hoffmann's son here, as master and companion for the children; he is only eighteen, but a charming, nice, young man; he is studying medicine and means to return to England when he is become doctor. I think it would be worth your while to keep your eye on him.[1]

---

[1] Professor Hoffmann is probably August Heinrich Hoffmann (1798–1874), the German poet and historian of literature.

From the Crown Princess

REINHARDTSBRUNN, JULY 7, 1868

Many thanks for your dear letter received yesterday. Your description of what you feel like is exactly how I felt in the month of March—the very rustling of a person's gown used to irritate me, and more than one person talking in the room made me feel as if I was going wild. I was ready to cry if I heard anyone speak for a few minutes together, and talking myself made a lump come in my throat! All this is so completely gone now that I have only the recollection left, but that is enough to make me sympathise with you. A complete change will I hope do you a great deal of good to diminish all these disagreeable and uncomfortable sensations—which must make you feel less up to anything. I believe nothing is better for the nerves than rising very early and having a walk before breakfast, and going early to rest—but this I think you do not like, and it does not suit you. For me it does wonders.

From the Queen

WINDSOR CASTLE, JULY 8, 1868

I am not as proud of Affie as you might think, for he is so conceited himself and at the present moment receives ovations as if he had done something—instead of God's mercy having spared his life. I am dreading the large family party at Osborne more than I can say, for I am longing and pining for rest and quiet. Parliament will soon be up which is a good thing. Good Alice and Louis tire me—they are not quiet enough and always are astonished that I cannot do what I used to do.

From the Queen

OSBORNE, JULY 10, 1868

Alix continues to go on quite well, but I thought she looked pale and exhausted. The baby[1]—a mere little red lump was all I saw; and I fear the seventh grand-daughter and fourteenth grand-child becomes a very uninteresting

---

[1] Princess Victoria Alexandra Olga Marie was born on 6 July.

thing—for it seems to me to go on like the rabbits in Windsor Park!

The present large family party is very far from enjoyable or good for me. Alice vain, and the others are exciting but as to Affie—he has become so noisy and excitable that it is all that I can do to bear it. We expect dear Uncle and Aunt today.[1] I rejoice to see both, but dear Aunt beyond measure. Going to bed early and getting up early would be a total impossibility for me. The night is the only quiet time for me—and I feel able for work then and not in the morning early. Darling Papa was very different and so are some people—but I find the greater part in this country do what I do. Walking before breakfast does not suit all—and never did me. However I shall try when I am abroad to modify it a little. I generally now have breakfast at a quarter to ten or half past nine (the last is what I wish to do—but I often can't get up early enough for that) and I generally am in bed by half past twelve. That is the time I wish to keep it—but it constantly is a quarter to one and even one o'clock, especially when we come home late and dine late which is unavoidable in this heat.

From the Crown Princess

REINHARDTSBRUNN, JULY 15, 1868

Many thanks for your letter received the day before yesterday—with the enclosed extract from your letter to the Queen which I think excellent. I am afraid your little hit against Catholicism will make her angry as it is a very sore subject. She has managed to get a Catholic bishop appointed especially to Berlin by the Pope—Minister Muhler (our donkey of a Culture Minister) and Count Arnim at Rome and the Radziwills[2] and above all Bismarck (who is delighted to be able to please her in one thing at least) have managed this and the King has been got round. I cannot tell you how indignant people are at this nor how

---

[1] The Duke and Duchess of Coburg.
[2] The Crown Princess is probably referring to Prince William Radziwill (1797–1870), the head of the influential Polish Catholic family.

much harm it will do. Fritz is furious at it. If you give a look at the liberal German papers you will see how serious a matter it is and how ill-looked upon. I regret it exceedingly!

From the Queen   OSBORNE, JULY 18, 1868
I am so shocked and so are Uncle and Aunt and your sisters and brothers-in-law at this shameful appointment of a R.C. Bishop to Berlin. Why did Fritz not protest? He should still now represent it in strong terms to the King and it might possibly be stopped. It is to me completely incredible what the Queen's object can be in wishing such things! She, who is so clever, and in other things so liberal-minded.

I find I am quite forgetting to tell you about Theodore's son—whom I saw on Thursday last and again on Friday (yesterday morning).[1] Lord Napier of Magdala (he has now been created a Peer) brought him—and he is under the charge of the gigantic but most kind officer Captain Speedy, who has been long in Abyssinia and knows the child's father and mother and speaks all those languages. The poor little boy, a dear, gentle, pretty, intelligent, little darling of seven years old, clings to him like an infant to its mother or nurse—can't bear him out of his sight, sleeps near him and sometimes even in his bed—as he is very nervous, and seems to have dreadful recollections of the murder of those people whom his father killed. Captain Speedy is really like the tenderest mother to him and it is quite touching to see

[1] Some years before this, the Emperor Theodore of Abyssinia had sent a strange (though not unfriendly) letter to Queen Victoria. This lay in the Foreign Office unanswered. Partly for this reason the Emperor imprisoned the British Consul. The Emperor withdrew to the natural fastness of Magdala, murdering many of his subjects who were in rebellion against him. A punitive expedition was sent against the Emperor Theodore by the British, and Magdala was stormed and burned. The Emperor Theodore committed suicide in Magdala. His son was educated at Rugby, died when he was 19 and is buried in St. George's, Windsor. Julia Cameron took a charming photograph of Captain Speedy and the boy prince. Captain Charles Speedy took part in Lord Napier's expeditions. His wife wrote an account of their journey in 1878 through the Sudan.

this great man of 6 foot 6 inches (!!) leading about this little child! The poor mother asked him to be a father to her child when she was dying.

From the Queen   OSBORNE, JULY 25, 1868
Poor Charlotte is worse again. She has refused to get up except at night; and she fancies poor Max was not dead but only said so, to enable him to marry again. I fear she will never recover entirely. You can write to me here up to the 2nd; but after that write always to Madame la Contesse de Kent, Pension Wallace, Lucerne. I travel under that name and nothing is to be directed to me—from here or elsewhere—otherwise.

From the Crown Princess
                REINHARDTSBRUNN, JULY 29, 1868
I hope you were not angry with me for making the suggestion about Brown through G. v. Normann. I know what an excellent impression it would make, and am convinced that dear Papa would have done something of the kind.[1] I have been painting a little here—but nothing very much. Countess Reventlow paints so beautifully that I feel the best thing I can do is to shut up paint brush and palette and admire her work.[2] I may say that I make progress in my judgment and understanding of art (for I give myself much trouble with that) but I have long ceased to think that my own daubs are worth looking at. Could I sit and study—day after day—in a real, business-like manner—having nature always before me—I feel that I could in time perhaps draw so as partially to please myself—but as it is, my drawing is a lamentable *hors d'oeuvre* and wretched dilettantism which only makes me sad to look at. Still it will ever remain a passion with me. I do love art more than

---

[1] This letter has not survived. Possibly it was a suggestion that Brown should be closely in attendance on the Queen in case of a Fenian attack or more probably concerned his position when the Queen went incognita to Lucerne.
[2] Count Reventlow had been friendly with the Duke of Coburg since the Schleswig-Holstein troubles of 1849. His wife was Countess Voss and was described by the Duke as "little, clever, and highly educated".

I can say and no occupation has so great a charm as even my small way of practising it. I am often months without ever looking at a pencil. It is no satisfaction to me now to scribble over sheets of paper as I used formerly. I have learnt that all the work one does out of one's head without looking around at nature is only the utterest waste of time.

What lovely sketches you will make in Switzerland and how you will gaze at those heavenly mountains. I envy you so much.

To appreciate really the beauty of nature and scenery one must be shut up during ten long winters at Berlin as I have. One gets to admire a poplar as much as a cypress, but I must end here, beloved Mama. Pray forgive all my nonsense.

On her way to Switzerland, the Queen spent the day in Paris and writing from the Pension Wallace, on 8 August 1868, she says:

I saw the Empress only for a few minutes and I thought her aged; she was very kind and I gave her your message. We took a drive through the town to the railway in Lord Lyons's carriage and not a soul made us out. Louise, Janie Ely and Lord Lyons were in the carriage with me. He is a very sensible, quiet, clever man.

From the Crown Princess

NEUES PALAIS, POTSDAM, AUGUST 8, 1868

I also rejoice at what you say about dear Bertie.[1] He has a kind good heart—and it always enrages me when I hear what is an *idée fixe* all over Germany that he is not a good son to you—and that you cannot bear him near you. I cannot say how I have contradicted this—even to my own mother-in-law who is convinced of it. (Please don't betray me.) If ever you can praise him in a letter to her I

---

[1] On 5th August the Queen had written: "Yes, Affie is a great, great grief—and I may say source of bitter anger for he is not led astray. His conduct is gratuitous! Oh! he is so different to dear Bertie, who is so loving and affectionate, and so anxious to do well, though he is some times imprudent—but that is all."

Interior of the tent erected at Balmoral for the Ball given by the Queen on Princess Helena's birthday, 25 May 1868.

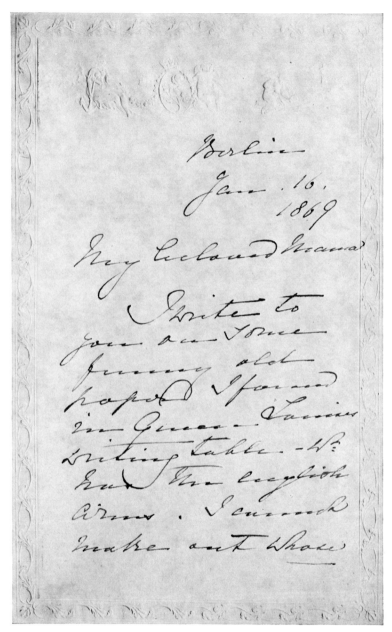

Part of a letter from the Crown Princess, January 1869.

am sure it will be a good thing as she will not believe what
I say.

From the Queen   LUCERNE, AUGUST 15, 1868

He (Affie) certainly is much more himself again; much
quieter, kinder and more amiable, but I fear little dependence is to be placed on him, and I cannot trust or even
feel happy or at ease when he is in the house. Marrying
may improve him but I fear, without principle, that he
may go on still as he does now—for how many do! I will
not, cannot think of it. I have done what I can—but more
I cannot do. I can't prevent the things. Of course much love
there cannot be for one who goes against all that his parents
thought right, and who shows you no confidence. I can
only give love and confidence where it is returned. But there
is a bright spot in another direction on which I love to
dwell, and that is dear Arthur.

From the Queen   LUCERNE, AUGUST 19, 1868

You may like to know how we go about. Almost always
in a (Scotch) sociable, the guide Hofmann sitting on the
box with the coachman, a safe but dreadfully slow man who
drives four in hand, and Brown in a dicky behind, which
has purposely been added and under which is a box which
I have to all my sociables these last two years, in which goes
the luncheons, tea baskets, etc.—sometimes, but for the
longer drives, I also use my wagonette and then no guide
goes. I thought you would like to know all about our ways.[1]

From the Crown Princess

NEUES PALAIS, POTSDAM, AUGUST 19, 1868

It is strange how good some children are—and how little
trouble they give. Ada's children are patterns of obedience,
gentleness—the best of dispositions. I do not wonder at
some of mine being so difficult when I think of the trouble
I was to everybody. I always tell the governess that I always

---

[1] Earlier in this letter the Queen says, "Brown and Archie go about
unmolested or noticed in their kilts". Archie was John Brown's brother.

feel responsible for all the bad qualities as it is certainly only from me they can have inherited them. Still I dote on Willy and think there is a great deal in him. He is by no means a common-place child; if one can root out—or keep down—pride, conceitedness, selfishness and laziness he may be a fine character some day; he takes an interest in everything he sees and is very quick of understanding besides having a will of his own, which is a great thing. I do not speak as openly of our little ones to anyone but you— as it seems cruel and unfair to pick out their little failings, but I let my pen run on and said what makes me anxious sometimes.

From the Queen   LUCERNE, AUGUST 30, 1868
    What you told me of dear Willy interested me very much. I share your anxiety especially as regards pride and selfishness. In our days—when a Prince can only maintain his position by his character—pride is most dangerous. And then besides I do feel so strongly that we are before God all alike, and that in the twinkling of an eye, the highest may find themselves at the feet of the poorest and lowest. I have seen the noblest, most refined, high-bred feelings in the humblest and most unlearned, and this it is most necessary a Prince should feel. I am sure you, darling, who never had any pride will feel and understand this well.

From the Queen   LUCERNE, SEPTEMBER 3, 1868
    Many thanks for your dear affectionate letter of the 31st with the enclosure from the Dowager Queen. I should much like to see her and think that I could manage to do it—if you would let me know the exact day of her arrival. I could manage to go quite privately in my drive to see her. Her case is really exceptional, and perhaps they would not put it into the German papers nor would I have it put into the English Court Circular.

From the Queen   LUCERNE, SEPTEMBER 6, 1868
    All you say of adored Papa is so true! But alas! he was

too perfect for this world; it was impossible for him ever to have been really happy here. I saw how dreadfully the wickedness of this world grieved his pure, noble, heavenly spirit, how indeed, like our Saviour, he wept over Jerusalem; he mourned over the vice and the strife and the bitterness and unchristian spirit of the world in general. And I think the loss of dear old Stockmar's company was dreadful to him. He used to complain so terribly of having no one really to talk to, and I felt alas! how little I, with my then—and still more than now even—very unscientific head, was able at all to compensate for this.

What you say of dear Charlotte I am sorry to hear, but I would strongly advise you not to speak of her or treat her generally as such a naughty and stupid child—but be very kind and encouraging though severe whenever it is necessary.[1]

From the Queen
THE BRITISH EMBASSY, PARIS, SEPTEMBER 10, 1868
I write to tell you that after all I had the pleasure of seeing the Queen Dowager for a few minutes last night at Lucerne. She only arrived in the afternoon but most kindly showed so much wish to see me that she offered to come up, or to meet me at the station, as our little house, with all the packages carrying out by the only door, was totally unfit for her to come to. I agreed to the latter. She was so very kind that I was much touched by it. I should have known her again, old though she has grown—only so much softer than she was.

From the Queen   BALMORAL, SEPTEMBER 29, 1868
Dear Affie left us early yesterday morning. His visit has been a very pleasant and satisfactory one—and he was quite himself again, affectionate, kind and amiable to

---

[1] The Crown Princess had complained that the child was backward and "far behind all other little children that I meet." The Crown Princess admitted that she was pretty, but was alarmed to observe a likeness to Prince Charles—the Crown Princess's particular *bête noire* in the family.

higher and lower. This is a great blessing. Ever since that severe letter of mine he has been quite different.

You will certainly see Bertie and Alix for they do not go till the beginning of December. I am to keep the children while they are away. It is rather a charge and I don't much like having the house for so long crammed full of children, but I think it is so important that they should be well looked after (which they are not) and their being with me may really be of great use, so that I never hesitated to consent. Alix is unfortunately most unreasonable and injudicious about her children.

From the Queen   GLASSALT SHIEL, OCTOBER 1, 1868
I write to you from this wild, lovely spot—where I have for the first time come to sleep under the roof of my own dear, pretty, little shiel which I had built as I told you, and which is only just finished and very prettily furnished and warm and comfortable. We have just had a house-warming in the shape of a dance in the little dining-room, in which we were 19 people including Ross who played. Louise, dear Arthur (who arrived here this evening straight from Geneva) and Jane Churchill which makes our party and all the servants including the policeman and the cook, made up the ball. After the first reel we all drank to "the fire kindling" and Grant made a little speech.

The unfortunate Queen is gone and fled. I have always felt for and pitied her—for she was so cruelly used. But I cannot understand her madness in governing as she did and bringing all this upon herself.[1]

We had Mr. Disraeli with us for ten days and he was most agreeable; he is so original and full of poetry and admiration for nature. No minister since poor Sir R. Peel (excepting poor dear Lord Aberdeen) has ever shown that care for my personal affairs or that respect and deference for me which he has.

---

[1] Queen Isabella II of Spain (1830–1904). She lived henceforward in exile in Paris.

From the Crown Princess   BERLIN, OCTOBER 7, 1868

I have not said anything to Aunt Alexandrine about the Putlitz's.[1] It was too painful to me. She knows how I valued and esteemed them and I relied on their friendship—and I can hardly bring myself now to tell her that both my esteem and my confidence are gone. You do not know how much I still suffer mentally from this business. Dear Marie Goltz has promised to do the duty of lady-in-waiting this winter for me. She is a friend of Fanny's and quite furious at the way she has been treated. I will speak to Lady Caroline when I see her about dear Fanny. I am happy to say that after a very disagreeable painful scene with Ditta's governess the latter has begged Fanny Reventlow's pardon—and is now on a good and proper footing with her.

From the Queen   BALMORAL, OCTOBER 10, 1868

The poor Queen of Spain is a most unfortunate woman. Every excuse must be made for her private conduct—on account of her cruel marriage. But her misgovernment is to me incredible.

From the Crown Princess   DRESDEN, OCTOBER 12, 1868

This town, though small and rather dull of appearance as almost all German towns are, is full of interest and of handsome paintings. I am so glad to have seen it. The splendid Madonna is worth a journey to see.[2] I think it is the finest picture ever painted by human hands. No print or copy renders its really overwhelming beauty and grandeur!

---

[1] There had been serious trouble in the Crown Princess's household, between Gustav zu Putlitz, his wife and Countess Reventlow. The cause of this is difficult to determine and perhaps it is of no great moment. It was however a matter of much concern to Queen Victoria. Countess Blücher seems to have been hostile to Countess Reventlow, but the serious thing was that the disagreement was magnified outside and did the Crown Princess harm. She was particularly anxious, as she wrote to her mother, that Countess Blücher should not listen "to the inventions of the Kreuzzeitung party and the friends of the Putlitz's".

[2] Raphael's Madonna di San Sisto.

The Crown Princess[1] is very nice and amiable. The whole Court has something very dignified and quiet—and the whole family is so respectable and united that the impression is a more favourable one than at Berlin where the *élégance,* confusion and *trouble* is not what I admire—there is a certain stately quiet wanting there which I see here and which pleases me much.

From the Queen   BALMORAL, OCTOBER 13, 1868
I can well understand what you must have suffered on account of this dreadful affair in your household. Though thank God nothing ever happened in mine approaching to this—still any little troubles, or any little disturbance at all—drives me wild and makes me perfectly miserable. But I never keep those that I find out are the cause of disturbance, and prefer quietly to get rid of them, even if they, in some respects, may have been good people or servants—and in this way I have effectually put a stop to all disturbances.

From the Queen   BALMORAL, NOVEMBER 1, 1868
I am very glad to see that you like St. Leonards. I dislike it very much and was very unwell there in the winter of '35 to '36.

From the Crown Princess
VICTORIA HOTEL, ST. LEONARDS-ON-SEA, NOVEMBER 2, 1868
This will perhaps be my last letter before we meet which seems like a dream! Darling Affie must have left today at daybreak; it was very sad parting from him the other day in London—he was in very low spirits himself. I went to see him at Clarence House—he was busy packing up all his things, paying his bills—the place was in great confusion.[2]
I enjoyed my day in London very much—particularly to see dear Bertie and Alix who were most kind. Those two

---

[1] The Crown Princess of Saxony was born in 1833 daughter of Prince Vasa, the descendant of the old Swedish ruling house.
[2] He was starting for the Far East, where he was cordially received by the Mikado.

dear little boys—how pretty they are, and how sharp and full of life and fun they seem! Dear little Louise and the baby are small indeed, the former will be like Alice and Victoria of Hesse I fancy. The baby is wee, but it looks plump and happy. I found darling Alix looking well and as bewitching as ever. She was so kind and really seemed pleased to see me again. And Arthur! I was so astonished to see his long legs—the dear boy—he looked so good and amiable. How old it makes me to see them all growing up! It seems like yesterday that I married and they were children and now they are men and women!

I thought Mary looking very well and made her husband's acquaintance and saw her little children. How handsomely and comfortably the rooms at Kensington are arranged. One is so glad to see her in a home of one's own, and happily married. She seems to be much quieter in her manner than she used to be. I wrote to Aunt Cambridge to say I was sorry not to find her in town and hoped I should see her later. Bertie says she would not receive Fritz;[1] if this is the case I cannot go to see her, as it would not be right for me to pay a visit to anybody who would not see my husband; but I fancy she cannot mean it in earnest, and perhaps my letter will mollify her. Uncle George came to see me at Marlborough House. I found him grown old and grey, but kind as usual. I had tea with dear Lady Jocelyn last night—her daughter is very near being very handsome and has a great look of Lady Gainsborough.[2] Today dear Tilla goes home—I was glad to have her here and to see something of her—but I do not think her at all well and I wish she would see a doctor.[3]

Vicky is so shy that I am afraid she will scream very much on arriving at Windsor. Every new face is dreadful to her—and you must kindly have patience with the little

---

[1] She was nearly related to the Danish Royal Family.
[2] Lady Jocelyn was the daughter of Lady Palmerston by her first marriage. She was much liked by the royal family. The daughter in question was Edith, who married the 5th Lord Arran.
[3] Miss Hildyard—the Crown Princess's old governess.

soul. I am sure when she sees you often it will wear off very quickly. She is particularly afraid of black gowns.

The following three letters are written by the Queen when the Crown Princess was staying at Windsor.

WINDSOR CASTLE, NOVEMBER 22, 1868

I wish just to say (as you may like to know) that Mr. Helps is a Whig, but very fond of and fair about many of the other party.[1] He was Lord Carlisle's great friend, also Lord Granville's and he knows an immense number of influential people of all kinds and positions. To me personally he has been most kind and I shall ever be grateful for it.

NOVEMBER 28, 1868

Mr. Disraeli is not coming tonight—and it is important that what I told you should on no account transpire till the moment it takes place.[2]

NOVEMBER 29, 1868

I had meant to come to you but was prevented by having to see the Lord Chancellor (Lord Cairns) and by having to write. Can you tell me which days this week Fritz will be absent from dinner so that I may know when to invite La Tour d'Auvergne?

From the Crown Princess   BRUSSELS, DECEMBER 29, 1868

Arthur will have given you my love and told you that he saw us safe across. The journey to Dover was very prosperous. The Bernstorffs got into the carriage at Brighton. At Dover the steamboat was jumping up and down, like a cork, in the harbour. I had just time to reach the cabin in safety, and was sick the whole time. I arrived so exhausted and shaken that I still feel ill today. We had a horrible passage. Even poor baby was very sick—he

---

[1] A tactful warning to the Crown Princess.
[2] This no doubt refers to the decision of Disraeli to resign without waiting to meet the new Parliament elected with a large Liberal majority a few days before this was written.

moaned and cried piteously. I thought the ship would turn right over, she lurched and rolled so frightfully. We got so knocked about that I am quite bruised. Your stewardess was the greatest comfort—I do not know what we should have done without her. Fritz and I have racking headaches this morning. The ladies all look like ghosts.

Poor Leopold and Marie look sadly dejected[1]—and Brussels makes a most melancholy impression. Marie of Flanders' situation is quite unmistakeable. She says her future sister-in-law is to have the rank and title of a Princess of Hohenzollern. Philippe said "the Duke of Hamilton is believed to be about to celebrate the event by making a scandal in the streets of Paris"—I fear it will not be the last either.[2]

I was much distressed to hear of the sudden death of Lauchert! Poor unfortunate Amalie what will she do with all those children and nobody to work for them! Can you not offer to do something for her—give her something towards the education of one of her boys? Will you write the poor thing a line? What have you heard about the Siamese twins? If it is very nasty please do not tell me.[3]

Goodbye, darling Mama. May God ever bless, support and protect you. This heart will never cease to pray for you and love you with all the love it has—and all the gratitude it can give. Far or near you are ever in my thoughts, dearest beloved Mama.

---

[1] Their only son was dying.
[2] The 12th Duke of Hamilton was grandson of the Duke of Baden and so connected with Napoleon III. He led a somewhat dissolute life in France and was the subject of the unbounded admiration (though they never met) of Maria Bashkirtseff. His sister, subsequently married to the Prince of Monaco, was presumably engaged at this time to one of the brothers of the Princess of Flanders.
[3] At this time the Siamese twins were nearly 60. They were married and had lived in one of the southern states of America, but were ruined by the civil war. They therefore reappeared in Europe to exhibit themselves, and the question was raised whether they should not be severed. Their appearance in Europe explains the Crown Princess's question. The problem of severance arose from fear of what would happen if one died. In fact one of the twins died in 1874 and the other died immediately—probably from fright.

From the Crown Princess   BERLIN, DECEMBER 31, 1868

Poor Leopold and Marie at Laeken—it was really too melancholy. What between poor Charlotte and their poor child, I cannot fancy anything more wretched and depressing. Charlotte looked as she always did—but she only talked on indifferent subjects and never mentioned Mexico or her husband. I perceived nothing strange in her manner —but thought her *baissée*—no longer making the impression of the very clever intellectual person she was!— Philippe's house is lovely, arranged with the greatest taste though almost too much splendour.

1869

From the Queen   OSBORNE, JANUARY 1, 1869

Our dinner on Wednesday with the Granvilles and Mr. Bright, though it made us all rather nervous and I had had one of my bad sick headaches, went off extremely well —and I had a good deal of conversation with him, both after dinner and the next morning and found him extremely agreeable—kind, large minded, full of sympathy and certainly very remarkable and quite simple.[1]

I asked Sir William Jenner about the unfortunate Siamese twins. Nelaton at Paris is to undertake to perform the operation, but till they try they cannot tell if it is feasible without endangering life to either. It is a most awful thing.

The Granvilles left this morning. She is so pretty and so very nice, distinguished, clever and sensible—but not a regular fashionable lady—which I so much dislike.[2]

From the Crown Princess   BERLIN, JANUARY 1, 1869

The King made no mention of the correspondence but I told the Queen what I thought about it.[3] Today we have

---

[1] The Queen is referring here to John Bright (1811–89). He was radical in his views and had warmly advocated the disestablishment of the Irish Church. He had just joined Gladstone's Cabinet as President of the Board of Trade.

[2] Lord Granville had married secondly in 1865 Castalia, daughter of Campbell of Islay.

[3] The Crown Prince and Princess had stayed with Queen Victoria over Christmas. The King had written confidentially to Queen Victoria, evidently commenting on the Crown Prince and Crown Princess's long absence from Prussia. Replying on 27 December the Queen pointed out that she had not seen her daughter for three years, and that she would expect to see her in England for shorter visits but at more frequent intervals. The King had also mentioned about social life, and the Queen promised that her daughter would do her best "only you and dear Augusta will certainly show consideration for her, for she does not really stand very hot rooms and late hours well". The King had also referred to the Crown Princess driving out without the customary four horses. The Queen would have none of this, explained that she never interfered

literally done nothing but see people, dress and undress, and drive about—I hope to the King's heart's content. It is to wind up with dinner and a theatre in the evening. I have not as yet had time to unpack a single thing or write a single letter. The heat of the rooms in the palaces and the smells and want of ventilation turn me quite sick. I wonder what you would say to it—and a remark upon it is taken very ill!

How can you say in your letter that you are a dull companion! I now reproach myself of having talked too much to you about here and our own affairs—for I know they cannot interest you and must bore you.

From the Crown Princess   BERLIN, JANUARY 5, 1869
After some account of the distressing circumstances in which the
  family of the painter Lauchert had been left the Crown Princess
  goes on:

Friedrich Kaulbach's prices are £214 for a full-length portrait. £125 for a half-length; £60 for only a head. I am sure Kaulbach would do Arthur beautifully.

The King is particularly kind to me—as if he felt sorry for his letters, and yours has most certainly had an excellent effect, and I thank you a thousand times for it. Bismarck maintains that the Austrians are instigating Greece against the Turks and agitating in Roumania, which they have succeeded in concealing from the French—whom he considers their dupes. Whether or not this be true I cannot tell. Perhaps you would just tell the General.

The dear flowers from sweet Osborne—camelias and laurestinus—are still fresh in my room and make me quite homesick.

From the Queen   OSBORNE, JANUARY 9, 1869
The Clarendons' visit passed off very well, and he was *des plus amiables* and most sensible and wise about politics—

---

with the Princess of Wales in such things, and that in any case driving with four horses "has quite gone out of fashion almost everywhere". *Further Letters of Queen Victoria*, edited by Hector Bolitho.

not at all French; but agreeable in society I cannot think him. I gave her your message. The Grosvenors come tonight till Monday. They bring their eldest girl—that Beatrice may see her—who they say is so lovely.[1]

From the Crown Princess   BERLIN, JANUARY 9, 1869

I miss poor dear Wanda so much—even more than last year because I went out so little—her sweet smile and kind heart, her beauty and charming manner do not exist in anyone else in society.[2] She was one of the few who was really attached to me and would never have said an unkind word against me, or allowed one to be said in her presence. The Putlitzs have filled the town with the most mischievous inventions about us and have done us a great deal of harm.

From the Crown Princess   BERLIN, JANUARY 12, 1869

The Kreuzzeitung party have been setting at me most violently since our return, painting me in the blackest colours. Bismarck told the children's tutor the evening before last that I detested Germans so much that I invited old gentlemen and old generals to ride out with me so as to tire them and injure their health. (This has never happened nor do I know what the man means.) This rather explains the King's letters to me;[3] that wicked man has been irritating the King against me. They treat me in the way the French did Marie Antoinette. If I had not so kind and good a husband I don't know where I should be. Luckily all this nonsense is restricted to a small but powerful circle. I do not care one bit about it; it is only spite and rage because Fritz and I are not of their politics, on the contrary it is rather a compliment than otherwise. But alas! the Putlitzs are the cause of a deal of mischief—that unfortunate story has done us a deal of harm. In time it will be forgotten I suppose.

---

[1] Elizabeth Harriet. She married in 1876 the 3rd Marquess of Ormonde. Her father was later the 1st Duke of Westminster, and her mother was the daughter of the Queen's friend—the Duchess of Sutherland.
[2] The wife of the Prince of Putbus. A brilliant woman and great friend of the Crown Princess; she had died in December, 1867.
[3] Meaning that it explained to her the King's letters to the Queen.

Please keep all this to yourself, the less it is talked about the better.

You will think we have gone mad when I tell you we are going to give a *bal masqué* at the end of the carnival. I am not at all keen after such like vanities; it amuses the young people who are fond of dancing which I have given up.[1]

From the Crown Princess

I write to you on some funny old paper I found in Queen Louise's writing table which has the English arms. I cannot make out whose paper it is, but I fancy it must be the old Queen of Hanover's—as she was Queen Louise's sister and they were so much together here.[2] I thought it would amuse you to see it—with that funny looking figure of Britannia leaning on an anchor.

The stories about me and Fanny Reventlow are the main talk of all the salons; there is nothing people do not say particularly Bismarck. I am very weary and discouraged. However it cannot be helped.

Poor Willy in his uniform looks like some unfortunate, little monkey dressed up, standing on the top of an organ— but if I were to say that I should give great offence.[3]

---

[1] The ball was finally held on 6 February, and the Crown Princess went as Jane Seymour explaining to her mother that her dress was based on Holbein's picture and that it was in "sombre hue". After the ball was over she wrote to the Queen "I fancied my cap very becoming (though you know that I am not given to great illusions on my personal appearance). It had something quaint and not undignified about it. . . ." The Crown Prince did not go as Henry VIII but simply wore a lilac-coloured domino. The King wore a blue domino with a Scottish feathered hat. The ball lasted till two o'clock and included special quadrilles in which the dancers represented figures from German fairy tales. See illustration facing page 228.

[2] Though she was not married to the Duke of Cumberland, afterwards King of Hanover, in Queen Louise's lifetime. Replying the Queen said, "The funny old paper reminded me so much of my childhood! Grandmama and I always used it. It belonged to the *Empire* style".

[3] He was shortly to be commissioned by his grandfather as a lieutenant in the 2nd Pomeranian Regiment. He was to be given this distinction on his 10th birthday.

I have been in some studios here where there are such lovely things, I wish you could see them! I enjoyed our little reunion where we have only artists, professors and authors. You cannot think how charming that society is, or rather you can because you have the same taste for it that I have; it is so refreshing after the other eternal, ballroom society which, seen every night, one gets so sick of. Berlin is peculiarly favoured in having so large a circle of clever men amongst whom there are some of the most distinguished people now alive, and those are not our enemies—on the contrary.

From the Crown Princess   BERLIN, JANUARY 20, 1869
    Dearest Bertie and Alix's visit is going off as well as possible; nothing can be more kind, amiable and good-natured than they both are.[1] I wish the visit could have been a little quieter but I was obliged to give way to the Queen—who wished them to do about twice what they have been doing and make them go to see all manner of things. I curtailed the programme as best I could, telling the Queen I thought you did not wish Alix to be overtired on so long a journey and that you wanted her to take rest etc. etc. They have been as well received as possible. The King quite touches me by the unfeigned pleasure he has in being as kind and cordial as possible to Bertie and Alix for your sake and dear Papa. He made Bertie a very pretty speech expressing the pleasure he felt in investing an English Prince with the collar of his Order particularly, as the son of a sovereign for whom he not only had the greatest veneration but the feelings of sincere friendship and affection. He said that the collar was the one he had received back from you and that he felt glad to think that he could give it to Bertie as it had belonged to his never-to-be-forgotten father.
    The Queen too is really most civil and kind to them both, and so anxious to do everything right and proper for them, and what would please you. The King gave Alix a

---

[1] They were *en route* for Turkey and Egypt.

nosegay last night for the ball; I do not think he has ever done such a thing for anyone before—not for the Empress of Russia even. The people who have seen Alix are all delighted—and I must say I had no idea she would *se tirer d'affaire* so well; she has a civil word for everyone and such a pretty manner. I am so happy to think of the pleasing impression they produced. I should be so grateful, dear Mama, if you would say a little kind word to the King and Queen when you write about their reception of Bertie and Alix.

I am dead tired. I never get to bed until the most unearthly hours—and have to be up and about the next morning. How long I shall stand this sort of life I do not know! I cry with weariness when I get to bed. The stupidity of a ballroom tries my nerves more than I can say! The Queen swims about every night all smiles—with a new gown every evening and the most beautiful phrases. How she can do it only shows how strong she is.

From the Crown Princess   BERLIN, JANUARY 23, 1869

The evening Bertie and Alix went away, after I had written to you how well everything had gone off, the Queen was in a very bad humour and was very rude to poor Alix, would hardly say goodbye to her which was very unjust as Alix was as civil as possible and in thanking the Queen for their reception said "I thank Your Majesty for all your kindness and friendship". This the Queen took violently ill as she wanted her to say "Aunt" and said "it is very impolite of you. By the way, you may call me as you wish, it does not make any difference to me", turned her back to Alix and walked away! I think she was sorry for it afterwards because she wrote me a note asking me to give Alix a very handsome set of china in her name—really a very pretty set for the chimney-piece, green and gold.

Alas! the Queen dislikes our poor Alix—this time quite without reason as Bertie and Alix both went out of their way to be civil to her and amiable. The King of course thinks her charming. Please take no notice of this when you write to the Queen. I merely tell it to you because you might perhaps hear about it and I wish you to know exactly how it was. Everybody here thinks Bertie so immensely come out and grown so much more manly, and expressing himself with so much sense. His kindness and his good heart seem to show more and more as he grows older. He seems so anxious to please you, dear boy.

From the Queen   OSBORNE, JANUARY 27, 1869

I am very sorry that there was a cloud at Bertie's and Alix's departure. I send you to read—what the Queen says of them to me. Poor Alix never will be liked by the Queen; that she should dislike the marriage I can well understand, but Alix herself, whom everybody likes, that's what I cannot understand. Bertie is indeed very much improved and has a most kind heart, but he is very thoughtless and after telling me he should take no one but Mr. Oliver Montagu, besides his two equerries, he has invited quantities of extraordinary people to meet him out in the East, which is very wrong, and will be very expensive. I am so glad Francy Teck went with him to Vienna as he is a very safe and good friend for Bertie in every way.

Poor Leopold B. writes me a beautiful letter. Marie feels quite as much—but she has wonderful strength of mind and great faith, and that helps you to bear what otherwise you could not. The thought of their beloved child's peace and happiness is now their great consolation. And there is so much to console in the thought of a pure child going to Heaven.

Marie of Flanders is rather abrupt and decided in her tone (she rules Philippe entirely, that I know from Captain Burnelle)[1] and then she is violently Prussian which of course cannot be pleasant to Marie Henriette (which one must call her to distinguish her) who is naturally a good Austrian.

Bertie wrote to me very much pleased with his reception and with your very great kindness. His poor children still

---

[1] T. F. S. Burnelle or sometimes without the final e. Aide-de-camp to the Count of Flanders.

look most wretched—excepting Georgie, who is always merry and rosy.

From the Crown Princess   BERLIN, JANUARY 29, 1869
Did I tell you about Willy's birthday? The poor boy really behaved very well, was not at all conceited or bumptious—but ready to cry. The King made him a little speech and then Willy reported himself to all the Generals, Colonels and Princes present. He does not look so bad in his uniform as I feared at first, and it has not had a hurtful effect on him at present. Of course he is very proud of it.

From the Queen   OSBORNE, FEBRUARY 3, 1869
I am quite against any idea of young Augustus of Portugal for Marguerite. The fever has left his naturally very weak intellect impaired and his health not good. It must not be thought of.
I send you an account of poor old Lehzen but I have had a better one since.

From the Queen   OSBORNE, FEBRUARY 6, 1869
Dear Fritz and Ada left here yesterday. They are most dear and amiable and dear Fritz is so sensible and excellent and deserved a different fate and better treatment. But justice and generosity are not in the King's or Bismarck's vocabulary. Nor I fear much in that of the Prussian Liberals either!
You ask me if I am going to open Parliament. No, I am not going to do so—purposely, and on sound grounds. I had intended not doing so when I still thought and hoped the late Government would have been in, and told Mr. Disraeli that I wished not to appear personally to take a part in this Irish Church question—which was the cry with which everyone went to the elections, and which resulted in a large majority against the very principle, which I cannot conscientiously but consider the right one, though I am

quite ready to give way to what may be inevitable.[1] But I will not give it the sanction of my presence. And this I have told Mr. Gladstone (who however had never asked or expected me to go) who is quite satisfied. I will do all I can to support my Government, but I will not appear to have turned quite round—considering the immense party who is entirely and conscientiously against it. I have explained this to Bertie—who will at once see it.

From the Queen   OSBORNE, FEBRUARY 10, 1869

I have just planted at The Swiss Cottage, with the three eldest grandchildren, four trees. The two little boys were very interested by it. They are improving fast in every way since they have been here—and are really dear little things. They go every day to Leopold who keeps them in famous order, and Mr. Duckworth thinks that Albert V. is not at all wanting but merely languid and listless at times for want of vigour.

I have had to write strongly to the King about this unfortunate Hanoverian sequestration which I must say I think a great iniquity.

From the Crown Princess   BERLIN, FEBRUARY 12, 1869

As for the Hanover business, dear Mama, the King is really not to blame as you may hear from the Hanoverians themselves who are here. It is a most unfortunate business and was mismanaged from the first. Bismarck made a treaty with the King[2] (which I think he never ought to have made) as he might have imagined that the money would be used in a manner which would only increase the difficulties of our Government. He soon found out his mistake, and saw how unpopular the measure he had taken was in the country. He is now forced to break the treaty—and thereby puts himself, the King and our country in the wrong and of course makes everybody cry out against such

---

[1] The Queen is here referring to a plan of Disraeli's to endow both the Roman Catholic and Presbyterian Churches in Ireland.
[2] Of Hanover.

an injustice. I know that the King has given himself the utmost pains to satisfy the King of Hanover indeed all the dispossessed sovereigns (with the exception of Fritz Holstein) that he has almost quarrelled with his Ministers on the subject; indeed I was almost afraid he would go too far in their favour. I think the whole affair as awkward and badly managed as possible—and am very unhappy about it as it puts the King into the position of the Emperor Napoleon *vis-à-vis* of the Orleans, and makes our cause unpopular which is not at all necessary. The public here were not pleased with the large sum of money allotted to the King of Hanover. Of course their point of view is a mere pounds-shillings-and-pence one and the fact of the Hanoverian legion in France exasperated people. Still I say a treaty never ought to have been made with the King of H. and then it would never have had to be broken. Our Government ought to have made a treaty with you and to have said—here is the fortune of the House of Hanover. The instant King George ceases intrigue against Prussia and pledges himself not to undertake anything against us you can give him this revenue. The English Government could soon have brought him to reason, and put away the dangerous people about him and have placed his money in safe hands. All this sad business would never have happened, but as for my father-in-law I must again repeat that he is actuated by no other motive than that of fairness and generosity. He is personally attached to the King of H. who is his own first cousin. I am sorry you have written to the King about it—as when you do write it ought to be with some chance of your wishes being carried out—and in this matter the King can do nothing.

The Crown Princess then refers at some length to Ernest Stockmar's approaching marriage to a widow of 50 with three grown-up sons.

He has engaged himself to a widowed lady whom he has known for twenty years. I should not wonder whether his ill health came in a great measure from feeling unhappy. You can imagine how glad and thankful we are for his sake as he is the best friend we have in the world. His mother, when dying, expressed her wish that he should marry this lady. I fear she is not good looking in any way but very good, clever, and agreeable, and highly accomplished. She is not very strong in health.

From the Queen   OSBORNE, FEBRUARY 17, 1869
    Ernest Stockmar's marriage does astonish me very much. I trust it may be for his happiness—but I feel rather doubtful. To begin a married life when you have been independent till fifty is very doubtful prudence. I am sorry he sold his old paternal home. It is a thousand pities that the Stockmars should desert their old "cradle".[1]

From the Queen   OSBORNE, FEBRUARY 20, 1869
    You will have received my telegram though I have no acknowledgement of it and I should think you must be anxious about our beloved Leopold. He was looking far too full and heated for several weeks past and I lived in dread of something. Medicine was constantly given and he seemed well, but was very foolish in running and jumping about and in over-exciting himself with the children. On Thursday evening after dinner, when everything almost was packed, I was told that bleeding had again shown itself and that Sir William Jenner had been telegraphed to, and that on no account must he move.
    You are in raptures about E. Stockmar's bride. Pray say everything most kind from me to *him*.

From the Queen   OSBORNE, FEBRUARY 24, 1869
    I have written to good Stockmar and would propose giving him a pretty breakfast-set for his new home, and perhaps sending his future a shawl? I hope he will be happy.

---

[1] In the Weber Gasse in Coburg.

From the Crown Princess   BERLIN, FEBRUARY 24, 1869

As you said the other day generosity was not in the King's vocabulary, I must mention a trait to you which is not known except to Fritz and myself, and a few others. You know the town of Frankfurt asks for three millions of guldens.[1] Bismarck and the Ministers flatly refused more than two millions. There was a council and the King sent for Fritz, and declared that as they would not grant the money he would give the third million out of his own pocket and pledged Fritz to do so if anything were to happen to him, the King. Of course Fritz agreed with delight; Bismarck was frantic. I thought it a noble and generous act of the King's and told him so. He can ill afford it as his revenues do not suffice for all he has to do, and he has more in the provinces which cost him a deal of extra expense. There are none of us here (except B. and his colleagues perhaps) who would stoop to look upon the new order of things in the light of pecuniary advantage—and I hope we may always remain poor enough to prove to the world that it is so. If we wish to see Germany united it is not from personal ambition or love of gain you may rest assured. A dynasty that thinks more of its own interests than of its nation's is sure to fall sooner or later.

From the Queen   BUCKINGHAM PALACE, MARCH 3, 1869

I fear I have written a very bad letter, but I have been often interrupted. Mr. Gladstone's speech is of a fearful length, and I have not yet read it through but I must try and do so. It is complicated, and in some parts not wise or judicious.[2]

---

[1] The City was in financial straits having had to pay a heavy fine for joining Austria in 1866.

[2] Gladstone's first Government had been formed in the closing weeks of 1868. This speech, delivered on 1st March in the House of Commons, lasted three hours and outlined his proposals for disestablishing the Irish Church. It was generally regarded as a masterly and luminous account of a highly complicated measure.

From the Queen   BUCKINGHAM PALACE, MARCH 10, 1869

How sad those deaths are! You call it diptheris but it ought to be diphtheria in English.[1]

Later. I am so very tired by the Drawing-room and all I did yesterday that I can do nothing but keep quiet this afternoon. I will just try and finish this letter, resting on the sofa in dearest Papa's room (where I generally rest and always dress and undress and sit of an afternoon and evening). My room I can't bear—it is too sad and gloomy and too full of recollections of all kind. I only sit there of a morning.

Well I saw at Philip's a memorial to Lord Elgin which is going to Calcutta—pretty but nothing very striking. Then I went to Mr. Boehm's studio; he is a young Hungarian (that is I suppose between 30 and 40), exhibited here since ten years, married and naturalised, full of talent, who does beautiful statuettes and groups of animals etc. and busts. He has just done an admirable statuette of me— spinning, also Louise on horseback (he does horses most beautifully) and another group for me; and he is going to come to Balmoral in the autumn to do (what dear Papa always wished) statuettes of the Highland Games for me, which I think will be very pretty. He is a very gentleman-like, clever, and excessively modest quiet person—known to many people in society but totally unspoilt. Then we went to Mr. Bell's studio to see his large group of America for the memorial; a fine thing—but there is too much sameness in the figures.

From the Crown Princess   BERLIN, MARCH 12, 1869

Many very affectionate thanks for your dear and kind letter by messenger also for the beautiful flowers! It is a sad pity we cannot raise such violets as the English ones. I have tried hard but find it impossible; the plants deteriorate so rapidly here in our sandy soil, which is so light and poor, and the violets we force are such small, pale, weak things which fade in a few hours—the stalks are so slender

---

[1] The family of the Crown Prince's coachman had suffered.

and the flowers themselves have hardly any smell and are very small. And yet no pains or care have been spared on the plants.

From the Queen   WINDSOR CASTLE, MARCH 13, 1869
     I went on Thursday afternoon to Argyll Lodge instead of Wednesday and a dreadful afternoon it was. It is a pretty place. The five daughters, Lorne and Walter were there.[1] Yesterday morning I went to Leighton's studio where he showed us four beautiful pictures and some lovely sketches just done on the Nile.
     Mr. Gladstone's measure may do well enough—but it was by no means a necessity. Reform yes, but not disestablishment. And every impartial person, and many Liberals will tell you that the Irish don't care the least for it. It is the land they want settled.

From the Queen   WINDSOR CASTLE, MARCH 17, 1869
     Lenchen is extremely well, better than the first time when she was very backward.[2] You seem to have written to her that she should be more careful than the first time, which has perfectly astounded me and very much annoyed her most excellent and skilful and careful nurse. Lenchen did nothing the first time but what every other English lady does, and who can have told you she was not careful I cannot imagine. That she was often complaining is partly her (unfortunate) habit, and her not having been very well, from one thing or another. But she is so inclined to coddle herself (and Christian too) and to give way in everything that the great object of her doctors and nurse is to rouse her and to make her think less of herself and of her confinement,

---

[1] Argyll Lodge was one of the secluded houses in their own gardens on Campden Hill. George, 8th Duke of Argyll, had married the daughter of the Queen's closest friend—the Duchess of Sutherland. His eldest son, Lord Lorne, was to marry Princess Louise. Lord Walter Campbell was grandfather of the present Duke of Argyll.
[2] Her second son, Prince Albert, had been born in February. He lived in Germany, served with the Prussian Army in the First War though refusing to fight on the Western Front. He died in 1931.

The Crown Princess dressed as Queen Jane Seymour for a fancy dress ball given at Berlin, January 1869.

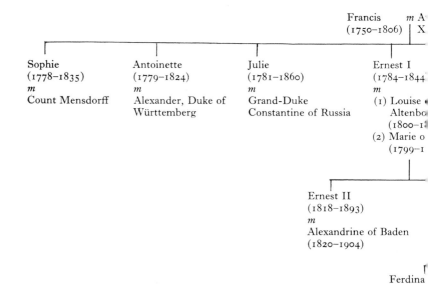

Francis   *m* A
(1750–1806)   X

Sophie	Antoinette	Julie	Ernest I
(1778–1835)	(1779–1824)	(1781–1860)	(1784–1844
m	*m*	*m*	*m*
Count Mensdorff	Alexander, Duke of	Grand-Duke	(1) Louise ‹
	Württemberg	Constantine of Russia	Altenbo
			(1800–1
			(2) Marie o
			(1799–1

Ernest II
(1818–1893)
m
Alexandrine of Baden
(1820–1904)

Ferdina
Portuga
(1816–1

THE HOUSE OF SAXE-COBURG AND GOTHA

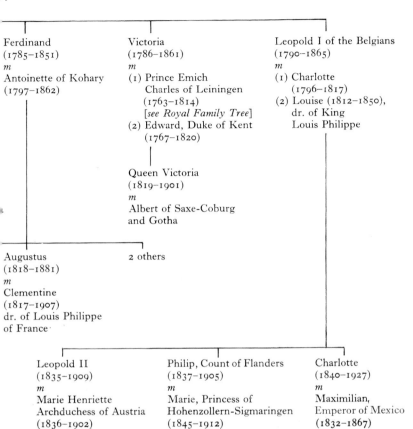

Ferdinand
(1785–1851)
m
Antoinette of Kohary
(1797–1862)

Victoria
(1786–1861)
m
(1) Prince Emich
Charles of Leiningen
(1763–1814)
[*see Royal Family Tree*]
(2) Edward, Duke of Kent
(1767–1820)

Leopold I of the Belgians
(1790–1865)
m
(1) Charlotte
(1796–1817)
(2) Louise (1812–1850),
dr. of King
Louis Philippe

Queen Victoria
(1819–1901)
m
Albert of Saxe-Coburg
and Gotha

Augustus
(1818–1881)
m
Clementine
(1817–1907)
dr. of Louis Philippe
of France

2 others

Leopold II
(1835–1909)
m
Marie Henriette
Archduchess of Austria
(1836–1902)

Philip, Count of Flanders
(1837–1905)
m
Marie, Princess of
Hohenzollern-Sigmaringen
(1845–1912)

Charlotte
(1840–1927)
m
Maximilian,
Emperor of Mexico
(1832–1867)

Prince William of Prussia in the uniform of the 2nd Pomeranian Regiment, January 1869.

which in England people do not make such a fuss with as in Germany and abroad in general. So pray, for Lenchen's sake, don't write to her to be so careful etc. for between her and Christian, who is so nervous, the fear is all the other way.

If you have not read that book on Ireland by Trench— you should do so, for it will make you understand the people and the real causes of the state of that unhappy country.[1] I send you today the Archbishop's charge which I am sure you will like.[2]

From the Queen   WINDSOR CASTLE, MARCH 20, 1869
The Crown Princess had sent her mother a photograph of Stockmar's bride. The Queen comments:

She is dressed like quite a young girl; is she not near fifty? A cap and, I think, longer sleeves would I think be more becoming, don't you? It's a nice face and, strange to say, strikes me as like E. Stockmar!

Constance Grosvenor had twin boys yesterday morning. A month before the time! It happened at St. Lawrence's, Ventnor and was to have been in London and poor Lady Alfred[3] has had her fourteenth! Thirteen alive. I suppose you will envy them?

You never mentioned the dear, sad anniversary of the 16th—but I know how you loved darling Grandmama's dear memory! Poor Lehzen is rather better or at least no worse, has written several times herself and is delighted with a wheeled chair I sent her.

From the Crown Princess   BERLIN, MARCH 23, 1869
Who should turn up here suddenly but Costa![4] He has come to settle about his oratorio which is going to be given

---

[1] William Steuart Trench (1808–72). Land agent to Lord Lansdowne. His book *Realities of Irish Life* was successful, and was published in 1868.
[2] At the confirmation of Prince Leopold.
[3] Paget.
[4] Michael Costa (1810–84). Composer and Director of Music at Covent Garden. He was knighted this year. Sir George Smart (1776–1867) was also musical director at Covent Garden. He was knighted in 1811 by the

here next November by one of the musical societies in the town; it was given last year at Stuttgart with much success. What a pity he has been obliged to give up the leadership of the orchestra at Covent Garden: he is the best *capell meister* there is and such a favourite with the British public. Could you not confer a distinction of any kind on him now he is going to retire as you did on Sir G. Smart and Sir H. Bishop and others? Is it impossible to confer a knighthood upon him? I merely mention this as I read a letter from England to somebody here saying how much it was wished that you should distinguish him in some way, and that dear Papa had wished it. This letter was written before I had an idea that Costa was here. I hope you will excuse my appearing to meddle in such things—but I thought I ought to mention it in the interest of the arts.

From the Queen   WINDSOR CASTLE, MARCH 24, 1869

The second reading of the Irish Church Bill was passed by a large majority. I fear it will do an immense deal of harm. The dis-endowment is the really bad, dangerous and unjust part.[1]

(Here the Queen gives an extract from a letter of the King of the Belgians.)

"The poor Charlotte goes from bad to worse. She wishes at all costs to go and fill the throne of Spain. It is necessary at Laeken to shut all the doors and exercise a close watch over her. My poor sister imagines that Max is not dead and that he is kept shut up in England; she writes to him without ceasing and has sent him some presents. The lamentable state of Charlotte makes us extremely sad."

Lord Lieutenant of Ireland. Sir Henry Bishop was a composer, and Professor of Music at Oxford.
[1] The Irish Church was to be disendowed forthwith (though not disestablished until 1871). The property of the Church was to be vested in Commissioners. The value of the Church's property was some £16,000,000. After the vested interests of the clergy and similar obligations had been satisfied, about half the £16,000,000 remained. The Government proposed to devote the remainder to those outside the Poor Law—the deaf, the dumb, the blind and the mad.

Then the Queen goes on:

Is this not too dreadful? May God in mercy release the poor troubled spirit—and let it recover its freedom and high aspiration in another and better, purer, freer world, where she will see all clearly and not as through a glass.

From the Queen   WINDSOR CASTLE, MARCH 31, 1869
I send you a curious photo of the Siamese twins (very horrid they look) for you to look at, which I beg for back. Should you wish to have one to keep I will get you another. I think it very sad to look at.

From the Crown Princess   BERLIN, APRIL 3, 1869
A Scotch bishop is coming here to hold confirmations. Lord Augustus calls him the primate of Scotland! Never having met a Scotch bishop I do not exactly know in what light to consider him and how to treat him as to rank etc. Can you not tell me what you wish I should do?

From the Queen   BUCKINGHAM PALACE, APRIL 7, 1869
Yesterday afternoon I went all over St. Bartholomew's Hospital which interested me very much; but it was a sad sight to see so many poor people and especially poor children —some such pretty ones—and so many suffering from burns, in a suffering state in bed.

I will see if I can give you a little for your church. The Scotch bishop is a mere dissenter in Scotland as you may tell Lord Augustus Loftus for me—and you must not call him by the name of his supposititious see. Those Scotch bishops are like the Roman Catholic ones in England! I can't bear the name of them.[1]

You will be pleased to hear that Costa is to be knighted. Mr. Gladstone sees no objection to it. But please don't mention it yet. I think he well deserves it. He will be much missed at the Opera.

---

[1] The Queen disliked the Episcopalians partly because of her liking for the Presbyterian Church, but chiefly because the Episcopalians had much in common with the High Church movement in England with which she was completely out of sympathy.

From the Crown Princess   BERLIN, APRIL 10, 1869

You may fancy my annoyance at finding the Putlitz affair in all the newspapers yesterday—of course turned in the light most unfavourable to me. It will go all over the country and do me a lasting mischief I fear.

If you want to read anything perfectly cracked you should see Richard Wagner's new pamphlet called "Jewish Influence in Music". I never read anything so violent, conceited or unfair. It is very much talked about here in Germany.[1]

From the Queen   WINDSOR CASTLE, APRIL 14, 1869

I have just knighted Costa who was very nervous but greatly flattered; and I think people will be much pleased by it.

From the Queen   WINDSOR CASTLE, APRIL 17, 1869

I yesterday drove over to poor, dear Cliveden and took tea (my own) there. It made me very sad to see the spot I last saw my dear friend in, and to miss, here and there, pictures which she has left to her family.[2] Otherwise all is the same, and it looked lovely and so green already! Mr. Fleming, the gardener, walked about with me and spoke of the interest HRH of Prussia took in flowers. Arthur has a perfect triumph in Ireland—even in the worst and most dangerous parts.

From the Crown Princess   BERLIN, APRIL 17, 1869

The Duchess of Manchester is here for the marriage of one of her sisters. As we gave a large dinner party yesterday we thought it right to invite her. She was at the Queen's soirée the night before last which soirée was so stiflingly hot and so late that I had a violent headache all day yester-

---

[1] This was an attack on the Jews, and was first published by Wagner in 1850. He reprinted this now, and explained that he did this because the Press was unrelentingly hostile to him and that it was in the hands of Jews. See Ernest Newman's *Life of Wagner*, Vol. IV, page 180.
[2] The Duchess of Sutherland.

day in consequence. I am really very tired of going out so much. The Duchess of Manchester has lost all her looks. The Queen is displeased that we are going to Potsdam on the 26th and thinks we ought to stay here longer on account of her, but really I am in want of a change.

From the Crown Princess   BERLIN, APRIL 24, 1869

These last few days have been very tiring for me. Fritz is away on a military tour, and I have been present two days running for two hours and a half at the sittings of the Congress of Geneva; I had all the delegates presented to me at the King's and tomorrow they are to be entertained at the Neues Palais. May I venture to recommend this Congress and their programme to your special consideration and that of your Government? It is, with the best of intentions and most important of objects, not proceeding in the most business-like and useful manner and cannot attain its most excellent and praiseworthy ends—unless the different governments take it up officially. That is to say the different war departments. I send you the printed programme etc. There is a great deal in it about the deaconesses and Roman Catholic Sisters of Mercy and religious communities being allowed to nurse the wounded, independently from any control from the War Office—which I think a great mistake but which the Queen approves of. Will you not kindly ask Sir William Jenner to see Dr. Longmore when he returns from here or will you see him yourself? He will be at Netley and you at Osborne. If wars are to continue and their art to be studied surely all the ingenuity the human mind possesses ought to be set to work to mitigate its horrors? And this ought to be done without delay. That is why I take great interest in the Geneva Conference.[1]

---

[1] This was a continuation of the Geneva Conference of 1864 which met to consider means of improving the condition of soldiers, wounded in the field, arising from the horror following the bloody battle of Solferino. Dr. Longmore (1816–95) afterwards Sir Thomas was at this time professor of clinical and military surgery at Netley Hospital.

The only thing I regret going away from here for are Professor Hoffmann's chemical lectures which are so interesting and amusing.

Yesterday I saw Mr. C. Wentworth Dilke and his son—they are here as tourists.

From the Crown Princess

NEUES PALAIS, POTSDAM, MAY 4, 1869

I was much shocked at the Mayor of Cork's speech.[1] The best way is to take such things coolly. They are sure to find the censure they deserve from every respectable person: those who approve such horrors are an unfortunate set of wretches—whom one must pity. I agree with you that the state of things in Ireland is at present very uncomfortable and that the Church measure will not satisfy the discontented. This appears to me to be, not the fault of the measure in itself or of the person who has introduced it, but the fault of previous Governments, who have allowed mistakes and mismanagements to accumulate until dealing with them becomes of an enormous difficulty. Surely our present Government, if any one can, is the one calculated to do most good at the present time. On the Continent it has won the greatest admiration for itself from patriotic, sensible and liberal-minded men who are attached to England and full of sympathy for yourself—indeed it has wonderfully increased your popularity.

Of course you can well imagine that among the short-sighted, narrow-minded and bigoted conservatives—of which there are alas! still many in Germany one repeatedly hears the phrases "England is fast becoming a republic"—"the English crown has lost its importance because of its radical Ministers" etc. All this stuff must be taken at what it is worth. A Liberal enlightened Cabinet has never yet injured a Crown—but throughout History—Conservative Ministers and measures have led to the downfall of dynas-

---

[1] He had described the assailant of the Duke of Edinburgh as "a noble Irishman", comparing him with "the noble Pole" who had fired at the Czar in Paris.

ties and the misfortune of nations, vide Spain, France, Italy, our own Stuarts etc. Therefore I am alarmed when I read and hear of dear Bertie's violence against your present Government. I hope he will speak to unprejudiced people when he returns.

From the Crown Princess
NEUES PALAIS, POTSDAM, MAY 7, 1869

Dear Alice has safely arrived with the dear children and Louis. The baby is a fine little boy, and looks so nice and healthy.[1] Victoria, Ella and Irene are in the best of looks. Our children are so excited and delighted that they do not know what to do with themselves. The little cousins agree very well together and do not quarrel. I am reading Trench's book which interests me so much.

I hear Mr. Boxall has resigned or will resign his place soon. You will remember that I was bold enough once before to speak to you in favour of Mr. J. Robinson—may I now again venture to call your attention to him? He would be so excellent at the National Gallery and is so highly thought of in the artistic world. I fear you have not much confidence in my judgment—but I think if you were to inquire you would hear how well qualified he is for that responsible and difficult post. Old Waagen used to speak to that effect too. Can you not speak to Mr. Gladstone about it? I hope you will not be angry with my interference.

From the Queen
OSBORNE, MAY 8, 1869

You do evidently not understand the state of affairs in Ireland or of parties here by the remarks you make. I think my experience of 32 years makes me capable of judging them very impartially and justly. In fact I am the *doyenne* of the Sovereigns, and I have much experience which public men nowadays (with the exception of a few) do not even possess. I will desire General Grey to write to you next Wednesday an account of the state of affairs. It is not

---

[1] Prince Ernest, afterwards Grand-Duke of Hesse, born 25 November, 1868.

satisfactory. I cannot blame Bertie for his feelings. There is so little true feeling of loyalty in many of these clever radicals. They would alter everything without being able to put better things in their place.

From the Crown Princess

NEUES PALAIS, POTSDAM, MAY 12, 1869

We saw some English gardeners yesterday. Sir William Hooker's son, Mr. Veitch's son, one from the Dublin Botanical Gardens and another. Sells did the honours of the place in the most extraordinary English and I hope they went away pleased. They are going to a horticultural exhibition at St. Petersburg.

From the Queen   BALMORAL, MAY 18, 1869

You, good child, I know never can or will believe how impossible it is for me to bear noise and excitement without feeling really ill, but so it is—and it gets worse each year. The noise in the streets and parks when driving out in London is what does me the most harm; I come back utterly exhausted—and quite trembling. And alas! any quiet and comparatively country drives, which I took formerly, are gone—for streets extend in every possible direction and make it most unpleasant.

I am in despair about dear Willy having to march past; it is very bad for him morally and physically—and in these days above all.[1]

From the Crown Princess

NEUES PALAIS, POTSDAM, MAY 20, 1869

The Crown Princess is writing for the Queen's birthday.

For us whose lot it is now only to love you from afar and to cherish the happy recollections of our sweet home and blessed childhood, as a something past and gone but never to be equalled—this dear day calls forth a thousand feelings —all centering in love and gratitude to you, our only

[1] There had been a big parade on the Sunday before her last letter, and the Crown Princess said that "Willy had marched past extremely well".

parent! In spite of all our different shortcomings and the annoyance we have, I fear, all of us often caused you in one way and another, you cannot doubt our deep love and devotion. A new home, new ties, new duties now fill up my life—but not my thoughts for they are ever stealing away to my home, which has a power—the power of love— over me which forever makes me long to be there and think nothing equal to it! It is never without a silent tear that I think of home now and of your saddened life, dearest Mama,—of what it used to be and what it is now. But since I last saw you the thought is not so devoid of comfort as it was, as I saw you were better—and I cannot say how grateful I am for it.

From the Crown Princess

NEUES PALAIS, POTSDAM, MAY 26, 1869

The dear day was celebrated by us in a quite unofficial manner. The five little girls appeared at dinner with wreaths of fresh flowers on their little heads and the lockets you gave them with your cypher round their necks.[1] The boys had sailors' clothes. We had the band to play "God Save the Queen" when we drank your health—in which Lord Augustus Loftus participated who had come to congratulate us. In the garden we hoisted the Royal Standard and some Union Jacks. The children all had a holiday. So you see your children and grandchildren made the dear day as festive as they could—in spite of there being no official rejoicing (which distressed the King very much).

From the Crown Princess

NEUES PALAIS, POTSDAM, JUNE 2, 1869

Fancy my astonishment at hearing of Mrs. Hobbs's marriage! I did not know whether to laugh or to cry. She will be a great loss to me and I fear impossible to replace. She has rendered us very valuable services, and I am much attached to her, and grateful for her devotion to the children. The parting with her will be a pang to me and

---

[1] Princess Alice, with her children, was staying at the Neues Palais.

to her too, I am sure. But she seems very happy and her prospects are very fair so I hope it will all be for the best. Will you let me say a kind word to her from you? You can imagine what a *remue-ménage* (hullaballoo) this will be in our household. My hair stands on end at the thought.

From the Queen   WINDSOR, JULY 3, 1869
The Queen is describing her visit to Aldershot.

I dined for the first time since nine years in the well-known dining-room. We were only ten—and I sat at the top of the table, and I dressed in beloved Papa's dressing-room. It seemed a strange dream to be there without him—and Bertie (who had never entered the house since darling Papa's days) was quite *impressionné* by it. He only slept there, dining with his own regiment. He was as affectionate and simple and unassuming as ever; I am sure no Heir-Apparent ever was so nice and unpretending as dear Bertie is.

We left again yesterday morning and visited on our way some huts of the Regiments including the Rifle Brigade which I had not seen since '60 (!!)—who were under canvas including all the women.[1]

No doubt you miss Alice—and as you like quantities of children and noise I daresay the house seems "desolate". That admiration of the King's provokes and annoys me; I can't understand it and think it very bad for Alice, who has already a too good opinion of herself; it spoils her and then she expects it elsewhere which she can't get. The little girls are dear little things.

From the Queen   WINDSOR, JULY 7, 1869
I think it is a mistake of Alice in her small establishment to have a lady governess. I should have taken one like you

---

[1] In those days most of the sergeants and about 7 per cent of the rank and file were allowed to marry. The women, to whom the Queen refers, are therefore the wives. When they were under canvas the single men were not necessarily segregated from the married couples: they were separated by a blanket hung over one of the ropes.

have and we have—and no lady superintendent at all. They are in fact great bores; we were always happiest when Laddle and Lady Car were away.[1]

From the Crown Princess   NORDENEY[2], JULY 11, 1869
This place is the most desolate, wretched corner of the world you can imagine—only fit for seagulls, as it is nothing but a sandbank without a single thing growing upon it. The paths to walk on are made of brick or tiles; the whole place is a fishing village of most primitive description, of which the greater part are let to the people who come here for the baths. We have got a largish house which is comfortable enough; it is the same one the King of Hanover used to have. The sands are very fine and the air excellent that is all I can say. Walks there are none—not a single tree—only one or two alder bushes and willows of a stunted and decrepit appearance. The children enjoy the beach and the sands, and I am never tired of looking at the sea but the place is not lively. The beach is perfectly smooth and flat; there is not a rock or a pebble and hardly any shells or seaweed. I took a ride yesterday with Fritz, on a pony we usually drive. I am sure we shall be happy and comfortable here, as we are together and can live in quiet and liberty. I have seen Fritz so little this spring and summer and shall see him so little in the autumn that it is quite a treat to have him to myself. It seems strange to be in a place which formerly was the King of Hanover's, but East Friesland had always been Prussian and only belonged to Hanover for fifty years. The people always had a strong Prussian feeling —amongst others they always celebrated the third of August (Frederick William III's birthday) even under the Hanoverian rule. The inhabitants of the little island received us very kindly. Getting in and out of the boats is not easy as the shore is so flat, carts have to drive into the sea, and one has to scramble up out of the boat into the cart

---

[1] Lady Lyttellton and Lady Caroline Barrington. An understandable comment but not to be taken too literally.
[2] One of the East Friesian Islands in the North Sea.

—the horses' heads looking into the boat has the funniest appearance.

From the Queen   WINDSOR CASTLE, JULY 14, 1869

Many thanks for your dear letter which gives anything but an inviting account of Nordeney. I think it must be very painful to live in the home of those one has despoiled. I may say this as you did not do it. But to be quiet is a great blessing and comfort, for which I am always longing and pining.

From the Queen   WINDSOR CASTLE, JULY 17, 1869

Lord Lansdowne dined here last night—such a remarkably nice young man—with such good manners, and very good looking.

From the Queen   OSBORNE, JULY 30, 1869

Has nothing further come out of that proposal of Victor Ratibor's son for Marguerite? She is very much depressed, and becoming peculiar—and altered really. Her family feel she will end in a convent if something is not done!

I am reading a very interesting book—just published; it is translated from the French and it is written by Madame de Witt (Guizot's daughter) and is in one volume—the memoirs of Charlotte de la Tremouille, Countess of Derby. I am sure it would interest you very much; shall I send it to you? She seems to have been a wonderfully heroic, courageous lady and so devoted to your "poor dear Charles I".

From the Crown Princess

                    ISLE OF NORDENEY, AUGUST 3, 1869

I should be charmed if you would have the kindness to send me the book of Charlotte de la Tremouille which I have heard about, though not seen but which out of devotion to my poor Charles the First I must read. Is he in any better favour with you since you have read it?

From the Queen   OSBORNE, AUGUST 7, 1869

Poor Charles I! My pity for him and my horror at his murder are great—but he was a bad King, and so false—alas! Such a bad friend.

The Grand Duchess Marie was most amiable, asked if you were not again in what you consider a delightful state —to which I replied I thought certainly not. She brought her son Serge, good-looking and very pleasing, but very delicate, with her. She went all over this dear, sweet place and was delighted with it. She certainly has *un grand charme* and is most easy to get on with. She is aged, but still very handsome so wonderfully like her father.[1]

From the Queen   OSBORNE, AUGUST 11, 1869

Last night Prince Albert of Solms-Braunfels, a nice young man, who was staying at Cowes dined here. The Princes are a real nuisance in the Island this year; for there is also a Prince Gunther of Schwartzberg-Rudolstadt, brother to the new Grand Duchess of Schwerin, at Ryde, whom I am going to see for a moment in the afternoon on Friday; and on Saturday once more the Grand Duke of Weimar.

From the Queen   OSBORNE, AUGUST 14, 1869

Dear Arthur left us on Thursday and it was a very sad parting, as we are all so fond of him. He is so beloved in the house and by everyone—for he is so good and unassuming, always cheerful and never makes mischief. We shall miss him much. He sails today. Mr. O. Russell and Emily were here for two nights—leaving today, and were both most amiable. She is much improved in looks and is very nice, unaffected and ladylike. He told us a great deal about the Pope and the monstrous things going on in this 19th century. Also of the extraordinarily good relations and coquetterie between Prussia and Rome! Why?

---

[1] Marie, daughter of Nicholas I, at this time widow of the Duke of Leuchtenberg, son of Eugène Beauharnais. Her son, possibly brought to reconnoitre Princess Louise, died young.

From the Crown Princess

Our journey was very interesting but very tiring. The weather wretchedly cold, blowing a north-west gale, and torrents of rain. We have not got our luggage yet. The "Grille", with all we possess on board, cannot get over the bar outside Nordeney until the weather abates. I have two gowns—that is all; the children no beds and no linen—pleasant is it not? I left Nordeney in a horrid old post-chaise —the pilot on horseback in front at 5 o'clock in the morning with Vicki, Waldy, Hedwig Brühl and Count Seckendorff.[1] For eleven blessed hours we posted in the pouring rain. It was so tiring; had not the children been patterns of goodness, and thought it great fun it would have been very disagreeable. East Friesland is a splendid country so green and fruitful, the pretty little towns so clean and Dutch looking. Fine cattle in the fields, fine crops ready for the harvest and rich, well-kept farmsteads in red brick—just what I admire. The type is very Dutch. Then you pass large moors covered with heather of all varieties which as it is in blossom made me think of dear Scotland. I picked some for auld lang syne—and wished I could have gathered it on the top of one of our own dear hills. We arrived at Wilhelmshaven where I had instantly to see the docks and harbour, and went across to the "König Wilhelm" and the "Friedrich Carl" in a very heavy sea—the men could hardly pull—and we found it very difficult to get up the accommodation ladder as the boat was tossing about so that one could hardly get on one's feet, and just as one had got prepared for the effort of mounting the step—the boat dived away again under one, and one came on one's nose. I thought of you so much—this is what Mama does not like I thought to myself. I was so wet and cold and tired that I did not like it either—the children (Willy, Henry and Ditta) screamed

---

[1] Count Seckendorff was a member of the household of the Crown Prince and Princess, and in later years was *chef du cabinet* to the Crown Princess in widowhood. He was the object of Bismarck's malevolence but was an accomplished and faithful adviser to the Crown Princess.

with delight and thought it the best fun in the world. I shall not enter into details of the ships—you know my enthusiasm about ships—and I am afraid to bore you. From Wilhelmshaven we took the train to Bremen, the children all went off to Potsdam and we stayed the night in Hilman's hotel—where I got your letter.

The next day we went sightseeing all over Bremen—in the pouring rain in an open carriage. It is decidedly by far the prettiest German town I have ever seen—the cleanest and most comfortable looking—there are some pretty old buildings and the wooden ones so nice and tidy and with such pretty gardens. I wish you could have seen it. I was charmed with it. We left at eleven for Hanover, where we stopped for a minute at the railway station. I had sent for Madame Brecht[1] to see her; she is looking unaltered.

At Hildesheim we left the train and Count Münster fetched us in his carriage (in the pouring rain). I never saw anything so fine and picturesque and well worth seeing as Hildesheim; it beats Nuremberg. I was immensely struck by it. The most beautiful old Byzantine churches, lovely old houses of the Renaissance period—I was delighted. We were very kindly received—though we had only come incog. and told the authorities to stay away. From Hildesheim we drove through a lovely hilly country to Dorneburg, Count Münster's place. It is beautifully situated, a fine old building formerly a convent—the gift of George the Fourth to Count Münster's father.[2] Fancy Reinhardtsbrunn on a much larger scale and on the slope of a hill with a river flowing down behind through the garden, which is full of fine trees.

---

[1] See page 162.
[2] Count von Münster (1766–1839) the Hanoverian statesman was the adviser and friend of the later English sovereigns of the House of Hanover. He was Hanoverian Minister in London (1804–41). The Crown Prince and Crown Princess are staying with his son Count George Herbert Münster (1820–1902) afterwards Prince Münster. He played an important part in easing the transition from Hanoverian independence to incorporation with Prussia. His second wife was Lady Harriet St. Clair Erskine, daughter of the 3rd Lord Rosslyn. His first wife was Princess Alexandrine Galitzine, widow of Prince Dolgorouky. They had married in 1847 and were divorced in 1864.

The house is roomy and well-kept—but made a gloomy impression upon me because of the dreadful dramas which it has been the scene of! Poor Countess Münster! Lady Harriet Sinclair's rooms—are all left untouched since her death—her chairs, books, pencils, pictures all just as if she was still there! Her husband worships her memory and cannot console himself! What makes it still more hard for him are the dark rumours which one hears from people who are intimate with him and his family that she is supposed to have been poisoned by a Russian maid (the servant of the first Countess Münster, who is a perfectly fallen creature—and goes about the world as an adventuress!) Her four daughters are charming pleasing girls well brought up and very ladylike. Of course they do not know all that has taken place, and how their father was used so that they pine for their own mother—though they liked their stepmother very much. There are two boys. There was a Miss Balfour, Lady G. Balfour's[1] sister-in-law staying with them and also her niece. The household habits are quite English—Count Münster is so fond of everything English. He is such a charming clever and amiable man; I know few so agreeable. He has been almost ruined by his first wife—so that his finances will only recover by degrees but with such large estates and a fine fortune it is thought that in a few years he will be all right again.

From the Crown Princess

NEUES PALAIS, POTSDAM, AUGUST 17, 1869

You may indeed ask what that ridiculous and dangerous coquetterie of our Government with Rome means. It is a source of disgust and despair to Fritz and to me. A certain lady, high-placed, keeps it going. Bismarck, who is delighted to know with what he can please her, gives way completely on this point to her; it is the only one on which they agree; Arnim at Rome is in my opinion a conceited fool who is bound to be jealous of Odo Russell, and fancies the more he

---

[1] Lady Georgina, daughter of Lord Cawdor, and wife of Colonel Balfour of Balbirnie.

is hand in glove with the Roman Government (the worst and most contemptible government there is almost) the better it is for him and for the country he represents. How much it is resented by the public here you do not know. Just at the present there is a storm in the press about a monastery which has been founded at Berlin—and to which the same lady has also contributed. I think all these demonstrations and advances to the Church of Rome are most absurd and injudicious.

May I ask a question in confidence? What do you think of the opening of the Suez Canal—and the quarrel of the Viceroy and the Sultan?[1] Do you think Fritz ought to go to the opening? For my part I should think not for many reasons. First on account of the expense of such a journey— it does not seem fair to spend so much money on a journey when money is so scarce as it is here at present. And then I doubt whether it would be prudent in going so far away at the King's age. The Queen is bent upon Fritz's going and angry with me for not wishing it. I cannot see that it is of any good politically. What do you think?

I am so sorry dear Arthur did not even write me one little line before leaving for Canada; he has not written a word for several months. How much you will miss the dear boy; it will be very interesting for him to be there where your father was.

From the Queen   OSBORNE, AUGUST 18, 1869

It must have been a most tiring journey. The nautical part certainly would not have suited me. I have a horror of those dancing boats, which are moreover dangerous for ladies and children. I never heard those suspicions about the Countess (Harriet) Münster's death; she had a heart complaint I was told. But it was terribly sudden; she was very peculiar but extremely clever.

---

[1] The Turkish Government felt that Egypt was acting too much as an independent power. The quarrel was made public by an exchange of letters between the Turkish Ministers in Cairo and the Khedive.

From the Queen   BALMORAL, AUGUST 4, 1869[1]

How is it that Elizabeth W. does not marry? I always fear Affie did not behave well there! And I often deeply regret Bertie did not marry her. He wants a cleverer and better-informed wife to amuse and occupy him. He is coming to Abergeldie on Thursday—and I believe later goes back to Wildbad to fetch Alix and the children who will probably come on here.

You ask me about Fritz's going to the opening of the Suez Canal. I should say certainly he should not go; and I do not intend any of our sons should go. It would only make matters worse between the Sultan and the Viceroy or Khedive as he is now called, and they are bad enough.[2]

I quite believe and expected what you said about who encouraged that incomprehensible intimacy with the Court of Rome. Here also people will not see the danger of encouraging the R. Catholics which is too foolish. You can never conciliate without their encroaching.

From the Queen   BALMORAL, AUGUST 31, 1869

I think it a misfortune that there should be such a fuss about rank always in Prussia and hope that in time more reasonable views will prevail. Here these things are of little difficulty.[3]

From the Crown Princess

BORNSTAEDT, SEPTEMBER 4, 1869

Many thanks for sending me Mr. Odo Russell's most

---

[1] I have assumed that this is one of the rare occasions when the Queen mis-dated a letter, and that it was written on 24 August, not on the 4th as written, since it clearly answers the Crown Princess's letter of 17 August.

[2] The Crown Prince went. By a firman in 1866 the Viceroy of Egypt was given the title of Khedive, with the succession in his family. The Sultan was especially offended by the Khedive inviting foreign monarchs to attend the opening of the Canal.

[3] The Crown Princess, commenting on the engagement of Princess Marie of the Netherlands, who was niece to the King of Prussia, said, "the Family here regret her future husband having no rank." Her husband was the Prince of Wied, who belonged to a royal but not sovereign or ruling House.

interesting letter which I return. He is quite right of course in what he says about the celibacy of the clergy—it is that which makes the machine so powerful. The one half of mankind is of course easier to govern alone than with the other half. The power and the thraldom of the Roman Catholic Church, with all its bad, corrupt principles so ruinous to a state, will only then be broken when the priests are allowed to marry. Perhaps at some future time, the French may branch off and become *"église gallicane"* with a married clergy and the German Catholics become an independent church of their own, but I doubt that happening in our day. The Pope's power is far greater abroad than it is at home— and to the German Roman Catholics he is still enveloped with the awe and mystery to which the Italians have long become indifferent—because *ils le voyant de trop prêt.* I only hope that the Pope and his government make themselves as ridiculous as possible with their Council, and shake the confidence of the German Catholics whose power is rising here. I myself do not fear their power—as what is built on such gross absurdity and error meets with the contempt it deserves from most reasonable people (particularly as a large majority of the educated German middle classes are free thinkers). Still they may do a deal of mischief in the schools, of which they are fast getting hold, for a time, by meddling in politics and creating a feeling of intolerance and hostility between Protestants and Catholics which I always think a melancholy and pitiable sight to see. A truly liberal government will always find the best means of dealing with them, by leaving them perfect liberty and by not appointing them as schoolmasters. At present the very reverse is being done here, and a great mess being made which causes a deal of excitement particularly amongst the public of Berlin, who are at this moment inclined to smash every Catholic's windows.

Anything you like to send Mrs. Hobbs would, I know, give her pleasure; perhaps a few dessert knives? She has a great deal of silver from me already.

From the Queen BALMORAL, SEPTEMBER 25, 1869

So long a separation from Fritz—and so far off—is a great trial and I feel for you, and wish it could have been avoided. Why not send someone else? In the meantime the quarrel between the Sultan and the Viceroy is not yet settled.

Mr. Gladstone left this morning. I cannot find him very agreeable, and he talks so very much. He looks dreadfully ill.

From the Crown Princess

NEUES PALAIS, POTSDAM, SEPTEMBER 25, 1869

Fritz's journey will be so interesting I would have given anything to go with him and see all the places I am so curious about, but in the first place I should have increased the expense, and in the second I am wanted for the children. I should not see Willy and Henry for seven months. That is too long and then as a new nurse is coming and Fanny knows nothing about little children's health I thought it would not be right to go away. Wally Paget is prettier than ever; I am so proud of her; but I regret that she is a little affected and grand sometimes. Becker and I play on the piano together. I am perfectly enchanted. There are some lovely things of Bach's (I think little known in England) some fugues and preludes and some smaller things of a beauty to which nothing is to be compared. I think the only drawback is that they are horridly difficult to play well. Have you read in the *Revue des Deux Mondes* "La Journal d'une Dame de la Court de George II"? Pray do, it is quite short and so interesting; it is the diary of Lady Cowper— who was lady-in-waiting to Caroline of Anspach as Princess of Wales.

From the Crown Princess

NEUES PALAIS, POTSDAM, OCTOBER 2, 1869

How very kind of you to say you would send Mrs. Hobbs a pair of candlesticks. Parting from her is very sad to me; I shall have no one to speak of my poor little Siggie to, and she is so fond of the children, and has been a very valuable and an excellent nurse in spite of all her faults, which certainly did a deal of mischief. I am sure she feels it very much herself and that she will miss us often. She is to be married on the 18th at Southborough not far from Tunbridge Wells where her home is to be. Will you send her your present on that day? The new nurse is called Mrs. Wakelin and arrived this morning.

From the Crown Princess

NEUES PALAIS, POTSDAM, OCTOBER 9, 1869

Please give my love to Aunt Clementine and Amalie and kindest remembrances to Uncle and Philippe? Is there no chance of poor Marguerite marrying? I do not know where on earth to find a husband for her there are no more Catholic princes with good fortunes to be had in our part of the world unfortunately. Is the King of Bavaria[1] impossible? He has done the maddest things lately—dining with his horse in his room, and having a golden crown put on the horse's head, and then looking out of the window with his horse! He has the strangest fancies. He told someone the other day that there ought to be two Emperors of Germany —one War Kaiser who could be my father-in-law and— one Emperor of Peace himself. He had a golden cloak made, embroidered with white doves and the crown of Charlemagne, and put it on and walked up and down his room in it! His fancies are so childlike. The Bavarians are in despair but all have told me, that I have seen, that they prefer having him a thousand times to his brother or cousin who are in the hands of the Jesuits.

From the Queen   BALMORAL, OCTOBER 12, 1869

I do feel for you the separation from dear Fritz, though you are so much more wrapped up in your children than I was, or ever could be, that to you it is very different to what it was—and is—to me. You say you suppose I am going soon South; thank God! not for another three weeks. I shall stop here till the 2nd or 3rd November as usual, and then

---

[1] Ludwig II (1845–86). Commonly called the mad King Ludwig.

go back to that dreadful old prison—where I shall certainly think of you and last year—but not more than I do everywhere, for you are always in my thoughts and I always look forward to your dear and so well-written and delightful letters.

The Crown Princess is staying at Cannes while the Crown Prince has gone for the opening of the Suez Canal. She has been joined by Princess Alice and Prince Louis of Hesse. It is interesting to notice that the Crown Princess is really a great peacemaker between Princess Alice and the Queen; the Crown Princess never fails to point out the many good qualities of her sister.

From the Crown Princess

THE GRAND HOTEL DE CANNES, OCTOBER 23, 1869

We have not seen Nice or Mentone; perhaps we shall do so next week. But we have been to Antibes, from where one sees the Alpes Maritimes and the sea and the islands opposite; it is a very fine view but I cannot feel any enthusiasm for the place. And I love every inch of dear Italy—it is tantalising to think one is so near—and yet not there. A trip to Genoa would be very enjoyable—but I fear too expensive for us. The expense of this place is frightful.

From the Crown Princess   CANNES, OCTOBER 31, 1869

We have not got such an "enormous caravan" as you say. As few servants as possible, and it would not be proper for me to be in an hotel in a foreign country with only one gentleman—besides Count Seckendorff is much too young for that. The boys make up a separate party altogether—as they are going to stay here. The expense is very great as the people here live on cheating the strangers who come here for the season. There is no one here yet we know, but Lord Dalhousie is expected also Princess Waldeck and her children. If it were not that dear Alice and I were so happy together and that we like living quietly I do not think we either of us would be enthusiastic about this place. There are some charming walks—but the poverty of the place— the absence of any nice building of any kind makes it monotonous. But I am glad we are not at Nice, which is

nothing on earth but a species of Baden-Baden and rendez-
vous for fashionable (and also bad) society of every kind,
and more expensive than here.

From the Crown Princess   CANNES, NOVEMBER 7, 1869
    I think I ought to trouble you for a moment with an
affair in our household which causes me great grief—indeed
has quite absorbed me these last few days. It is Valerie
Hohenthal's sudden departure.[1] She has left my service—
saying her duty forbid her staying. She came here the day
before yesterday and took leave of me—having only had a
few lines from her the day before to the effect that she
wished to retire from Court. I was thunderstruck. She
would not explain her motives but has completely broken
with her family and all her friends—and will not even say
where she is going and what she is going to do. All this is a
complete mystery to us. You may imagine what will be said
—and how dreadful a scandal will be made of it. I dread
going home to Berlin more than I can say. Wally Paget is in
utter ignorance of all this. I am sure you will feel sorry for
her. If you had seen her, you would I am sure have pitied
her as I did—she is so dreadfully altered. Of course the less
this sad occurrence is talked about the better. I have written
to tell Lady Caroline who always takes so much interest in
her. And I thought I ought to tell you who have always
been so kind to my Ladies when they have been in England
with me. I was much attached to her; she has been with me
for nine years, and was good and kind to me in 1866 when
I was in such distress. I cannot think without a pang that I
am never to see her again, and hardly ever hear of her as
I am afraid she must be thinking of some very mad act.

---

[1] She was lady-in-waiting to the Crown Princess and younger sister of
Walburga Lady Paget. After living for some time with Count Üxküll
she eventually married him. She died in Hungary on 19 March 1878,
her husband having died shortly before.

From the Crown Princess   CANNES, NOVEMBER 19, 1869

I have had letters from Mrs. Hobbs who seems very happy and is settled at Tunbridge. We have had a lovely walk to a place called "Notre Dame de la Vie". There is a lovely view over the sea, the hills, villas and gardens. Perhaps Leopold knows it? There is a friend of Leopold's here, who is very kind to us and whose garden we walk in sometimes—(Mr. Washfield) a nice old gentleman who reminds me of Sir William Jenner. He is very generous and benevolent and does a great deal for the place. He has a very pretty house and has built a lovely little church to which we go on Sundays. We saw poor old Countess Calorada yesterday.[1] She talked to us unceasingly for an hour—and knew all the news of Vienna, Nice, Rome and Paris and edified us in a quiet way with a little scandal about the Duke of Hamilton etc. The Duke and Duchess of Newcastle are at Nice. These lines will reach you on my birthday which is, as Bertie writes to me, "no longer a subject for congratulations" (I suppose he thinks me too old already). They are to ask your blessing for the coming year—the last one the wrong side of thirty—and to beg you on that day to think a little bit of your most dutiful and affectionate daughter Victoria.

From the Queen   WINDSOR CASTLE, NOVEMBER 26, 1869

You mention in your letter that Abbat has been with you. I think it right to state now finally to you that this alliance is out of the question. Louise and I have other views for her, and it is well that he should know once for all, that all idea of this is at an end. I mention this to you and Alice and Louise will tell you this herself if you should ask her. I think you ought to tell this to the King.

---

[1] This is probably Chretienne, Princess Colloredo-Mannsfield. She was a widow, born in 1801.

1870

From the Crown Princess   BERLIN, JANUARY 1, 1870

The carnival of this year will perhaps see an addition to our family. I mention this to you now—though it is very soon to speak of it, but the last time when I did not tell you till later, you said you wished me to do so earlier. So I do so reluctantly, knowing as I do how much you dislike such announcements. I have not told my mother-in-law—she seemed so ill-tempered that I preferred putting off imparting news which she usually receives very badly.[1]

From the Queen   OSBORNE, JANUARY 8, 1870

I am glad that you told me of the impending event. I could have wished indeed a longer rest for you. And (what you do not yet know and feel) the anxiety and trouble of a large family (and especially of a royal one), is very very great, and when one has so many as you have, I can hardly look on it as a matter of congratulation. Those are my reasons (from experience) for being anxious and not joyful when such events are announced.

Now to come to your long and interesting letter about poor Valerie.[2] I quite believe all you think and say about her. I can quite understand and imagine it—and that she thinks things right, which a cold heartless world—or the very severe and religious ones, with naturally established usages—will not understand—though God will! To me there is such a vast difference between heartless, wicked immorality, like one sees, alas! constantly—especially in the higher classes, and one noble passion when all the feelings and aspirations are pure and noble—and when only, perhaps from impossibility of money, or rank, or God knows what, the outward earthly form cannot be given by

---

[1] The future Queen of the Hellenes was born in June.

[2] This letter does not seem to have survived, but it is clear from the Queen's reply that Valerie had eloped. In a later reference to the correspondence dealing with this matter, the Queen writes, "Yours shall certainly be burnt."

man! In God's eyes, I believe as surely as I write this, that this will be considered as holy and right—as what may receive the sanction of man and the world, often without one really noble and holy aspiration! This I firmly believe. But the world as it now is constituted—and above all in days when all that is not merely conventional is scoffed at and condemned—cannot sanction or approve this. It would lead—as the world now is—to the encouragement of all that is bad. It could only do—away from the world—unknown to it.[1] And yet what wickedness and immorality is tolerated! How many are seen, and even liked, who have no high views but disbelieve in all that is noble, pure, disinterested, and above earthly considerations! You will, I am sure, dearest child, understand me! I believe that I enter into your feelings about poor Valerie though I do, for your sakes, deeply lament the half crazy notions she has got. I hope you will continue to tell me what you hear. Don't worry yourself too much, dear child, not to make yourself ill.

The poor Duchess of Argyll resigned three weeks ago— and I have appointed her sister-in-law the young Duchess of Sutherland in her place—a very loyal, kind hearted, though not perhaps very wise little woman; but that is not very necessary in her place. She is no stranger which is a great thing and there was no one else I wished for. The Duchess of Grafton is too delicate; the Duchess of Cleveland, odd and not pleasant—and the Duchesses of Norfolk and Somerset —impossible. Constance Westminster and her husband came here yesterday and stopped till Monday. Augusta Stanley and the little Dean are also here. Have you seen Tennyson's new volume? Augusta S. has been reading a little out of it to me and it seems beautiful. Shall I send it to you if you have not got it?[2] Now I must end this volume.

---

[1] A difficult sentence to unravel. The Queen evidently means that things, in themselves right though wrong to the conventional, would have to be concealed from the world.
[2] *The Holy Grail*, which included "The Passing of Arthur", was published in 1869.

From the Queen   OSBORNE, JANUARY 12, 1870

I cannot tell you how much grieved I am at the sad, and distressing accounts you give me in your dear letter of the 8th for which I thank you very much. Believe me, darling child, that I do feel for you both and for the poor, unfortunate girl more than I can say—and that you have my warmest sympathy. The duel is dreadful. I must say, that though they are dreadful things in themselves, the absence of them in this country has led to a total want of all chivalry and high tone amongst men, and to a very bad tone amongst women, and a total want of regard and respect towards them. There are positions which require duels, I really think, and many gentlemen have said the same. General Grey is greatly distressed about poor Valerie—thinks her mad. If only she could go to her sister or a friend.

I send you "The Holy Grail" but must say—beautiful as are passages in it—it is still more unclear than any of his writings and leaves me quite bewildered. I have only read "The Coming of Arthur" and "The Holy Grail". I shall go on with the others today. Another poem in the book "The Golden Summer" is very beautiful.

The Queen wrote rather hotly and bitterly about Valerie and you for the first time by this messenger and I have merely answered as follows—"the sad affair of poor Valerie is very regrettable and the poor girl and Vicky are much to blame. Vicky herself must be spared in her present condition, and I do ask for allowance to be made for her."

From the Crown Princess   BERLIN, JANUARY 14, 1870

I am sure the Queen will write you a letter of complaint about me. She, in the most peremptory way, commanded me instantly to take a *Grande Maîtresse* and another lady. We had a most disagreeable and painful scene with her the night before last, and she was very violent—saying she had written to me to Cannes instantly to fill up those two vacancies and appoint new people, she had given me three weeks time and it was very disobedient of us not to have done so before now, and now she and the King would insist. And the King, who has all along been so kind and sensible and easy about all these things, suddenly wrote us a flaming letter, which was directly recognised as having been dictated by the Queen. We told her very decidedly that we had not yet found anyone or made up our minds and that we could not after all that had passed make a choice in such a hurry. Marie Goltz does all I want for the present in the way of representation and when I want more ladies than one, I have recourse to Fanny. The Queen thinks this arrangement highly improper. You cannot think what trouble, annoyance and vexation the Queen has caused us, and we so sincerely wish to satisfy her whenever we can and to live in peace and quiet with her—for our own sakes as well as for hers. Year by year she becomes more autocratic—the King is ten times easier to deal with in these things. However I trust your letter will have done a deal of good[1] and perhaps she will come round as she often does when she sees violence is of no use, and that we have the interest and the dignity of the Court just as much at heart as she has—although we do not think ceremony, etiquette, Court life and society the first consideration in the world, as she does—and do not attach so immense an importance to the existence of a *Grande Maîtresse*. As the Queen will not allow me to have a few, quiet, married ladies as all my friends advise me, I shall try and find an elderly spinster of demure and unobtrusive habits—and then perhaps I may hope to carry the point of the *Grande Maîtresse*. I would make any compromise to save me from that *fleau*. I would surround myself with one aged hunchback if that would do any good, and prohibit any colour except black—instead of a *Grande Maîtresse*. Fritz had better have brought back one of those overseers of the harem from Constantinople, as the Queen thinks supervision and discipline so wanting. I think such a person should be appointed to look after all the females in the establishment. Do you not think that would be still more efficacious?

---

[1] Writing a few days later the Crown Princess said that the Queen's manner had greatly changed for the better since receiving Queen Victoria's letter.

I have just looked into Tennyson's new poems of which I had heard a good deal—but I own they are beyond me. I cannot quite understand them. Many thanks for sending them to me.

From the Queen OSBORNE, JANUARY 15, 1870

I can't help feeling that poor Valerie must have been very foolish. Nothing makes me more indignant than the abuse of those who, as I said last time, have no noble or high feelings, are roués and yet fall upon others who do not merely conform to the principle usages of the world!

The Queen certainly is not very particular about her friends—but if the proprieties are kept, anything is overlooked. This shows the miserable imperfection of the world! I quite agree about the difficulties of the unmarried ladies. Their position is a very false and bad one—and really untenable. You can't make a young unmarried girl quite independent. Think what it would have been, if it had been so with my Maids of Honour? General Grey does know, but I don't know whether he had told his sister. But I can suggest his saying something to her.[1]

From the Queen OSBORNE, JANUARY 19, 1870
After further comments on Valerie, the Queen writes:

But I must now tell you that not only the story of the duel but poor Valerie's name are known in London, and we are asked what it means to which we answer we don't know. But I think you ought to find out for else if you go on, kindly and as a true friend, to defend Valerie, you may find out that things are worse after all—and then you might suffer for taking her part. Why don't Count Üxküll say what he has to do with it? Surely she has a friend whom you could ask to tell you the truth.

The Government are busy about a land measure for

---

[1] Lady Caroline Barrington.

Ireland, which I think they will be unsuccessful in—as in the Irish Church. Ireland never was in a worse state.[1]

From the Queen   OSBORNE, JANUARY 22, 1870
Prince Christian had had Scarlet Fever. The Queen writes:

Today is Christian's 39th birthday, but he looks like 50! It is quite extraordinary that he should look so old of his age.

From the Crown Princess   BERLIN, JANUARY 29, 1870
Is it indiscreet if I ask for a drawing and the measurements of the meat larders (out-of-doors) at Osborne and Balmoral? Here there are no such things, and I am afraid to trust alone to my description.

Today there is a dinner at Charlottenburg for the Archduke Charles Louis. We find him aged a good deal. He is very stiff and distant to us all and everybody, but everyone feels for him how unpleasant it must be for him to come here after 1866.

In announcing this visit to her mother the Crown Princess had said that she was glad it was not the youngest Archduke Louis Victor 'who is so ill behaved'.

From the Queen   OSBORNE, FEBRUARY 1, 1870
What you say about Tennyson is most true.[2] That Byron scandal is too shameful; I have not read it as I have a particular horror of scandal and gossip, and it is quite untrue. Mrs. Stowe has behaved shamefully.[3]

---

[1] The Irish Land Act of 1870 "was not a success, though it did much to save tenants from the worst kind of eviction." E. L. Woodward, *The Age of Reform*.
[2] In her letter of 29th January the Crown Princess wrote, "I have been reading the 'Holy Grail'—some bits are very fine—but others are affectedly confused, which is such a pity. I wonder how such disgraceful things as the 'Byron Controversy' get into print. Really I am quite ashamed of having read it."
[3] *Lady Byron Vindicated* by Harriet Beecher Stowe had just been published and handled the poet's supposed relations with his half sister.

I do hear more music than I did sometime ago, and ever since this autumn have played myself again, with Beatrice and Leopold—to please them as they read so well at sight and are very fond of it. I am as fond as ever of it when I hear it, but I don't feel any very great enjoyment in listening to it. No that is gone. As for travelling, it is the act of travelling which tires me so—as I can't travel quietly and stop anywhere unobserved, when I am tired, and abroad in the sun where the heat is so frightful. Perhaps in a year or two—I may be better able to bear it!

From the Queen   OSBORNE, FEBRUARY 5, 1870
I had anticipated your wishes—telling the Queen that I thought you ought not to go out of an evening, that it was bad for you, and that I never could bear it at those times. I do regret for your health, dear child, that this should be the case again. It is very exhausting. I believe the poor Duchess of Argyll's illness is entirely the result of over exhaustion from having 12 children. Lady Lyttelton the same—also Lady Hardinge and Lady L. Brooke.[1]

From the Crown Princess   BERLIN, FEBRUARY 5, 1870
The cold is intense here, and we are quite shut up. We cannot get a drop of water in the house as all the pipes are frozen, and all the chimneys smoke terribly which is very uncomfortable when one has a cold. I am better, but have no voice at all.

From the Queen   OSBORNE, FEBRUARY 9, 1870
Parliament opened yesterday. Mr. Gladstone looks very ill and seems weak—a bad beginning. And Mr. Bright is so unwell as to be obliged to go down to Scotland for some weeks. He left London yesterday.

---

[1] Lady Lyttelton was the wife of the 4th Lord Lyttelton and had 8 sons and 4 daughters. In eight years of married life Lady Hardinge, wife of the 2nd Lord Hardinge, had 5 sons and 3 daughters. Lady Louisa Brooke, wife of Sir Richard Brooke, had 6 sons and one daughter. All three ladies died while they were still comparatively young.

From the Crown Princess   BERLIN, FEBRUARY 9, 1870

We had a dreadful fright with this horrid fire, and have every reason to be thankful that it was no worse for it might have been very serious. The floor just above our bedroom was burnt almost through in one place, and an immense bit of the loft and of the roof is gone—and this in the midst of this intense cold, when hardly any water is to be had and the pipes all frozen and bursting! The whole place is so filled with bad smells and smoke that the windows are obliged to be open in spite of the cold. We are wrapped up in furs and shawls as if we were out of doors. The house is full of work people and we cannot get out. It is more than a week since the children or I have been out and the colds and coughs have no chance of disappearing. I was too excited (and too anxious to appear quite calm and unconcerned) to feel the effects of this fright at the moment but now I perceive that my nerves have been shaken and my general health a little upset but this will come all right in a few days. I was not sure whether Charlotte was in safety for a few minutes, but she soon turned up. As the fire was discovered at night no one was up and all the doors to the staircases locked, which of course caused some confusion. The firemen were excellent and did all that was required very quickly and very cleverly—and most of our servants had their wits about them and behaved very well. Of course the female part of the establishment indulged in more screams and wails than was necessary. But there is something very frightening in seeing the whole landing-place in flames—and the whole passages and staircases with volumes of smoke pouring out of them. Had we not been woken by a man from the bank, who got into the house and rushed into all the rooms—screaming "Fire", we might none of us escaped in time! But the man's screams in the dead of the night at our bedroom door gave me such a shock that I felt my heart jump into my mouth, and consequently forgot to put on slippers or dressing-gown, and had no command of my words for the moment to ask for them. When all was over these adventures are very funny—but at the instant it seemed no laughing matter.

A shooting party in Windsor Great Park, 1869. *Left to right*: General Grey, Major Grey, General Seymour, the Prince of Wales, Prince Christian, Sir James Clark.

A contemporary sketch of a Drawing Room at Buckingham Palace in March 18

A family group in 1870. *Left to right, in front*: Princess Beatrice, Prince Albert Victor of Wales, Queen Victoria; *behind*: Prince Leopold, Prince George of Wales, Princess Louise, Princess Louise of Wales, The Princess of Wales.

From the Queen   FEBRUARY 12, 1870
No heading but presumably Osborne.

Poor Mr. Bright is very unwell and he must keep perfectly quiet for a month, and it is doubtful whether then even, he will be able to resume his duties. Lord Granville is not well and Mr. Bruce laid up, and Lord Clarendon very far from well and Mr. Gladstone looks wretchedly ill.

From the Crown Princess   BERLIN, FEBRUARY 15, 1870
The horrid cold has relented a little so that we can go out in a closed carriage. But it has done a deal of mischief, and has been a terrible time for the poor who have suffered much. The chickens and fowls have all died in most people's hen-houses, engines on the railway have been spoiled without end—many poor engine drivers disabled for life by frost bites—and some workpeople killed by the cold. The air is so wretchedly dry that though we could hardly get our rooms to a reasonable temperature we have not a cupboard or table that has not split, or a book or box that is not warped. As for our paper-hangings they have all cracked. All the woodwork comes unglued and the tilestones all cracked and bent. What a state my skin is in I am quite ashamed of—and can hardly show myself I am such a figure. My forehead, nose and chin are covered with large red blotches and so chapped and stiff that it is very uncomfortable and yet I never was out in the coldest weather. I should be heartily thankful for damp and a thaw—for this dry cold is very unwholesome. There are inflammations of the lungs, croup, pleurisies etc. all over the town and parents are afraid to send their children to school.

From the Queen   OSBORNE, FEBRUARY 16, 1870
I grieve to think I shall not see your dear boys this year, and also not see you for so long. I have rather a horror of planning things a year beforehand. But it would be very nice if you could come this year and occupy Osborne Cottage and Albert Cottage (formerly Kent Cottage) which has been enlarged and newly done up and where the Greys

are now. If you came with not too enormous a household then the two, which are close to each other, would hold you nicely. Those enormous families are too much for me now, dear child, I must honestly own. In that way it would be very nice indeed and we could see each other very pleasantly. Osborne (I mean my house) is not made for large parties and in the summer it is quite dreadful. I had an experience of it in '68 and could never try it again.

From the Queen   WINDSOR CASTLE, MARCH 2, 1870
   Many, many thanks for your dear loving letter, so full of good and right feeling of the 26th. Bertie's appearance did great good—but the whole remains a painful, lowering thing not because he is not innocent, for I never doubted that, but because his name ought never to have been dragged in the dirt, or mixed up with such people. He did not know more of, or admire, the unfortunate, crazy Lady Mordaunt more than he does or did other ladies. The husband is a fool urged on by a bad brother and mother who wished the property to come to them—and certainly B. has been vindictively and spitefully used—though why and wherefore I can't tell.[1] He may have said something about Sir C. M's usage of his wife, which came back to him as poor B. is not very discreet. He has however received many warnings now. You read I hope *The Times* article of the 24th—and a still finer one in *The Daily Telegraph* of the 26th. Have you seen that? B. feels now that these

---

[1] Sir Charles Mordaunt, 10th Baronet, of Walton Hall, Warwickshire had petitioned for divorce citing Lord Cole and Sir Frederick Johnstone. An application was made to stay the proceedings on the ground that Lady Mordaunt was insane. Amongst others the Prince of Wales was examined as to his conduct with Lady Mordaunt and denied in the witness box that there had been undue familiarity between them. The brother was John Mordaunt (1837–1923) and the mother was widow of the 9th Baronet and daughter of George Murray, Bishop of Rochester. The Crown Princess's letter appears to have been destroyed. The Mordaunt case made an exceedingly bad impression in Germany, and was a contributory cause of the disfavour in which the Prince of Wales was viewed by the Prussian Royal Family.

visits to ladies and letter writing are a mistake—to say the least. But they lead far too frivolous a life, and are far too intimate with people and with a small set of not the best or wisest people who consider being fast the right thing!! I hope we shall get him to change but it is difficult; still I never give up reminding him of this dreadful trial.

I see daily more and more that the best parents, the best upbringing (as the Scotch term it), the best advice and example are of no use—if the character is weak and unprincipled, and beloved Papa could have done but little and would have suffered dreadfully. Believe me, children are a terrible anxiety and that the sorrow they cause is far greater than the pleasure they give. I therefore cannot understand your delight at the constant increase of them! Mr. T. Martin said to me the other day that he had quite ceased regretting having none, from the knowledge of the number of parents whose hearts were broken and lives rendered miserable by bad or thoughtless children. Believe me a large family is a misfortune.

From the Queen   WINDSOR CASTLE, MARCH 5, 1870

You will be deeply grieved to hear our beloved Countess[1] is alarmingly ill. Sir William Jenner has been telegraphed for—and I will let you know as soon as I hear. May God spare that dear and valued life. Please tell the Queen.

Dear Alix has just left us, and with increased love and affection and regard on my part. We agree so well, and she is so good and honest and right-minded. She is looking wonderfully well—quite fat for her. She has felt everything, that passed lately, deeply—but she is I think quite easy as to Bertie's conduct; only regretting his being foolish and imprudent. The dear children I do not think improved. They are not well trained or managed.

From the Queen   BUCKINGHAM PALACE, MARCH 9, 1870

First of all let me tell you about our poor, dearest Countess. She has been more or less unwell ever since she came to England—nay even been very ill on first arriving

---

[1] Blücher.

at Brighton. Since then she has been down in Cumberland alone with her sister, who is nervous and very much depressed, and this seems to have affected the dear Countess. She was to have come to town last week when Sir William Jenner heard that it was put off for two days, and then came a letter to say that she was very alarmingly ill. Sir William went down on Saturday and on Monday I saw him. He said the dear Countess was very ill and dreadfully altered—that it was disease of the liver as well as jaundice, that he left her a little better and hoped she would improve —but feared she would never entirely recover. Is this not very sad?

With regard to what you say about children and large or no families I quite agree with you and understand you. No doubt to see none growing up at all is sad, but the higher the station—the greater the difficulty to keep the family united. Where the children have to earn their livelihood and support their parents it is a much finer and more natural relationship. I have seen in the working-classes whole families grow up to be the pride of their old parents. But, just as you said in your previous letter, Princes know that they have nothing to gain by work, or if not well disposed there is nothing to keep them straight. While children are small, they cheer and enliven a house very much and are an object of great interest and pleasure, mixed with anxiety. But when they grow up and you can no longer help them and they resist your advice and help— then you wish you had had none! Still there are many bright exceptions. But I am equally shy of marriages and large families. To be happily married is indeed the greatest of blessings; but the contrary is dreadful—and better a thousand times never marry than marry for marrying's sake—which I believe the greater number of people do. You are wrong in thinking that I am not fond of children. I am. I admire pretty ones—especially peasant children— immensely but I can't bear their being idolised and made too great objects of—or having a number of them about me, making a great noise.

From the Crown Princess　　　BERLIN, MARCH 12, 1870

First let me thank you for your dear letter by messenger. Our correspondence on the subject of married and single life and large or small families is very amusing. The great majority (with some exceptions) of younger sons in royal families (still more in poor princely families) are the most unhappy and useless of creatures. I wish indeed there were fewer of them, still more I wish that their position might in many things be modified so that they should be able to enter honourable professions, earn their own bread and distinguish themselves—instead of being a burden to themselves and their families, and a disgrace to their relations. The French society is a flagrant example of what becomes of family life when children are considered merely as an obstacle to amusement; two are too many, and the daughters must be sent to convents to be brought up—are sent away into the country with their nurses' babies—because Paris air is supposed to be bad for them but in reality because their mothers will not be bothered with them. It is a fact only lately brought again before the public that many never return, that there are no end of changelings, and that the population in France is less than necessary and increases very slowly. The gay mamas and reckless selfish fathers, the absence of home existence, family duties and family ties brought on the great revolution and has at present produced a total ruin of morals. This would not be had they larger families and were obliged to take care of them and educate them; there would not be so much money left to spend on dress, theatre etc. and they would be an easier nation to rule.[1]

---

[1] After this the Crown Princess gives the Queen a political message from the Crown Prince, and this part of the letter is printed in *Letters of Queen Victoria*, Second Series, Volume II, page 10. The Crown Prince wished the Queen to know that the head of the Spanish Government, General Prim, had approached Prince Leopold Hohenzollern to know if he would accept the Crown of Spain. The Prussian Royal Family wished to know privately the opinion of the Queen. The British Foreign Secretary, Lord Clarendon, advised her that she could not express an opinion on a subject where no British interest was concerned.

From the Crown Princess   BERLIN, MARCH 15, 1870

The boys write that they have lovely weather at Cannes. They play with two English boys, the one a son of Mr. Knatchbull Huggesson and the other a son of Mr. Dudley Ryder. I believe the fathers are Members of Parliament.

Does Mr. Odo Russell write very amusing and interesting letters about the Ecumenical Council? It really is next to a farce in our days, and the excitement it produces in the Roman Catholic world is very amusing to watch.[1]

Is it really true that all that awful business about Lady Mordaunt is coming out again and that Bertie's name will be mixed up again? I think it shocking.

From the Queen   WINDSOR CASTLE, MARCH 17, 1870

Enclosing a copy of Lord Clarendon's letter the Queen says:

I at once spoke to Lord Clarendon about the secret communication you made me, and I enclose the answer in German to Fritz. You will, I am sure, see that I cannot do or say more. The neighbour would be very suspicious.

The poor Duke de Montpensier is quite blameless in this dreadful affair. Don Enrique[2] was a horrid, low, republican scamp and forced poor Montpensier who is as myope as a mole and totally unaccustomed to pistols into this duel. But it is most painful for him.

I agree in the great part of what you say. And now one of the new fashions of our very elegant society is to go in perfectly light-coloured dresses—quite tight—without a particle of shawl or scarf (as I was always accustomed to wear and to see others wear) and to dance within a fortnight of their confinement and even valse at seven months!!!!

---

[1] The involved and often uproarious proceedings which marked the opening of the Vatican Council to define Papal Infallibility.

[2] Don Enrique was the brother of Queen Isabella's husband. The Duke of Montpensier was King Louis Philippe's son and had married Queen Isabella's sister. Both Princes aimed at the Crown after Queen Isabella's expulsion. Don Enrique called Montpensier "a puffed-up French pastry-cook". In the duel Don Enrique dropped dead at the third shot. Montpensier was banished from Madrid for a month, and fined 6,000 dollars.

Where is delicacy of feeling going to! Sybil St. Albans danced a quadrille under these circumstances.

This visit to Kimbolton (which is an old engagement) is a great misfortune.[1] If this trial comes on again I don't think there is the slightest fear of Bertie's name being again mixed up in it. I had a very kind and sensible letter from the Queen of Denmark about the whole business. I think it is so dreadful for them both!

From the Crown Princess   BERLIN, MARCH 18, 1870

Fritz thanks you very much for your memorandum. He has sent it to Prince Hohenzollern. Nothing is decided on this subject, and we quite feel that for you it is impossible to offer a decided opinion. No one here likes to give one either, so what will become of the business I have not an idea!

What you say about ladies going about in light dresses, without shawls, in my condition is just what I think. How can they have so little delicacy and dignity? I never put on light-coloured things if I can help it, and never am in my own room without a lace shawl or a shetland or black mantilla. I am much too shy of showing myself before the children and the servants. As for dancing I do not think it nice at all.

From the Queen   WINDSOR CASTLE, MARCH 19, 1870

Where can I find words to say what I feel! Our darling Countess—the truest and best of friends—has been taken to the world where all she loved best is gone, and where she so firmly trusted she would meet them. Yes, we must not repine, but for us, for you, dearest child, and for the poor Queen her loss is quite irreparable. And for her poor sick sister who depended upon her and looked to her for everything, and to whom she meant to devote her remaining days, it is too fearful. I cannot find words to say what I feel.

---

[1] Kimbolton Castle, the home of the Duke of Manchester who was, by repute, fast.

Every, every one feels grieved. She was universally beloved by high and low. But too much was put upon and expected of her. All poured out their troubles to her and her health could no longer stand it. To me this is again the loss of one of the few remaining true and devoted friends I have left.

From the Crown Princess   BERLIN, MARCH 22, 1870
You had not a more loyal, loving, devoted subject and friend than our dearly beloved Countess. Though she was so attached to the Queen and had been so true and devoted a friend to her for so many years, yet I know that her feeling for you was tempered with that peculiar affection which every English heart feels, and this was a strong tie between me and her. Out here in a foreign land which had become the land of her adoption and of mine we both felt that special compound of fond tenderness and pride when we thought of home and of you. How invaluable that was to me in the first few years of my married life! How I shall miss it! She was the only person I had in this world to whom I could talk about our dear home! I think of her goodness. What a noble nature her's was, and it is comforting to see in this world where evil so often triumphs and where the wicked seem so often to get on the best, how goodness is a power! What an influence our beloved Countess had over those she came near, and what a wholesome and cheering influence it was. How strongly one felt oneself drawn to her by her motherly kind heart. All those, who knew her well, grieve sincerely—the King and Queen, Fritz, Louise of Baden, Stockmar, my ladies, the Queen's ladies and even people who had only seen her occasionally. She was loved as she deserved to be, and her unselfishness is in every mouth. She was always doing a kind action, helping or serving someone else. No one ever turned to her to ask her advice or assistance under difficulties in vain, and never was confidence more surely placed than in her! As discreet and wise as intelligent, as cautious and prudent as she was quick, determined and courageous, when necessary, throughout so generous, forgiving, lenient, and charitable, so easy to please and, in spite of all the sorrows and trials she had gone

through, so cheerful and ready to be amused and even to enjoy. All these qualities made her so delightful to live with, and I always felt a blank when she left the house after she had been with me! She was a very remarkable person and we may all consider ourselves honoured to have known her as we did.

From the Queen   BUCKINGHAM PALACE, MARCH 23, 1870
Many thanks for your two dear letters. I knew at once how you would grieve and indeed we shall feel her loss more and more. For you especially I do feel this most deeply. The beloved Countess was so attached to you, so anxious about you, for your difficult position. I know well how you stand in need of such a dear, true and wise friend —and I too (though of late years her bad health and her sister's sorrow and still worse health prevented my seeing her as often as formerly, and she was so much aged the last few times, and her nerves seemed very much shaken). I am to see Count G. Blücher here tomorrow; and also poor faithful, devoted Fanny Schuster whom the Countess loved much—as well as the rest of her family. She knew the inestimable value of attached, devoted, faithful and trusty servants. There is nothing like it—for you depend so much on them and you expect so much from them.

From the Queen   CLAREMONT, MARCH 26, 1870
I was just going to write to you—when I received your dear, long letter of the 22nd. Before I answer it let me tell you that we have a fresh sorrow in poor General Grey's very alarming illness. Ever since we came back from Osborne, he has been complaining of a total want of power in his legs, of great weakness and depression and looked so ill and was so sleepy. Sir William Jenner was alarmed at this, and said the influenza he had had was not enough to cause this, and he feared there must be something very wrong—premature old age coming on. Mrs. Grey was dreadfully alarmed. However he went on much as usual, when at a quarter to eleven this morning, we heard from Sir William Jenner that "General Grey was seized with epileptiform convulsions

and insensibility at soon after seven this morning; he has had three attacks of the convulsions since that time (it is now nine o'clock) and is in very great danger. I am called away by a fourth attack." This is I fear very bad! He has been failing much the last year and grown terribly irritable but would not take care. I have telegraphed you to tell you of it.

Since I wrote to you I saw first of all the dear Countess's devoted maid, Fanny, who has nursed her with the tenderest love and devotion and who says she had been long very ill, and very suffering—but concealed it from everyone. And in the afternoon I saw young Count Gustaf Blücher, whom the Countess loved most dearly and so often spoke of to me with the greatest affection as one of the best young men she knew. And I never saw anyone more touchingly affected than he was; he loved her more, as Fanny said, than his own mother, and he sobbed like a child in speaking of her, and of her sorrows and sufferings, and in reading to me her beautiful letter in which she thanked him for all his love and affection to "the poor widowed, childless, old, old woman" and prayed God to reward him. In this letter she says that she wishes in case "I should die in my own country" to be buried in the vault where her brother-in-law lies—at Cressingham [Gressingham] near Capernwray and there she was buried and he means to have a marble cross—plain just like the one she had raised over her husband's grave! If she had died abroad she wished to be buried at Baden near her husband and child. He also spoke so touchingly of her great love for me—her great affection for you. The German property including the house at Baden all belongs to him. All her English money and her silver goes to the Passys for whom this loss is quite irreparable.[1]

---

[1] The Countess died at Capernwray Hall, the home of her brother-in-law, George Marton, who had been Member of Parliament for Lancaster. She is buried just outside Gressingham Church, in North Lancashire close to the Marton tomb. The Queen and members of the Royal Family sent wreaths of immortelles. The poor, sick sister, to

What you say about her is most touching and true and I feel that it was a great privilege to have been her friend. She had however greatly changed during the last three years and while her loving nature and affection, her unselfishness and discretion were ever the same, the strength of mind, the courage and firmness had decreased and this we here observed and thought a bad sign of health. Her hand-writing altered too and she had much anxiety, worry and sorrow. For you, dearest child, I feel and understand all you say most completely. That cutting off, which is the death of those who were a link with home and the past, is dreadful! No one has experienced more of that than me. It is dreadful indeed and makes one feel very lonely and dreary.

From the Crown Princess   BERLIN, MARCH 29, 1870
     I forget whether I told you that we have engaged an English governess for this autumn called Miss Byng.[1] I wish we could have done with Mlle Darcourt alone, as it causes us a deal of extra expense and trouble, but everyone was *d'accord* that it would not be good to put another child with Charlotte on account of the peculiar difficulties in her education, which might injure another child. They all hope in a few years she will change and improve. So I gave way, at first against my will but I now think they are right. When we return to Berlin next November (if we are all alive) Vicky will go to Miss Byng. Having an English governess saves my having English masters and mistresses

whom the Queen refers, is almost certainly Giustina Dallas who did not marry. Another sister married Major Passy.
     The Court Circular of 20 March contained the following paragraph— "the death of Countess Blücher (née Miss Dallas) of which the news reached Windsor Castle yesterday morning has caused the Queen and the Royal Family the deepest sorrow. The Countess was one of her Majesty's truest and most valued friends, and her loss will be irreparable not only to the Queen, but to the Crown Princess of Prussia, to whom the Countess was ever truly devoted".
[1] Augusta Maria Byng, governess to the Crown Princess's children from 1870 till her death in 1882. The Crown Princess thought very highly of her and in a later letter to the Queen (1 September, 1881) she writes "How often I had made her promise that if I died she would never leave the children until they were grown up and married".

who are very difficult to get here—and with whom we have had a deal of trouble. The children must be able to talk and write good English.

From the Queen   CLAREMONT, MARCH 30, 1870
We have travelled and driven about a great deal in this really lovely country where the air is extremely good from the lightness of the soil and the heather and many commons and fir trees. The quiet, and the absence of court and many people are a great relief to me which I much needed.

If the Queen wishes to come to England why does she not do so—on her own accord—like the Queen of Holland and then I could invite her down occasionally—and we should be independent of one another? But she always will come on a visit to me, which is what I cannot often bear, from the great fatigue it causes me—though in November I am quite ready to undertake it.

From the Queen   WINDSOR CASTLE, APRIL 2, 1870
Referring to General Grey's death the Queen writes:

His spirit is now free from all the shackles of this wicked, weary world, and knows all which interested his mind, so full of faith but not fettered by bigotry. He had very much altered of late, and it was very difficult for one to get on with him—often very irritable, and excited, and impatient of any difference of opinion. He could not have gone on long and wished to retire already three years ago—feeling old age creeping on, he said—though he was not more than sixty-three then and just sixty-six when he died.

Last year again he represented his wish to retire, but there was a great difficulty in making a suitable arrangement. He then consented to go on for a time. The arrangement which he strongly recommended and which Sir Thomas Biddulph and the Dean (who has remarkably good judgement) also suggested will then be carried out viz--that Colonel Ponsonby should succeed the General as Private Secretary, aided by the advice and experience of Sir Thomas. He was Private Secretary to three successive

Lord Lieutenants, has excellent abilities, great facility in writing, great discretion and very good temper. A stranger I never could take. Of course the experience dear General Grey possessed cannot be replaced—but that is the dreadful misfortune which all encounter as they grow old and no one feels that more acutely than I do. But it is God's will it should be so, and I must make the best of it and not lose courage.

I went up yesterday morning with Louise to see poor dear Mrs. Grey who is quite admirable in her great calmness and Christian resignation—and struggles not to break down. We saw the dear General looking so unaltered without that ghastly, yellow white which, often or indeed generally, gives the greatest alteration—looking younger and so peaceful and like himself. His bed was covered with flowers.

The dear old Baron had a great opinion of Colonel Ponsonby and often said to me "You should make more and more use of him".

From the Crown Princess   BERLIN, APRIL 2, 1870

Fritz Carl has had a threatening of a stroke, is very red in the face and suffers from giddiness; he has gone to his place to be quite quiet and drink some waters. I am not quite happy about Fritz's health. He is over fatigued with perpetual *soirées*, standing in hot rooms for five hours together almost every night, in consequence of which he looks very yellow and his liver is a little out of order. He has a bad knee; a slight inflammation in the joint, Langenbeck says—and is going to put a blister on it. Fritz looks thin and tired; but the Queen will not admit the real reason which is his life which the King and Queen make him lead when he is here.

I had the grief of hearing yesterday that there is no doubt about poor Valerie. She had a son on the 24th March —born at the right time. Count Ü. is with her—they live in the same house; but she persists in saying she will not marry him. Marriage was wrong and she alone in the right, and having the right principles can make no concession for the sake of the world! Was there ever anything so mad, perverse and foolish? It is a shock to me—as I had no reason to believe that she had carried on a *liaison* ever since the month of June last year. I never had any proofs of it that were convincing during the autumn. I was with her every day and all day long and certainly such an idea never passed through my mind. And all that was told me here when I returned from Cannes was so untrue that of course I disbelieved everything I heard—as her own brother and everybody in the house here thought it absurd and out of the question.[1] I can no longer defend and excuse her—but only say that she is really unlike other people, and that we who know her well cannot indiscriminately class her with many who have carried on the like misconduct. I pity her as I am sure she will live to see the folly of her theories and repent her having departed from what she will some day be forced to acknowledge is the right path!

From the Queen   WINDSOR CASTLE, APRIL 6, 1870
    Sir Thomas[2] is gone down to Howick for the last sad ceremony which takes place at ten tomorrow.

I have sent five wreaths from myself, three daughters and Leopold and a bunch of lilies of the valley, which I could just get and which were his favourite flowers—as they are also mine, to be laid on his coffin!

I am much grieved to hear the account of dear Fritz's health! It is so precious that every possible care should be taken of it, and it is too bad to let it be used up for such miserable, frivolous objects. The older the King and Queen grow the fonder they seem to become of these worldly things which they overdo—sadly.

That sad story of Valerie's is only, I grieve to say, what I expected from what I had heard, though I recognise she really must be mad to have such extraordinary ideas. Such

---

[1] Count Maurice Hohenthal-Hohenpreissnitz. Lady Paget (Wally) evidently alluding to this liaison said, "it darkened and embittered my life for many years." *Embassies of Other Days*, page 252.
[2] Biddulph.

things are only to be understood when for reason of one kind or another people cannot marry—but when they can, over and over again[1]—unless (which I cannot believe) the report that Count Ü. was not the father of the child should be really true—it seems to be so incomprehensible and so devoid of all romance!! It is very distressing for you. I pity her for she will some day waken to a sense of her extraordinary position!

From the Queen   WINDSOR CASTLE, APRIL 9, 1870
Referring to Fritz's health, the Queen writes:

Would a change of air do him good? I would have offered sea bathing at Osborne in July for a fortnight but then I fear that for the liver the sea would be bad, or a fortnight or three weeks Highland air in August or September. In short if I can be of any use to one so dear to me—and so precious to thousands—I should be too glad and you would not grudge his being with me as you know that I should take the greatest care of him.

Colonel Ponsonby is a very decided Liberal, but he never has mixed in politics—and is very discreet which our poor, dear General was not, I must own, though it may appear very strange to you.

From the Crown Princess   BERLIN, APRIL 12, 1870
The "Grille", the yacht on which we have spent so many summer days and taken so many expeditions, is at Plymouth and will go to Spithead. It would give me so much pleasure if you could order her to Cowes Roads and see her in any way—she is only a little thing like the "Fairy". If you would allow Beatrice or Leopold to see her. I have quite a sentiment for the little vessel and it would be such a pleasure to me in future to think you or any of the brothers and sisters had been on board her. Last year we dined and had tea on board every day and the boys spent

---

[1] These words are difficult to read, but if this reading is correct the Queen means that an attractive girl (such as Valerie) has chances of marrying over and over again.

so much of their time there; on Henry's and Ditta's birthdays we have had dances on board. The "Grille" has taken us repeatedly to the Baltic and she took Fritz and Louis through the Suez Canal and into the Golden Horn. She is neither as pretty nor alas! as clean and well-kept as the "Fairy", nor are the cabins very comfortable. I have spent many a night on board. It would be very kind of you if you would give a look at her.

From the Crown Princess   BERLIN, APRIL 26, 1870

You will be glad to hear that all thoughts about Spain are entirely given up and a complete refusal has been sent. What a shocking thing has happened in Greece! The murder of these unhappy English travellers, if it be true, may produce political complications. May it not?[1]

From the Crown Princess   BERLIN, APRIL 29, 1870

My children had a great fright this afternoon—a madman jumped into the carriage, and sat down on Mrs. Hawes's lap. The children were soon got out—but the man would not leave the carriage and bit the footman's hand. However he was soon marched off in safety and nothing else happened fortunately. Of course the poor nurses were horribly frightened.

From the Queen   OSBORNE, APRIL 30, 1870

Bertie is having the whole thing well sifted and so should everyone where their characters are slandered.[2] It is the greatest mistake to say "it makes it too important".

---

[1] A party consisting of Lord and Lady Muncaster, Mr. Frederick Vyner, Mr. Herbert, Count Boyl and Mr. and Mrs. Lloyd, with a child of 5, left Athens in carriages for Marathon. On the way back they were ambushed by brigands, and Vyner, Herbert, Boyl and Lloyd were later murdered. Lord Muncaster was allowed to go back to Athens to arrange a ransom.

[2] The 4th Lord Sefton had married a daughter of the first Lord Hylton. There was a report in a Sheffield newspaper at the beginning of this month that Lord Sefton was bringing an action for divorce against his wife citing the Prince of Wales as co-respondent. The report was without foundation.

Unfortunately the children have only a day governess, and no regular one. Alix spoils them terribly.

From the Crown Princess   BORNSTAEDT, MAY 2, 1870
     I do not wonder at everybody thinking and talking of little else than this appalling tragedy in Greece. It is really dreadful but I cannot help pitying Alix's brother, who has a pleasant position of being responsible for mischief he is too weak to prevent, as he cannot depend on his ministers or his army. The thrones of Greece and Rumania seem to me the most wretched and unenviable of positions. I believe Charles Hohenzollern's affairs are going on as badly as possible—he makes one mistake after another which I suppose he cannot help, cannot keep a single German or reliable person about him—and is said to be very much out of spirits.[1]

From the Queen   OSBORNE, MAY 4, 1870
     That Greek tragedy gets worse and worse. It was no mere act of brigandage; people high in position at Athens were implicated in it. The Muncasters and poor Mrs. Lloyd are expected back on Friday. I hope to see them soon after. King George is in the greatest distress about it. He has given Mrs. Lloyd £1,000 and a pension, for she is very poor; her husband was a Civil Engineer engaged in the railway there.[2]

From the Queen   OSBORNE, MAY 7, 1870
     I am very sorry indeed for the bad accounts from Rumania; but we have heard just the same, only I did not like to say anything about poor Charles H. How can any people long for such thrones?
     Poor Willie (King George) is much to be pitied—for to be unable to prevent these horrors is so dreadful, and he is

---

[1] Charles Hohenzollern, 1839–1914, younger son of Prince Hohenzollern, elected Prince of Rumania in 1866.
[2] The Queen here was misinformed. He was a member of the Bar, and correspondent for the *Standard* in Athens.

quite distracted at it. The accounts are more and more distressing.

From the Queen   BUCKINGHAM PALACE, MAY 11, 1870
Don't press poor dear Henry too much; it will not do any good and he will learn none the better for it. Believe me, dear child, more harm than good is done by forcing delicate and backward children.

From the Crown Princess
                      NEUES PALAIS, POTSDAM, MAY 11, 1870
You ask how the madman got into the children's carriage the other day. The carriage was leaving the door at a trot, the man jumped at the horses and caught the reins. The coachman pulled up, as quick as he could, to prevent the man being driven over, who was however already knocked down by the horses. He jumped up again in a minute and opened the carriage-door and took possession of the seat, but it was not easy for the nurses and children to get out. The man was mad—had done almost the same thing with the Archduchess Gisella in the streets of Vienna; he is a Bohemian.

From the Queen   WINDSOR CASTLE, MAY 18, 1870
We had Lord and Lady Muncaster here with us for Saturday—most interesting to hear—but they are both dreadfully impressed with all they have gone through, and the loss of their poor companions, and Lord Muncaster being the sole survivor. He looks very sad and is becoming as dark as any brigand—an interesting countenance; she is a pretty person, very tall with beautiful eyes, and seems to have shown immense courage. That ride home with poor Mrs. Lloyd on the horses of the wounded with the poor little child—in danger of meeting with another band of brigands—losing their way and only reaching Athens at twelve at night, not knowing what would become of their husbands must have been dreadful! You will see all the public despatches in the papers and will be much interested in the deposition of the German courier who behaved

beautifully.[1] Yesterday I saw poor Mrs. Lloyd, who is a little woman, rather stout, who was much overcome when she saw me. She said she never thought she would see her husband again "Oh if you had seen those brigands" she added, "you could have had no hope". The poor little girl still wakes up at night in a fright with the recollection of being woke out of her sleep, pulled out of the carriage and surrounded by those horrible men!

From the Crown Princess   BORNSTAEDT, MAY 28, 1870

We are much astonished to read in the "Independence Belge" a letter said to be from Bertie to Affie written on the 4th March. Either the letter is not authentic or if it is how on earth has it got into the papers? Of course it is much commented upon—really poor Bertie is very unlucky and what one brother may say quite naturally to another sounds very different when in print and before the public. Besides the French translation has to a certain degree altered the sense of the words supposing the letter to be real and not a work of fiction.[2]

---

[1] Probably Lewis Gleissner, Lord Muncaster's Swiss courier. He went to the camp of the brigands and offered to exchange himself for Frederick Vyner. See *The Dilessi Murders* by Romilly Jenkins, 1961.

[2] Prince Alfred at this time was in India and was the first British prince to visit that country. The exchange of letters between the two brothers found its way into the *Madras Mail*. In his letter the Prince of Wales begins by saying that he hopes one day to go to India "if la mère approves". He says that the Mordaunt divorce case had given him a good deal of annoyance and that "la mère begged Mordaunt to leave my name out of the proceedings". Another of his vexations was that "poor father's name is constantly held up. . . . I must not do this or that, I must always be goody because he was so good. . . . Here nine years after poor father's death I am expected to sit in sackcloth and ashes to his memory." The letter contained several allusions to Ireland, to the improvements at Sandringham and to the convivial habits of the two brothers. The whole is spiced with much chat about Alix, Bertiebus (his eldest son) and the beauty of his unmarried sister-in-law Thyra.

The letter is palpably a joke—though a well-informed one—and the curious thing is that the Crown Princess should have even thought that it might be genuine. But it was this kind of thing which did the Prince great harm in Germany. On 6 June 1870 *The Times* declared that the letters were forgeries. See also the additional note on pages 281 and 282.

Willy gives much promise. The poor arm is no better, and Willy begins to feel being behind much smaller boys in every exercise of the body. He cannot run fast because he has no balance, nor ride nor climb, nor cut his food etc. I wonder he is as good tempered about it. His tutor thinks he will feel it much more, and be much unhappier about it as he grows older and feels himself debarred from everything which others enjoy—and particularly so as he is so strong and lively and healthy! It is a hard trial for him and for us. Nothing is neglected that can be done for it—but there is so little to be done,

From the Queen   BALMORAL, MAY 31, 1870

I am quite at a loss to understand about this letter of Bertie's. Very often I think things are invented abroad—or translated from obscure papers which no one heeds or dreams of here and unfortunately you all see them and think they are of importance. This is a great misfortune. You should always ask me or your sisters and they would at once tell you. I will enquire about this.

Poor Louis of Portugal showed neither strength of character or courage on the occasion. He absolutely stopped all the faithful troops who had been sent for and told them not to come—as he wished no disturbance lest it should wake the Queen!! (Probably out of fear at being scratched and beaten by her—which has often been the case.) And he told Saldanha to do what he liked!! How deplorable![1] I am afraid a good deal of the same conduct would be pursued if I died. This is why I have learned to wish to live, and try and keep myself tolerably well—for the sake of my people, children, friends and country! It is a sad and anxious thought to me—often.

---

[1] The Duke of Saldanha (1791–1876) a stormy figure in Portuguese politics expelled the Government by a show of force, and was believed to favour the joining of Spain and Portugal. King Louis had married Marie-Pie, daughter of King Victor-Emmanuel II of Italy. She had perhaps inherited some of the rough qualities of her father.

From the Queen   BALMORAL, JUNE 6, 1870
   I did not know Lord Lorne was gone to Berlin.[1] *Il ne faut pas disputer des goûts* but I do not fancy him. He has such a forward manner, and such a disagreeable way of speaking but I know he is very clever and very good.
   Those letters are fabrications. Bertie denies both of them absolutely and indignantly. You can certainly deny them.
   That story of the Duchess of Hamilton's daughter is too disgraceful.[2] Really what many of the nobility are now-adays, no one can tell.
   Only imagine our astonishment at seeing in the village this morning an Italian pifferaro (in singular I suppose) and two boys dancing. The last I had seen were on the Devils Bridge on the St. Gothard!! And come all the way from Naples! The people here were so astonished to see another kind of piper and dancing.

From the Crown Princess
                    NEUES PALAIS, POTSDAM, JUNE 8, 1870
   I am so glad that fabrication of Bertie's letter has been contradicted in *The Times*—now the foreign papers can deny it also and really things of this kind are most mischievous to our family and to English interests—that is why I am on the *"qui vive"* as soon as I hear anything unpleasant, being in a manner the first one to suffer by it, and naturally being very jealous of our family honour and anxious to be of service to you in that respect.[3]

---

[1] In her letter of 2nd June the Crown Princess said "Lord Lorne has just been here. I was so glad to see him; he came for the wedding of a friend of his, which took place at Berlin yesterday, a Mr. Talbot—who is a Prussian officer, and who married a Miss Broadhurst, a pretty American lady." Gerald Francis Talbot was also a colonel in the Staffordshire Yeomanry.
[2] Lady Mary Douglas-Hamilton married the Prince of Monaco in September, 1869. Their son was born in July, 1870. They were divorced in 1880, the marriage being declared nul by the Papal Court.
[3] On 6 June 1870 *The Times* published the following paragraph: "Certain letters purporting to have been written, the one by the Prince of Wales to the Duke of Edinburgh, and the other by the Duke of Edinburgh to the Prince of Wales which, we believe, appeared originally in

From the Crown Princess

Do you not think the Queen of Spain's manifesto rather touching? I cannot help pitying the poor creature for whom no one feels pity or respect. She would never have sunk to what she now is had she had another mother and another education and had she not been made to marry such a wretch of a husband.[1]

For several weeks the Queen had been largely engrossed by domestic matters—the approaching confinement of the Crown Princess, the illness of Prince Leopold, the death of Lord Clarendon, the death of Sir James Clark and the slight nervous illness of Princess Helena. Of Sir James Clark's funeral she writes on 6 July 1870 from Windsor:

All went off very quietly on Monday at Kensal Green— the idea and publicity of which I do not like.[2]

I will write more about this another day. Let me however say today that we are much startled by the news of Leopold of Hohenzollern's election as King of Spain, and above all at a telegram from Paris saying that France will resist this and hopes we will also, which is quite preposterous but alarming. I thought that that was all given up.[3]

---

an Irish paper, have obtained circulation in the Provincial Press, and have even been translated in the *Independence Belge*. Though written with a certain smartness, they were so evidently intended as a hoax that it was scarcely necessary to deny their authenticity so long as they were only circulated at home; but, as foreign readers can not be expected to discriminate, it is necessary to declare, as we have authority for doing, that both letters are forgeries."

[1] The Queen formally abdicated, from Paris in exile, in favour of her son, the Prince of the Asturias, afterwards King Alfonso XII. Her husband, the Spanish Duke of Cadiz, was said, according to the gossip of the day, to be impotent.

[2] The Queen is doubtless referring to the funeral procession through the streets to Kensal Green, contrasting this with a funeral in a graveyard, close to or adjoining a church, where burial was still possible even in London at this time.

[3] The Queen is referring to the previous offer to Prince Leopold of Hohenzollern in March (see page 265). But the Spanish were unable to find another candidate so after canvassing a number of possible princes they offered it once again to Prince Leopold.

I pity the poor Queen of Spain very much for it was not her fault that she turned out so badly.

From the Crown Princess

NEUES PALAIS, POTSDAM, JULY 8, 1870

Though I think everything ought to be avoided which might wound the susceptibility of the French nation or make the Emperor's position still more difficult than it already is I do not quite see what right the French Government has to call upon England to resist Leopold Hohenzollern's election. It is surely the affair of the Spanish nation and no one else's?[1] With General Prim originating the idea of Leopold Hohenzollern, nobody was more taken aback than the Hohenzollerns themselves who had never dreamt of such a thing. It is needless for me to repeat again that Prussia had nothing to do with the Spanish revolution or any sort of connection with any of the different parties. Indeed I do not think that there was any interest felt in Spain or the Spanish affair. Leopold Hohenzollern is an independent Prince, though he is a member of our family. But the Government has nothing to do with his decision. I fear the French will not understand this— though they might easily as the Hohenzollerns are related to the Emperor and always keep up a sort of intercourse with Paris.[2]

From the Queen

THE PAVILION CAMP, ALDERSHOT, JULY 9, 1870

I have come here early, to avoid the great heat which

---

[1] Two days previously the Crown Princess had described the Hohenzollern acceptance as "a sad mistake". The change in her opinion is the indication of the heightening of national feeling. The reader is referred to Professor Michael Howard's *Franco-Prussian War* for an analysis of the Hohenzollern candidature and of Bismarck's part in it.

[2] Napoleon I's wife, Josephine, was the link between the two families. Her daughter by the Vicomte de Beauharnais was the mother of Napoleon III; her niece Stephanie (Grand Duchess of Baden) was the mother of the Princess of Hohenzollern and grandmother to Leopold Hohenzollern.

tries me so dreadfully, and have the troops out this afternoon at five returning to Windsor Castle later this evening.

This unfortunate affair of Leopold H. may set Europe in a blaze. If only he would retire of himself it would be a blessing, though the conduct of France is most preposterous and shameful. If the King too would say he had nothing to do with it.[1]

From the Queen   WINDSOR CASTLE, JULY 13, 1870

Late last night we heard that Leopold H. had given up. It is the only thing he could do, for though the conduct of France was perfectly monstrous, still what chance had Leopold to succeed or do Spain good if his acceptance set Europe in a blaze? Though no doubt it is madness to look upon him as a Prussian candidate (considering his near relationship with the Emperor's family) it reminds me most forcibly of the old Spanish marriage question, which brought on the downfall of Louis Philippe when he and Guizot were so violent against Leopold Coburg on the ground that he was an English candidate—whereas he was the brother of the King's daughter-in-law and son-in-law, and might have been considered as too French by us!!![2] Paris[3] said to me two days ago "It speaks much for our civilisation that we should wish to have a war of succession in the nineteenth century."!!!

I send you the copy of a confidential memorandum of Lord Granville in consequence of which I wrote the substance of it to Philippe Flanders asking him to communicate it to Leopold H. I communicated in strict confidence Fritz's

---

[1] An important sentence, and added by the Queen as an afterthought.
[2] The Queen is here referring to the family of her uncle Prince Ferdinand of Coburg-Kohary. Prince Leopold, 1824–84, was the youngest son and subsequently made a morganatic marriage. The eldest son married Princess Clementine, Louis Philippe's daughter: the only daughter, Victoria, married Louis Philippe's son, the Duke of Nemours.
[3] Louis Philippe's grandson, Louis Philippe, Count of Paris (1838–94).

The Crown Princess's children in 1870. *Left to right*: Prince Henry,
Prince William, Princess Charlotte and Princess Victoria.

The departure of the German Emperor from Berlin on 31 July 1870 for the campaign against France.

to Lord Granville.[1] Respecting the steps taken by the Orleans Princes you shall hear later.[2]

During the period of the fighting in the Franco-Prussian War the Crown Princess's letters are naturally dominated by patriotic feeling. Many of them are printed in "Letters of the Empress Frederick" by Sir Frederick Ponsonby and there seemed therefore no advantage in republishing them here. The reader may however be glad to have this very short summary of some points in them.

On 18 July, immediately after war had been declared, the Crown Princess wrote to her mother "the odds are fearfully against us". Later, when the Queen asked why she had said this, she wrote that she and most Germans had expected the French to overrun the Rhine "before we could get our troops ready". This expectation of disaster explains why the Germans in the early stages of the War were so indignant with English neutrality. The Crown Princess herself did not endorse this but she reported it to the Queen and said that in consequence of it "I am looked upon with suspicious eyes". She frequently contrasts the frivolous life of the French under Napoleon with the more humdrum existence of the Germans—"our poverty, our dull towns, our plodding, hard-working, serious life has made us strong and determined—is wholesome for us. I should grieve were we to imitate Paris and be so taken up with pleasure that no time was left for self-examination and serious thought".

The Crown Prince left the Neues Palais for the Front at half past five in the morning of 26 July, husband and wife having agreed that they would bid one another "no formal farewell". He was to command the Third Army, which was made up of south German troops and two Prussian Army Corps. He won the battle of Wörth, and his Army took part in the victory at Sedan. The Crown Princess left alone in Berlin did what she could to organise

---

[1] Lord Granville's Memorandum is on pages 24 and 25 of *Queen Victoria's Letters*, Second Series, Volume II. The Crown Prince's on pages 22, 23 and 24 of the same volume. The Hohenzollerns accepted, but emphasised that the King of Prussia, as head of the family, only gave his consent with reluctance. The Crown Prince's memorandum was written after Prince Leopold had accepted and before his eventual withdrawal. Lord Granville's memorandum suggests urging Prince Hohenzollern to persuade his son to withdraw since the violent reaction of France made the prospects for Prince Leopold unpropitious. The Count of Flanders was brother-in-law to Prince Leopold.

[2] The Orleanist princes had appealed in the previous June against their exile from France.

hospitals for the wounded but the Crown Prince had sadly to write in his diary "all her endeavours and offers of help in the matter of tending the sick were contemptuously rejected—presumably on account of the anti-British feeling".

However when she moved nearer to the frontier to organise hospital work much of the criticism died away. In the early autumn of 1870 she went to live in the old castle at Homburg (once the home of her great-aunt Elizabeth, George III's daughter) so as to be near the battlefields; here she turned the old military barracks into a hospital on modern lines. She built new wards at her own expense and her husband was gratified to learn how generally her efforts were appreciated. Florence Nightingale sent out Miss Florence Lees (one of her friends and pupils) to help the Crown Princess and she was warm in her praise of all that was attempted. In Washington a model of the Victoria ward at Homburg was exhibited for many years as an example of the latest methods in nursing and hygiene.

From the Queen   OSBORNE, JULY 16, 1870

Beloved child, I cannot say what my feelings of horror and indignation are, or how frightfully iniquitous I think this declaration of war![1] My heart boils and bleeds at the thought of what misery and suffering will be caused by this act of mad folly! And just when all that we and Leopold B. were asked to obtain to settle the question had been obtained.[2]

Poor good Sir C. Lewis would have been delighted at the idea of one of my grandchildren being called Sophia on account of the Electress Sophia.[3] Else I think the name ugly.

---

[1] On 15 July France declared war on Prussia. "There were many among us even then who believed Prussia and Count Bismarck—the terrible Chancellor, as Mr. Carlyle called him—to be the real mover of the war, and, among military men especially, a chivalrous if not very logical feeling, founded on our former alliance, created a strong sympathy for the cause of the French. But the expressed feeling of the country at large was undoubtedly German, a feeling which subsequent events went far more than to modify." The Annual Register.

[2] The Emperor Napoleon had asked the King of the Belgians to intervene with the Hohenzollern family.

[3] Sir George Cornewall Lewis (1806–63), scholar and statesman. He was obviously an admirer of George I's mother the Electress. He was a close personal friend of the Queen and Prince Consort. The Crown Princess's third daughter (the future Queen of the Hellenes) was born on 14 June.

If you wish to send a letter safely send it under cover to Löhlein or Emilie Dittweiler as W. Sahl is in Germany.[1]

From the Queen   OSBORNE, JULY 20, 1870

My poor, dear, beloved child, words are far too weak to say all I feel for you or what I think of my neighbours!!! We must be neutral as long as we can, but no one here conceals their opinion as to the extreme iniquity of the war —and the unjustifiable conduct of the French. Still, more publicly we cannot say but the feeling of the people and country here is all with you—which it was not before. And need I say what I feel? My whole heart and my fervent prayers are with beloved Germany! Say that to Fritz—but he must not say it again—and that I shall suffer cruelly for you all—thinking of beloved Papa too, who would have gone to fight if he could. Most anxious shall I be to hear what your plans of defence and attack are—for till now we know nothing!

That story about Bertie is quite untrue—so he declares and he is furious with Bernstorff who certainly is a shocking mischief maker.[2] He ought, for the interests of both countries to be removed. My heart bleeds for you all! The awful suddenness of the whole thing is so dreadful! Do not over worry yourself—not to make yourself ill. Poor Alice makes us all very anxious—and she seems anxious not to leave Darmstadt. I have no doubt that you will both advise her for the best. My thoughts are constantly with you— wishing you the daughters could be safe here! These divided interests in Royal Families are quite unbearable. Human nature is not made for such fearful trials—especially not

---

[1] German members of the Royal Household in England to whom it was safe to write without the risk of post-office espionage.
[2] At a dinner at the French Embassy the Prince of Wales was supposed to have congratulated the Austrian Ambassador on his country's neutrality, and to have expressed the hope that Austria would join France. The unpopularity of the Prince of Wales in Germany did not— as is often mistakenly imagined—derive from the Kaiser. It dated back to the Prussian Royal Family's dislike of his supposed immoralities, and to such mischievous stories as this, circulated by Bernstorff—that "ill-conditioned man" as the Prince named him.

mothers' and wives' hearts. But God will watch over you all, I doubt not. You have the warmest sympathy of all— and all the people in the House take the deepest interest in you.

From the Queen   OSBORNE, JULY 22, 1870
    I enclose a few lines from me and also from Arthur for the King but must ask him not to say publicly I have written for I am bound, for the sake of my own country, to be neutral.[1]
    I send here a copy of a memorandum of Mr. Knollys' which Bertie sent me, and an extract of Bertie's. And Lord Granville tells me that Count Apponyi is furious—as B. never spoke to him upon political matters. I hope the King will soon remove him[2] as this really is too abominable and outrageous, and he has done incalculable mischief by all the gossip and lies—he has invariably retailed and sent to Berlin to poison all your ears. Many things you have heard in former years I can all trace to his inventions—treating idle rumours as real facts!! It is too wicked and, in Bertie's case, very ungrateful for he and Alix have taken his and her part against the Cambridge ladies who are so very rude to them. Bertie starts early tomorrow morning for Copenhagen to bring Alix back immediately. He is only to stay four or five days and return at once. It would never do for either of them now to be there.
    Christian is heart and soul with Germany!
    I see that in my confusion I never thanked you for your dear, touching letter of the 18th with its anguish and its heartfelt appeals—which cut me to my heart! Oh my darling child if you knew how my poor heart is wrung! I feel and understand all!

---

[1] The Queen's letter to the King was written on 22 July at Osborne. She said, "Dear Brother. As an old friend I cannot see you go to war without crying 'God save you and bless you' from my whole heart! My heart is indeed heavy. May God protect all those dear to us and especially our dear Fritz! More I am unable to say, but my task is a heavy one. Ever your devoted sister V." *Further Letters of Queen Victoria*, edited by Hector Bolitho, 1938.
[2] Bernstorff.

From the Queen   OSBORNE, JULY 27, 1870

The feeling here is very strong, and the appearance of that Treaty has aroused very great indignation and alarm though many people would not believe it.[1] I have had a few kind touching lines from the Queen who I know will be full of courage and patriotism.

From the Queen   OSBORNE, AUGUST 1, 1870

How fully I enter into your feelings! How my heart bleeds for you all! But you know I have great duties to perform—and I must not swerve from the path, steep and thorny though it be! As it is—I shall be suspected of every sort of thing and of course everyone knows what my feelings and sympathies must be! Doubly difficult therefore is my task and doubly hard to bear! These divided family interests are fearful—almost unbearable and untenable in our days!

I fear it would be very difficult to supply you for the same reason ostensibly with anything, and besides the difficulty of sending anything is so enormous—still I will see if we can, under your and not my name, send you some old linen and oilskin.[2]

There is a Society established in England for the purpose of aiding the wounded, which I hope to be able to subscribe to.[3]

I must tell you that Christian wished to go to Germany to serve as a good German but as he is nationally my son-in-law and as we are neutral it was thought better he should not, as it might lead to difficulties and complications.

From the Crown Princess

NEUES PALAIS, POTSDAM, AUGUST 1, 1870

The question everybody is asking is whether England will not at least prevent the blockade of our ports—and

---

[1] Bismarck published in *The Times* the terms of a draft treaty agreed between the French Ambassador and himself at the end of the Austro-Prussian War that, in return for recognising Prussian conquests in North Germany, France would take possession of Belgium.

[2] The Princess had asked for some old linen for the wounded.

[3] The National Society for giving Aid to the Sick and Wounded in the War with which Florence Nightingale was closely associated.

keep our coasts clear for the sake of her own, as well as for our commerce, and whether an English garrison is not going to Antwerp? People are in a frenzy against poor Lord Granville,[1] and say that England sides with the French against us, and has interpreted her neutrality to the exclusive benefit of France. One hears nothing but the bitterest complaints of England's partiality etc. How wretched it makes me I cannot tell you; it is the one drop of gall, in the cup of national enthusiasm, which is very grievous to those who love England with all their heart and soul. The French are so little to be trusted that the day may come when they will seek a quarrel with England alone— and then our being beaten now will not be an advantage. It is still hoped here that the American fleet will join the English on account of American commerce which will suffer so much from this war. We took leave of the King yesterday; he was looking ill and care-worn; he was frantic about the cartridges which are furnished the French from Birmingham, and about the coals which the French ships have obtained and the horses bought, for the French cavalry, in Ireland—saying England furnished the French the means of carrying on war against us instead of trying to prevent it! I have only a few lines from Fritz from Munich but he gives us no news. The difficulty of getting letters and parcels is very great.

I cannot get my medicine chest back, which I sent to be filled some time ago; it is at Buckingham Palace since three weeks also some medicine which the doctor has ordered me a fortnight ago I cannot get, and am in want of it.

How glorious it would be if the English helped us to our victory and if our two nations stood once more as in the great days of old—side by side in the field of honour. This present Emperor is not the scourge of Europe as his uncle was—he has done much that is good, wise and useful. I am

---

[1] Lord Granville (1815–91) had succeeded Lord Clarendon as Foreign Secretary at the end of June. As the spokesman for the British policy of neutrality he was inevitably attacked by both belligerents.

sure in his heart he would like better to be at peace but if the French are to be allowed to fly at their neighbours' throats whenever they think fit, to be jealously disposed, or to have a thirst for *gloire*—the kindest of Emperors is not only no use but a dangerous individual, as he wields so great an instrument as the French army and into the bargain makes use of it to keep it from "looking too near unto his state" (as Henry IV says in Shakespeare).[1]

Poor Mlle. Darcourt is very sad of course but she is very sensible and thinks her countrymen much to blame; she hates the Emperor and hopes for his downfall and that of his dynasty.

Potsdam is like a large convent of melancholy and excited women!

From the Queen   OSBORNE, AUGUST 3, 1870

I wish in confidence to ask you a question, which I am sure you could ascertain. The Emperor N. maintains that Bismarck told Prince Napoleon at Berlin that they (the French) wished to have the Rhine which they could not. Why should they not take Belgium? He (B). would help them were it not for *l'entêtement* of the King!!! and that Count Goltz[2] had repeated this to the Emperor. Is this last possible? But you must not please mention me, or that I told you this, for this has been told me (as yet) in confidence and I should like much to know if Goltz ever could have said such a thing. As for Bismarck I don't trust him ever.[3]

Lord Granville suggested that there should be a cypher between you and me, and between Alice and me—but I don't know how to manage it. Lord Granville does extremely well—firm, calm and conciliatory.

---

[1] Second part of *Henry IV*, Act IV, Scene V, where the King, on his death-bed, speaks of his plans for a crusade to occupy the people "lest rest and lying still might make them too near unto my state".

[2] Count von der Goltz (1817–69) Prussian Ambassador in Paris in 1866 when these matters were discussed.

[3] This letter marks the beginning of a weakening in the Queen's feelings for Prussia in the war, there was also a shift of opinion towards France in the country generally.

From the Crown Princess

His (Fritz's) first victory was of course a great happiness to me, that his army should be the first to win is an intense satisfaction to me, and it will give the poor southern Germans courage.[1] They have not had a taste of glory for so long, and it will raise them in the eyes of the Prussian troops which is also a great blessing. It will make the South feel still more confidence in Fritz and in that respect it is a happy event.

How cruel it seems to take that dear little boy the Prince Imperial to the war; it is enough to make the poor child strange for life.

I send you some photographs—two of little Sophie, one for yourself and one for Leopold, and a group of the four eldest. Poor Henry has not grown prettier, he is the image of the Princesses Frederick and Marie of the Netherlands— which mortifies my feelings.

From the Crown Princess

NEUES PALAIS, POTSDAM, AUGUST 9, 1870

I know how harrowing and dreadful war is to him (Fritz), how he hates it, and how little ambition he has to become a military hero. On the other hand I know that he is considered our best leader—and that it was not thought necessary to give him the best officers on his staff whereas they were kept for Fritz Carl—so great was the confidence on the part of Moltke and the King in Fritz's genius. He is always quiet and self-possessed and determined; having no personal ambitions he only thinks of what is best not of what makes most effect, and the difficulty of commanding a motley army, whose leaders one does not know, is very great.

I have tried to ascertain what you wished about Bismarck. I asked Baron Schleinitz, who was Goltz's confidant

---

[1] The Crown Prince was in command of the Third Army, which included contingents from the south German States, and this force routed a division of the French at Wissemburg, on 4 August.

and is Bismarck's enemy and always knows what is going on better than anyone, as he was a diplomatist and Minister of Foreign Affairs. What Bismarck may have said—Heaven knows! What does he not say? The wildest and most extravagant things which he could never own to! But he never acts in a foolish fashion in moments of imminent danger. Goltz I am sure never said anything of the kind to the Emperor N. Goltz was a careful, wary, shrewd man—and served his country extremely well; he often had to repair the scrapes Bismarck's imprudence got him into. Goltz never told the Emperor an untruth and that was why the Emperor liked and trusted him (G. never trusted the Emperor). Goltz was devoted to the Empress most sincerely and loyally, though he was never a moment blind to the political mischief she did by her violence, her Catholic and Spanish sympathies, her hatred of Germany. In short Goltz, who was a very clever man, behaved as well and honourably to the Emperor as he did to his own government. Whereas Bismarck behaved very ill to the Emperor when it suited his purpose and at other times was so amiable that the Emperor and his friends let out (most imprudently) all the dark schemes they were meditating for their own purpose. I know a great deal of what came out and cannot help being shocked at the Emperor as his intentions towards England were too abominable—all the while he was seeming so staunch a friend. The Emperor seems to me a man who would like to behave well whenever he could—but whose determination to found a dynasty leads him to do whatever seems expedient without the slightest scruple. He has consequently got himself into the most awful fix—one cannot help feeling the justice of his present fate and pitying him.

I have fought many a battle about Lord Granville—indignant at hearing my old friend so attacked, but all parties agree in making him out French! I picked a quarrel with Bismarck about it on the day of the christening. Tired and miserable as I was, I sent for Bismarck up into my room on purpose to say my say about Lord Granville but he would not believe me. Fritz of course does not believe it, but I think the King and Queen do—but one must not be too hard upon people here. You know that with a pistol on one's breast one is not inclined to investigate much and may judge by appearances and, in the state of fevered excitement and anxiety, hasty judgments, which after all seem very plausible, must be excused. All eyes were turned to England for help as one turns to a friend one loves, and the first positive indication of England's feelings was the unfortunate sale of coals, ammunition and cartridges! The blow was so keenly felt that it will be long before people will believe that England means well and kindly by her sister Germany.[1]

From the Crown Princess
NEUES PALAIS, POTSDAM, AUGUST 16, 1870

Matters seem as if they would take a turn—and most likely a very bad one—for the Emperor. His system—alas! one of corruption, supported by corrupt men, in spite of his undoubted genius and capacities, seems to be crumbling and tumbling to pieces, and Paris, which is a Sodom and Gomorrah, is in an attitude of frantic excitement, rage and disappointment.

I think the most incurable hater of the Prussians would be converted into an admirer if he heard and saw all we do; the spirit of discipline and obedience is so beautifully combined with loyalty and enthusiasm and devoted sense of duty. I can only say that they have my respect and affection. It is owing to their moral qualities that they are so invincible—as the French have the same advantages in all purely military things.

From the Queen   BALMORAL, AUGUST 19, 1870

Just as I was starting I received your dear long letter with those interesting accounts by dearest Fritz on the second, great bloody victories (so touchingly and so beauti-

---

[1] There was no breach of neutrality in trading with the belligerents. In an exchange of letters with Lord Granville Bernstorff argued that England ought to display "benevolent" neutrality to Prussia.

fully described).[1] I hope you will allow Sahl to copy them for me, as they are very fine and I feel so proud of him. But oh! the loss of life is too dreadful! The cause of quarrel seems too small for such sacrifice of life. How can such numbers and numbers be sacrificed! How is it to go on!— It makes one shudder.

There is the greatest sympathy for the poor wounded here and everyone is occupied in trying to help, including ourselves—our ladies and all.

The Emperor is in a dreadful position and no one in France pities him. Lord Lyons writes "The dynasty falls lower and lower; the Empress has much pluck but little hope." All our papers speak of the great kindness of the Germans to the poor French wounded and prisoners. One fears however that there will be more exasperation in each battle.

From the Queen   BALMORAL, AUGUST 22, 1870

The position of the French seems to get hourly worse! Such a complete tumbling to pieces of their empire and its far famed army has really never been seen! It does seem like a judgement from heaven! Everything seems to fail! Odiously impertinent, insulting and boastful as the French have always been, one cannot help feeling for them; for to see a great—or at least a powerful—nation so utterly crushed is a fearful and a sad thing! And how awful is this loss of life!! And for what? One shudders! Most unhappy Emperor to have this sin, and these thousands of innocent lives on his head!

How nice and kind of you to have the children give bread and bouquets to the wounded and prisoners. Really it is quite marvellous how the Germans carry everything before them and how wonderfully well the campaign is being conducted. Everyone is in admiration of it. How

---

[1] The Crown Prince kept a journal during the war which was published after his death.

pleased the King must be at his victory!—It is wonderful at his age![1]

From the Queen   BALMORAL, AUGUST 26, 1870

On this blessed day, still kept and treated as a holiday, I write these few lines, having just returned from giving a number of presents to our good people and families, to thank you for your three dear and most painfully interesting letters. How dreadful these losses are! How can it go on! In mercy I pray it may soon end and dear Fritz be able to make peace at the walls of Paris!

All you mention interests me and all so much. You know what I feel. I feel too that in all this I see a just judgement—a just retribution on a very guilty government and a very frivolous vain-glorious people, and the fulfilment of beloved Papa's most earnest wishes.

From the Queen   BALMORAL, AUGUST 30, 1870

I should be sorry if Paris were to suffer much, on account of art and its beauty. No one knows where the Emperor is. What will the terms of peace be? If only the French would give up this needless struggle! It would save such thousands of lives! People think it would be far wiser if Germany were not to ask for Lorraine and Alsace because peace would not be lasting if the French had, after so many years, to give them up. Morier is of that opinion and told Fritz so—who seemed to concur. But will Germany and the army ever be satisfied without them? What do you think, dearest child? I am so anxious for the power, unity and permanent security of Germany and Europe. Lord Halifax who is here, is a staunch supporter and admirer of Germany! He is very clever and sensible.

---

[1] The Queen is referring to the double-battle of Regonville-Gravelotte. The Germans lost 20,000 officers and men. At one stage of the battle the King and his staff personally rallied the Prussian II Corps which had fallen back in disorder on Gravelotte. See Michael Howard, *The Franco-Prussian War*.

From the Queen   BALMORAL, SEPTEMBER 2, 1870

Let me say how deeply, truly I grieve with all the poor afflicted and that I should take it very kindly from you if you would let your poor afflicted friends know how, though unknown to them, I feel for them in their terrible trials and afflictions.[1]

You need not be under any apprehension that this government wish to interfere in trying to mediate or make peace. It would be folly. And though I am sure I would give anything to stop this frightful massacre, which in these times of civilisation is really too monstrous, I would think it very unwise and unjust to attempt to interfere. Neither party could accept it, certainly not now.

From the Queen   BALMORAL, SEPTEMBER 6, 1870

These news[2] take one's breath away—and I rub my eyes to ask myself whether one short month can have changed everything so wonderfully!! Unfortunate Emperor and Empress and what a fate! I had wished to answer fully your dear, long letter of last week and now I have no time. But I will write all I think about the events of the last few years down for you and then send it. Beloved Papa—much as I miss his help and sympathy which kept me up in '48 and during our war—and I could not wish him back to this world of trouble and strife—(and probably to be attacked and mistrusted on account of being a German) and I can do much and say much more than he could.

I know you will feel for the poor Emperor and Empress and think of '55 and '57 and yet what are their sufferings compared to those of thousands and thousands of unhappy innocent subjects of his who have been killed or wounded or ruined for ever! Whether he was dragged into it or not, he ought to have abdicated rather than have consented to a war—for to say he would not have undertaken it, if he had known he would have failed entirely, is no excuse for the

---

[1] In writing on 26 August the Crown Princess referred to her friends who had lost husbands or sons.
[2] Sedan and the surrender of the Emperor.

wickedness of risking so many, many lives! Still it is an awful fall! How I long for details, how '48 comes back to my mind and '55! And I can remember '30! Therefore three revolutions in thirty years in that luckless France.[1]

I thought, knowing the Empress as I did,—she having been twice my guest, and we hers and the Emperor's, I could not be so unfeeling as not to say one word to her, so I have desired the following messages to be conveyed to her "That I was not insensible of the heavy blow which had fallen upon her or forgetful of former days." I wish Fritz to know this—in case he should hear of it and I have also told the Queen.

From the Queen   BALMORAL, SEPTEMBER 9, 1870

Many thanks for your dear letter of the 2nd, received yesterday from Homburg in the palace of my poor old Aunt.[2] I can but too well understand all you feel and suffer. I am very thankful to hear that you think dear Alice well, for really she has gone through and is going through so much. But I really believe that women can go through much more than people think—both in that state and when nursing—certainly the working classes do—though I sometimes fear your baby may suffer from the terrible anxiety and suspense and emotions you must endure.

Someone (no one of importance at all) wrote to Bertie describing the awful state of corruption in the French government and the want of patriotism in the country— and then he went on to speak of the savageness of the Germans and of their dreadful conduct towards the women!!! Now I am sure that all this is false for all our newspaper correspondents have praised their conduct. Of course amongst so many thousands there must be some black sheep. But I am sure that Fritz's *armée corps* is not guilty of such things.

---

[1] This may not be quite clear. The Queen means that she can remember three revolutions 1830, 1848 and 1870. She adds in parenthesis '55— the year of her triumphant visit to Paris.

[2] Princess Elizabeth, 1770–1840, daughter of King George III, Land-gravine of Hesse-Homburg.

From the Queen   BALMORAL, SEPTEMBER 13, 1870
   I so entirely agree in what you say.[1] You are so moderate
and generous and sensible. I have nowhere seen, nor can I
find what you say about Joinville. No one has seen that
letter here. Is it not perhaps a fabrication? He and the
whole Orleans family are very anti-Prussian I know—far
more so than the Emperor—but Joinville is so clever and
amiable I can hardly believe his doing such a dreadful
thing.
   In England I can assure you the feeling is far more
German than French, and far the greater part of the press
is in your favour. All reflecting people are. The Pall Mall
has excellent articles.[2] You should take it in.

From the Queen   BALMORAL, SEPTEMBER 17, 1870
   In one of your former long letters you said you thought
now of many things which dear Papa had said—which
showed that all was after all not so entirely unexpected in
France!! The system of corruption, immorality and
gaspillage was dreadful. Nothing annoyed dear Papa more
than the abject court paid to the Emperor and the way in
which we were forced to flatter and humour him, which was
shortsighted policy, and spoilt him. No one was worse than
Lord Clarendon and also Lord Palmerston for that—
though the latter had his eyes opened latterly. However
once that it was thought politically necessary, dear Papa
was the first to wish and see that it should be properly
done, and the Emperor treated with respect and confidence,
and he did all he could to keep him straight. But when in
'59, in spite of all our endeavours and warnings, he made
war in Italy against Austria and deceived us, Papa was most

---

[1] Commenting on the fall of the Emperor, the Crown Princess wrote on
6 September that the downfall was melancholy, but "may we all learn
what frivolity, conceit and immorality lead to". The Prince de Joinville
(1818–1900) was the third son of Louis Philippe. He was supposed to
have incited the French population to murder Prussian soldiers.
[2] The writer of the articles on the War in the Pall Mall Gazette, which
were widely noticed, was Engels who was introduced to the editor
by Karl Marx.

indignant and broke off all friendly, personal intercourse and had the worst opinion of him which was never removed till the Empress came over in '68 to Osborne. Your elder brothers unfortunately were carried away by that horrid Paris (beautiful though you may think it) and that frivolous and immoral court did frightful harm to English society (that Papa knew and saw) and was very bad for Bertie and Affie. The fearful extravagance and luxury, the utter want of seriousness and principle in everything—the many crimes in France all show a rottenness which was sure to crumble and fall, but certainly not so soon or so suddenly when it did come.

From the Queen

GLASSALT SHIEL, LOCH MUICH, SEPTEMBER 20, 1870

Though I wrote to you only two days ago, I cannot let the messenger go without writing a few lines to say that I had the pleasure of getting a letter from dear Fritz himself which has given me great pleasure. I wish to tell you also that I—entirely of my own accord and after much careful reflection—have sent—though it will not go as fast as a telegram[1]—the following telegram to the King which I felt as a friend and as a woman it was almost a duty for me to do. "In the name of our friendship and in the interests of humanity I express the hope that it may be in your power to offer terms which your defeated enemy can accept. Your renown will only be the greater if at the head of your victorious army, you decide to conclude peace with generosity."

If it is of no use, it can do no harm. J. Favre is going to see Bismarck. We don't wish, and don't think it right in any way, to interfere—though many would wish us to do so, but as a friend—in the interests of Prussia and of the King—I wish it were possible to stop. The French are half mad and will not be more likely to yield after Paris is bombarded than now—that is my honest conviction.

---

[1] Probably meaning that as the King was with the invading army, the telegram would take longer than usual.

A contemporary drawing of the Crown Princess in the hospital barracks, Frankfurt, during the Franco-Prussian War.

The Crown Princess in 1871.

A photograph of Queen Victoria taken by Downey in 1871.

My poor dear old Lehzen is gone to her rest—peaceably and quietly—on the 9th within less than a month of her 86th birthday! I owed her much and she adored me! Even when she was quite wandering she spoke of me.

From the Queen   BALMORAL, SEPTEMBER 24, 1870
    Lady Ely arrived at the Glassalt Shiel on Wednesday and told me a good deal about the poor Empress whom she saw this day week at Hastings, and who expressed herself as most grateful for the King's great kindness to the Emperor. She looks dreadfully ill and altered, coughs very much and was very poorly dressed in black, but there was no murmuring or complaining of others—only great sorrow and distress at the loss of life. She is in an uncomfortable, smelling hotel at Hastings with hot, disagreeable rooms[1]. The boy is well but talks with certainty of returning to Paris.

From the Queen   BALMORAL, OCTOBER 3, 1870
    I must now tell you that I have changed my opinion of Lord Lorne since I have got to know him (he has been here since Thursday) and I think him very pleasing, amiable, clever—his voice being only a little against him. And he is in fact very good looking.

From the Queen   BALMORAL, OCTOBER 4, 1870
    I wish to say that the Government here remains firm and stout not to meddle in the contest going on, by advice on either side—though there have been various attempts made to urge it on us. I have done all I could to point out the uselessness and dangers of such a course and I have invariably found them of my opinion. The stupid, radical peace party here who would drive us into war to make peace are quite contemptible and harmless and will have no effect whatever.

---

[1] The Marine Hotel.

From the Crown Princess   DARMSTADT, OCTOBER 9, 1870

My mother-in-law comes the day after tomorrow morning! What a cram and a crush we shall be! She brings between thirty and forty people with her—and is only a single person. I have the same number with six children.

From the Queen   BALMORAL, OCTOBER 11, 1870

Dear Fritz's letters and journals are most interesting.— How dreadful this long war and yet how can it stop while these mad French will not understand a reason or come to terms. God grant that 'ere long this may happen.

I now write to you an event which has just taken place in our family and which, with the blessing of God, will I hope conduce to dear Louise's happiness. She is engaged to Lord Lorne. I know well that abroad such a marriage, until it is thoroughly understood, may startle people but it is what I have long thought it must come to. Great alliances like yours are right and well for some of the family— though I fear they have little political weight inasmuch as they do not and cannot influence any more the actions of governments and nations, and thereby often cause incalculable sufferings to the Royal Families themselves—as we both know—being suspected of undue leanings and undue influence. But small, foreign Princes (without any money) are very unpopular here, R. Catholics illegal and totally repugnant to our feelings; therefore one naturally turns towards those in one's own country, who possess large fortunes and rank certainly equal to small, German Princes. The Marriage Act, which many people suppose forbids such a marriage, only forbids any marriage of one of the Royal Family with anyone without the sanction of the Sovereign; except after they are twenty-five when, even in spite of the Sovereign's opposition, if after a year parliament does not petition against them, it can take place. A marriage here with a subject is just as good as with any other person, and the children born of such a union can just as well succeed to the throne as those born of one with a Prince.

Lord Lorne was only thought of amongst others—and

I always wished for him, though I did not like him so much, till I got to know him and now I do so much. Louise however wanted to judge for herself, and very properly said she could not and would not marry anyone she did not really like. And so I asked him to come here for a few days (I had had several other visitors here before) and he arrived —strangely enough for I had never thought about it—on 29th September.[1] And the more Louise saw of him the more she liked him. His devotion to her is quite touching. He is as you know most superior and quite excellent, and so are his parents. And, dearest child, I doubt not, whatever your feelings at first may be, that you will rejoice at the prospect of dear Louise's happiness—which I think is very great—and will write lovingly and affectionately to her. Will you send this letter to dear Alice as I don't wish to announce it to her till I really think she is fit to hear it?[2]

There is not a doubt that the country will hail this marriage with joy.

From the Crown Princess   DARMSTADT, OCTOBER 13, 1870
The Queen has arrived at Homburg! She is very kind and amiable to me and we get on very well. She comes to dinner and tea, which is rather trying for my servants and kitchen but if I can be of any use or comfort to her I am only too glad—for nothing gives me greater pleasure than when she is happy and satisfied. Alas! with the King it is not so. He has written me a very unkind letter which gave me a great deal of pain. He says I am to go back to Berlin—and that he did not give his consent to my taking the children, the travelling was bad for their health and education, and that I did not understand my duty etc. I think it very hard to be used in this way—when I am doing all I possibly can to do what is expected of me! He does not see why I should go to see Alice etc. etc. This perpetual interference with my children and household is enough to try the patience of a

---

[1] The day on which the Crown Princess herself was engaged.
[2] Her son, Prince Frederick William, had been born prematurely on 6 October.

saint in Heaven. I shall certainly stay a little while longer at Homburg before I am shut up for so many months at Berlin.

From the Queen   BALMORAL, OCTOBER 18, 1870
It is too bad and too foolish and senseless of the King to write such letters. Pray be firm and say you and the children require change and that they can pursue their studies as well there as elsewhere. Lorne (who left us yesterday morning) spoke much of the dear children whom he saw at Cannes. He is really most amiable. All the papers express great satisfaction at Louise's marriage and there is but one opinion in the nation on this event.

As regards Louise's engagement I am much vexed that the newspapers announced it to you before my letter. As the newspapers themselves could not reach you until the Saturday 15th or Sunday 16th, I certainly hoped and felt sure my letter would have been beforehand—but I suppose it was telegraphed which I could not help.[1] I did not guess what your feelings would be; certainly not that they would be so very contrary to the feeling of the whole nation, as you know that the one marriage which was tried to be forced upon Louise and me—was out of the question.[2]

After what occurred last winter it was impossible for me to renew the subject of her marriage to you or I would have earlier mentioned the subject—though as regards Louise it was quite uncertain until the day that the engagement took place. Lorne was only one out of five young gentlemen who had been asked here and whose names were all in the papers; Lord Rosebery, Lord Stafford, Lord H. FitzRoy and Albert Grey. The date of the marriage is not yet fixed. I shall declare it in Council on Monday.

[1] Meaning that the English newspapers could not reach the Crown Princess before the letter from the Queen, but that in fact the news was telegraphed to the German press by their correspondents in London.
[2] To Abbat. The Crown Princess had favoured this, and the following sentence alludes to her efforts to bring about that marriage.

From the Queen   BALMORAL, OCTOBER 25, 1870

I yesterday gave my consent in Council to her marriage which has called forth a great burst of delight. People call this "The most popular act of my reign."

From the Queen   BALMORAL, NOVEMBER 1, 1870

Darling child, before I answer all you say[1]—and which I will do with the same openness and kindly spirit with which you have written to me—I wish to tell you that poor Louise's knee (which Alice will have told you of) keeps her completely confined to the house and to a chair, and laid up and totally helpless! It is at this moment very hard, but she is good and patient and we must all take it in patience as God's will. She was so well and able to take so much exercise—though she had felt this knee which she must have knocked or strained all summer—then she had one or two little accidents, probably over-tried the knee walking downhill which has led to what has now ended in this sad, tiresome, swollen joint though without any inflammation. It will of course prevent our moving from here for almost another fortnight.

I certainly did expect that there would be surprise and, on the part of the King (who was so determined, flattering as this was in some ways, to have another daughter of mine in the Prussian family) much displeasure, at Louise's preferring to remain in her own country and lead a quiet, domestic life in preference to a foreign court and foreign land full of trials and difficulties. But I thought you would greatly prefer this to a small German Prince, who would have been the only other alternative. A second Prussian marriage—popular as yours is and proud of Fritz as they are—if I would have allowed it even—would have been very unpopular here, and a poor, small, German Prince also.[2] That I have known for many years. Whereas the popularity of this step and this marriage all over the empire, including Ireland, is quite marvellous! And, when the

[1] The Crown Princess's letters have not survived.
[2] The Queen means here that marriage to a small German prince would have been no less unpopular than the Prussian marriage.

Royal Family is so large, and our children have (alas!) such swarms of children, to connect some few of them with the great families of the land—is an immense strength to the Monarchy and a great link between the Royal Family and the country. Mind my words and you will see that this will have to be done elsewhere also. Besides which, a new infusion of blood is an absolute necessity—as the race will else degenerate bodily and physically.

Unity in this family is of great importance—but it is very difficult with large Royal Families, which I think—and Papa did also—a real misfortune; and I do not think that the two elder brothers—for different reasons—add to that. Alix is not clever and her feelings are so anti-German and yet so little really English that she is no real help—good, dear and kind as she is and much as I love her.

The fall of Metz is a great event—indeed the surrender twice over of two such enormous armies (the one at Metz as large as the forces commanded by the Duke of Wellington in the Peninsula) is totally unheard of in the history of the whole world!! From Herodotus downwards—such success and such complete crushing of another country has never been known.

From the Queen   BALMORAL, NOVEMBER 4, 1870

There are I think real hopes of an armistice; but what is ever to be the fate and state of France for a long time to come? Mr. Cardwell (who has been with us here since the 23rd) speaks more sensibly than anyone. He (who was accused at the beginning of being French is more German than any of the Ministers) and is so much distressed at the bad feeling against us, which is really too unjust for the sympathy has been all on the side of the Germans in England, but now I fear it will go the other way if they show, as (excepting Fritz and his immediate staff who are all kindness) they do, rudeness towards the English. It annoys and worries me very much and has done so for long. Those two nations misunderstanding one another, which for those like you and me and dear Papa who knew the merits and faults of both, is enough to drive one wild.

From the Queen   BALMORAL, NOVEMBER 12, 1870

What you say of the very shamefully unjust feeling against England is what I quite believe and understand. But I fear there is a grudge and ill-will and a total misunderstanding between the two countries which little circumstances, which I must say the Germans care for much more than we do, for they are much more punctilious, unfortunately confirm. The German press is so ill-natured—but I must repeat Bernstorff is a serious misfortune and a great danger; he (I know it) writes and has done so now for years every sort of stupid, ill-natured gossip which he enlarges on, and is delighted to retail, of the Court and England—and though you say you don't believe his reports I have perceived that something of them remains behind and that you are constantly totally misinformed as to the true state of the case. You will I am sure admit that yourself. Let me therefore repeat here first that no good understanding can exist between the two countries as long as Bernstorff continues here, and secondly that you are never to credit anything he writes about our family whom he seems to dislike. Now Lord Augustus is not very bright and I dare say blunders—but he never repeats any ill-natured reports or stupid, gossiping rumours and stories or anything but what is kind and respectful towards the King and Queen and the Royal Family. This is a fact as much as the other. Let me therefore again ask you to turn a deaf ear to what Bernstorff writes. Unfortunately poor Bertie gives much cause for remarks of no good-natured kind. Instead of being more careful since that dreadful business in March he is more and more careless. No one looks up to him, though all like him.[1]

---

[1] In writing to the Queen on 7 November, the Crown Princess had said that the feeling against England in Prussia rose because the Prussians felt that if England had spoken firmly to the French "France would never have dared to make war, and all those lives would have been saved". She added that if a great German Empire did result from the war both Bernstorff and Lord Augustus Loftus should be moved. "A charge of such importance ought to be confided to the very best heads, both countries can produce. I am sure nothing would set matters straight sooner."

From the Queen   BALMORAL, NOVEMBER 15, 1870

On Sunday last I witnessed (one is allowed to look on) the dispensing of the Communion here. I never was so impressed with anything, and hope the time may come when I may also take it there as well as in the English church. The great simplicity was touching and the wonderful devoutness and reverence of the dear, old people was most beautiful and moving to witness. Old and young—amongst the former, people of 81 and 86, who had walked through deep snow to take it.

From the Queen   BALMORAL, NOVEMBER 16, 1870

These lines are to greet you on your dear birthday—your thirtieth, which I can hardly believe possible,—but which I fear will be very sad, far away from dear Fritz, full of anxiety for him and with the shadows of the cloud of much mourning and sorrow around! But I pray that God may shower his choicest blessing on your dear head, preserve and bless you, give you strength and patience and humility to bear the great position which is and still more may be your lot! Great power and great position is a terrible trial and temptation, and I always dread it for those I love most.

I send you the copy of a picture painted of dear Beatrice last year, a warm Scotch cloak with the Prussian colours and a new biscuit box of Aberdeenshire granite which I hope you will like.

From the Crown Princess   HOMBURG, NOVEMBER 16, 1870

We are horrified at those tiresome Russians beginning to try what they can get out of the war for themselves;[1] it would be too awful if the blaze were to spread and become general! What you say of Bernstorff is very true to a certain extent, but not as to his giving us news of the Court which we go by. To begin with I very rarely see or hear

---

[1] By the Treaty of Paris, at the end of the Crimean War, the Black Sea had been neutralised. The Russians denounced the Treaty when, after the fall of Metz, it was clear that the French could not retaliate.

what he writes—perhaps twice a year! And he seldom mentions the Court, as each time he does the King tells us and asks us, and it is then some very stale, old bit of news or report, which I have long before heard about from England. His news would be the last we should go by! Alas dear Bertie is so incautious and makes himself so much talked about that it comes from all sorts of sources—and does a deal of damage to us all! These reports are not of Bernstorff's making. The stays at Petersburg, Paris and Wiesbaden and the stories of last January did the mischief— and established a species of public opinion which is very difficult to destroy.

From the Queen   WINDSOR CASTLE, NOVEMBER 30, 1870
The Queen returns again to the question of Princess Louise's marriage.

In your letter of 6th November you spoke openly to me of your feelings about her marriage and your reasons for having wished another and I will answer equally openly. You say you could not be enthusiastic about Louise's marriage. I never intended or expected you should, but I thought you would rather have this marriage than one with a poor, small German prince. The more so, when you know how immensely popular it is here in the whole Empire. The feeling against foreign marriages has long been very strong here, especially if the princes are poor or if they were of a nature to bring us in political collision one with another. A second Prussian alliance would have been very unpopular here—for while admiring and loving dear Fritz and being proud of him and admiring the wonderful organisation of the Prussian army—their bravery, endurance, discipline, all—the English do not like the Prussians, and instead of its bringing the two nations nearer together it would have the contrary effect. Abbat (whom I never at all liked and who I am sure would never have suited our family in any way) could not have lived much with me without my being subject to every sort of suspicion of undue, foreign influence, and I should have been unable to see them but very rarely. In dear Papa's time this was in many ways different, but he was entirely aware of the dislike felt here to any long visits from abroad entailing large suites of foreign ladies and gentlemen—a great deal of German being spoken at table—and was always afraid of these being too long at a time and too frequent—still he could manage all that for he knew exactly what they ought and ought not to do, and helped them in every way which I cannot do. Of course I can Fritz and Louis, who to a certain extent know all this, and are quite at home here—but newcomers whom I cannot instruct and guide or have with me (with my endless occupations) as he could, would find much greater difficulties; besides my being constantly suspected of German leanings etc, which of course is but natural—though I am sure I should never be biased by this to the detriment of my own country's interests. These divided interests are so dreadfully painful for me and my children that I could not wish for their and my happiness to continue them, and saw therefore the prospect of comfort, peace and unity and a quiet domestic life for my daughter, with the same interests and living in the same country, secured by a marriage with a subject.

My visit went off very quietly and well.[1] It is a country house, reminding me of Orleans House,[2] furnished entirely as a French home, and the whole thing—the ladies and gentlemen—reminding me of our visits to Claremont and Twickenham. The poor Empress looked very pale and aged and sad, but sweet and gentle, full of tact (reminding me of what she was in '55 at Windsor for I thought she altered later) without the slightest bitterness. She spoke of her dreadful departure from Paris; of the incomprehensible mission of Bourbaki[3]—and said she prayed for peace and enquired after you and Alice. She was dressed in the very plainest possible black, silk dress—with no ornaments—and a little net over her hair. The boy is a very nice child

---

[1] To the Empress Eugénie at Camden Place, Chislehurst.
[2] At Twickenham. The home of Louis Philippe from 1800, and acquired again by his family after their expulsion from France.
[3] General Bourbaki was allowed out from Metz by the Prussians to carry some kind of peace terms to the Empress—still ostensibly Regent.

but excessively short—shorter than Beatrice who is a year younger than him.

From the Queen   WINDSOR CASTLE, DECEMBER 3, 1870
    I fear the fighting these last three to four days has been very severe and much life lost. Oh! how dreadful it is that it still goes on. How this must depress you all. I can well understand the children cheer you and that without any you would feel very sad and lonely—and would like to turn nurse. But so many are a terrible anxiety when they grow up and cause more sorrow often than pleasure— especially in Royal Families. Then when one idolises one's children, as you do, what will you suffer when you have quite to give them up and feel how little they care for you and all your care and anxiety! To see one's child totally independent and constantly wishing to go quite contrary to their parents' wishes, convictions and kind advice is very dreadful.

From the Crown Princess   BERLIN, DECEMBER 9, 1870
    The Queen showed me part of your letter about the poor dear Empress whom I pity so much. I always thought her a sweet, graceful, attractive creature—interesting and lovely! I wonder whether it is true that she pushed her husband into the war as much as she could and said *"celle-ci c'est ma guerre"*. I hardly believe it—still it is related on very good authority.
    I myself have nothing to complain of except a dreadful feeling of not being able to do all that is necessary—all my business, my letter-writing, seeing people etc.—it is a superhuman strain on one's temper and 1870 has decidedly not improved mine, which never was a first-rate article.

From the Queen   WINDSOR CASTLE, DECEMBER 10, 1870
    You say that the Germans are convinced that the French will try and begin a new war as soon as they can, and that therefore Alsace and Lorraine are necessary to rectify and fortify the frontier. Whereas here everyone says—that the

only objection to the taking of Alsace and Lorraine is that there never will be a durable peace, if they are taken, as the French will always wish to have them back and never rest until they get them back! What everybody had hoped when the war began and what I remember you also wrote to me was that this war was to be the last and that the French should once for all be made to feel they could not again become an aggressive power or threaten the peace of Europe, and now unfortunately, from the length and bloodiness of the contest, this bitterness and hatred of the two countries will make matters worse than before.

From the Crown Princess   BERLIN, DECEMBER 25, 1870
A charming young English lady is staying here with me in the house for Christmas—Miss Florence Lees. She has the nursing and superintendence of my sick and wounded at Homburg, and is second in skill experience and devotion to Miss Nightingale only. You would be much taken with her if you saw her—or if you could see her at her work! I asked her here as I thought she would be lonely at Homburg at this season.

From the Crown Princess   BERLIN, DECEMBER 30, 1870
Many thanks for your dear letter which arrived today. It is so kind of you to break lances for the Germans in England; the mutual distrust is too dreadful.[1] It must be the aim of our statesmen to dispel these feelings—so unjust, unnecessary, and injurious to all that is useful! Here the feeling is getting much better. The nasty Americans boast everywhere of having got up a *brouille* between

---

[1] In her letter of 28 December the Queen wrote "I hear that they have begun to bombard Paris! If only it would soon end. To my despair the feeling is becoming more and more bitter here against the Prussians, and unfortunately the officers are so rude to ours (not at Headquarters) that it increases the irritation, which is so unjust on both sides. I can't tell you how it worries me, and what lances I break for them. But I am very powerless." The Queen is referring to the English officers attached to the Armies as observers. See *Days of a Soldier's Life* by General Beauchamp-Walker, who was British Military Commissioner at the Headquarters of the Third German Army.

England and Germany. It seems just what they desire. That the Prussian officers should be rude to the English ones is too bad; but I fear our dear countrymen are a little awkward and ignorant of the forms which Germans are accustomed to. I know they quite neglect to have themselves named, and this the Prussians misunderstand and take for intentional rudeness which they then fancy it their duty to return; this is too stupid but I know it is the case. It all comes from an imperfect knowledge of one another's national habits, for I have found those Englishmen and Germans who have lived much in both countries get on particularly well together and be the best of friends. Prussians are really very civil but they expect this formal introducing and presenting, and if it is forgotten are offended. I do not think half the English that go abroad have an idea of their being necessary and, on the other hand, that Germans do not know that it is not the custom in England, and this always creates little disagreeables. And when there is so much excitable matter in the air, feelings are so irritated; every trifle is taken at more than it is worth; hence these eternal squabbles and misunderstandings, which make me utterly wretched.

1871

From the Queen

I am so fond of painted flowers and have taken to do them myself which I don't think I told you—and really I was surprised at my own comparative success. I will try to do some for you.

What you say about this dreadful irritation between the two nations is alas! just what I feel, but your officers, who are unfortunately very overbearing, have been very rude and then this affair with the ships has caused the greatest anger.[1] It will take so long to get this right again that both sides must be forbearing. Do tell this to dear Fritz. I have just croche'd him a comforter which it gave me much pleasure to do, and sent it him today and hope he may use it.

From the Queen

The long, long separation must be very painful to you. I have had such a dear, kind, wise letter from dearest Fritz this morning; only far too complimentary to me, it is a great satisfaction to me to see that he recognises and understands my actions and conduct and England's too. What hurts and pains me is the violence and bitterness of dearest Aunt Feodore against England. She won't try to understand things. How odd some people are about that!

I am so very glad that you and the Queen get on so well and see so much of each other. Such times of trial and anxiety draw people together. I send you some new books to read. "The Minister's Wife"[2] is most beautifully written and most interesting. People ask me so constantly why Fritz Carl is called the Red Prince. Is it on account of his uniform?[3]

---

[1] Six British vessels were seized by the Prussians, and sunk in the Seine. The crews, it was believed, were treated with brutality.

[2] By Mrs. Oliphant and published in 1869. It gives a picture of the cottar's life in western Scotland.

[3] His favourite Huzzar uniform. The Crown Princess explained that he was Colonel of the Ziethen Husaren (Red Hussars of the Guard) "who have red coats with silver—and a red Kolpack".

From the Queen   OSBORNE, JANUARY 14, 1871

The bombardment is a sad thing and I cannot say how I pray for the ending of this dreadful slaughter, which seems alas! so useless, for the feeling in England is becoming sadly hostile to Germany. Everything will be done to calm this, and Parliament in this respect will do good they say, though things will be said which are painful and may have a bad effect. The fact is people are so fond of Paris—so accustomed to go there that the threatened ruin of it makes them furious and unreasonable.

From the Crown Princess   BERLIN, JANUARY 20, 1871

I was just taking up my pen to write to you when your dear letter of the 18th arrived—with your two dear photos for which I am specially grateful. It is such a pleasure to have a peep at your dear face; though the features be but imperfectly rendered, the ensemble of the photograph is good and pleasing—though my own dear Mama's face has a charm that none but Winterhalter's pictures have ever approached and that no photograph can reproduce— precious and valuable as they are for the truth of many little details.

From the Queen   OSBORNE, JANUARY 25, 1871

I can't resist sending you a copy of a really insane letter of Aunt Clementine's. Send it to Alice but don't show it the Empress. It would only irritate[1].

From the Crown Princess   BERLIN, JANUARY 30, 1871

Although tomorrow is my day for writing I cannot resist doing so today—as our hearts are all so full of joy and

---

[1] The writer of this letter was the daughter of Louis Philippe and wife of the Queen's first cousin Prince Augustus of Coburg, and she let herself go in a way which explains why the Queen, who was fond of her, called her insane. She appealed to the Queen to put an end to "the ambition and barbarity of the new Emperor of Germany" and said that she was writing as a descendant of St. Louis and as the wife of a descendant of Wittekind. The letter is printed in full in *Letters of Queen Victoria*, 2nd series, Vol. II, page 111. The King had become German Emperor on 10 January.

gratitude at the news from Versailles![1] Peace must surely be soon coming—and the thought that many poor creatures are relieved of their sufferings and that the sword is not always hanging over the head of those we love—is inexpressibly soothing. Everyone is glad, and all hope that the horrors which have maddened us for six months are now at an end! No one will be more intensely thankful than the Emperor! I have hung out all my flags, and were I a Roman Catholic, I should burn wax tapers on the altars of the churches—as I am not, I have given vent to my feelings in sending a great bucket of spiced, hot ale to the guard-house for the men, which will be very welcome as the cold is so intense that we cannot leave the house! Many affectionate thanks for your dear letter of the 27th written on dear Willy's birthday.[2] You need not fear that he will be brought up in a way to make him proud and stuck up. I hope to instil all that is most Christian therefore most liberal into his mind—and at the same time, with a sincere desire to be of use to all fellow creatures be they who or what they may, give him a horror of low company, which has been the ruin of so many princes *vide* Louis VIX,[3] the ex-King of Hanover and many other German princes whom I could name—one alas is not far off (and whom we love but who has lost all respect and esteem by the company he chooses).[4] Willy is very shy by nature and that often makes him look proud. The ladies and gentlemen who tried to nurture a mistaken pride, in the idea that it was patriotic, are no longer about him. Not to avoid all familiarity—and till now I must say we have had no difficulty on that score with him. His companions are chosen without regard to rank or family, and the continual contact into which our princes are brought with soldiers—there is not a more democratic institution in the world than our army—the nation under arms—is a safeguard against their growing

---

[1] The King had telegraphed to his wife on 29 January, "Last night an armistice for three weeks was signed".
[2] Seemingly missing.
[3] So written but presumably Louis XV.
[4] Presumably King Ludwig of Bavaria.

— *316* —

up in ignorance of the wants and interests of the lower classes. What you say for me especially I can only say amen to, but do not fear that my poor head could be turned by "so-called greatness". First of all to my mind an English woman and your daughter is far greater than any foreign Crowns, though I do not say so here. Then the greatness here is tremendous hard work. I do not think there is a greater slave than the sovereign, and with my love of ease and liberty, my fondness for travelling, and following up my favourite pursuits, the golden chains of the future— heavier than those which weigh uncomfortably upon me already—have nothing very attractive! I have a passionate love of liberty, and an idea and a passionate wish to see the ideal of a free and truly cultivated state become a reality. For this end I would suffer much and give up much— one must however have a cause to which to devote oneself and for which to live. Oneself—one's own comfort are too small, too narrowing and paralysing to all one's capacities— "Man grows with his higher aims" says Goethe and I firmly believe that little interests cripple the mind. I hope with you that humility may never forsake me—but that it may grow in me more and more! Fritz and I are equally devoted to Germany and feel ourselves equally German! I copy a few words from a letter of Fritz I have just received it is written on the 26th "the hope for peace is such a ray of light completely blinding me too, and—after the many disappointments we experienced so far—I would rather not deceive myself with joyful plans—but philosophically wait."

I hear the joy of our army round Paris is not to be described. I must end here dearest Mama—pray excuse this abominable writing I have been so often interrupted. Ever your most dutiful and devoted daughter Victoria.

From the Queen   OSBORNE, FEBRUARY 1, 1871
The pride of your position is one sense I can share and understand, in the other I wrote on dear Willy's birthday what my feelings are. Every day and hour shows me here,

in this very free speaking and liberal country, our difficult duty is in that sense!

God be praised truly and really for this blessed capitulation and armistice which will soon dissipate the sentimentality here. It came so suddenly at last but the wretched people must be in a terrible state, and that sortie on the 19th fearfully bloody! I am sure peace will follow.

From the Queen   OSBORNE, FEBRUARY 4, 1871
Here the terms (which are not authentic) have created a bad feeling. But I should think they will be abated—at any rate the money part, which would be quite impossible for the wretched French to pay.[1] It seems they did suffer much more from want of food, than was believed, in Paris and look wretched. Our Consul informed Mr. O. Russell that they (the Parisians) wished for peace at any price. But then there is that violent Gambetta who excited people so dreadfully, and he of course profits by these extravagant terms, which should not have been published if they were not authentic.

From the Queen   WINDSOR CASTLE, FEBRUARY 10, 1871
I wish just to touch on your answer to my observations and hopes respecting Willy. The vehemence with which you speak of "the horror of low company" would make it appear as though I had advocated it!!! The low company you speak of—consisting of actors, actresses, masseurs, barbers (in one case at least) are the very reverse of what I suggested, for those sort of people are the proudest and unkindest to those below them, and to the poor. What I meant (but what I fear your position in Prussia living always at a palace, and with the idea of immense position of kings, princes etc.) is that the princes and princesses should be thoroughly kind and helpful, should not feel that they were of a different flesh and blood to the poor—the peasants and working classes and servants—and that going amongst them—as we

---

[1] Under the Armistice the French were to pay 200,000,000 pounds within a fortnight. This was agreed.

always did and do—and as every respectable lady and gentleman does here—was of such immense benefit to the character of those who have to reign hereafter.

To hear of their wants and troubles, to minister to them, to look after them and be kind to them (as you and your brothers and sisters were accustomed to be by good old Tilla etc.) does immense good to the character of children and grown-up people. It is there that you learn lessons of kindness to one another, of patience and endurance and resignation which cannot be found elsewhere. The mere contact of soldiers never can do that, or rather the reverse. For they are bound to obey, and no independence of character can be expected in the ranks. The Germans must be very different from the English and above all the Scotch, if they are not fit to be visited in this way. But I fear they are from what dear Papa often said—and the English even are in this respect—especially in the south—for in the north they possess a good deal of that great independence of character and determination, coupled with real, high, noble feelings which will not brook being treated with haughtiness. The Germans have less of this. Dear Papa knew how to value and appreciate this, and so do our children as much as I do—and all reflecting minds here. This is what I meant and maintain is essential for a prince and princess of our times. Regarding the higher classes— the way in which their sins and immoralities are overlooked, indulged and forgiven—when the third part in lower orders would be highly punished—is enough to cause democratic feeling and resentment. I am sure you will watch over your dear boy with the greatest care, but I often think too great care, too much constant watching leads to those very dangers hereafter, which one wishes to avoid. It is a terrible difficulty and a terrible trial to be a prince. No one having the courage to tell them the truth and to accustom them to those rubs and knocks which are so necessary to boys and young men.

What you said about your dear self in answer gave me much pleasure. Any high, great position, the result of great success is very dangerous and ought to fill one indeed with the deepest humility. I am glad to see that you feel prouder than of anything to be an Englishwoman or rather more a Briton, for you may be as proud of the Scotch blood in your veins as of any other. One of the last walks I took with darling Papa, he said to me "England does not know what she owes to Scotland". She is the brightest jewel in my crown—energy, courage, worth, inimitable perseverance, determination and self-respect. This it is which has brought them on in the world in the most wonderful way—and which urges them always onwards and forwards till they get to the top of the tree. If the Germans are properly led and feel they are one, they will also get on and become more independent. But I often despair of getting the two nations ever to understand each other.

From the Queen   WINDSOR CASTLE, FEBRUARY 15, 1871
Upon the whole on foreign matters things have gone quietly enough in Parliament. There is no wish for war except for the very smallest fraction. In confidence I may tell you that Mr. Gladstone is very much excited about Alsace and Lorraine, though this is not shared by the rest of the Cabinet—though I think they all think it would be unwise if Germany took them but he says there never will be a cordial understanding or feeling between England and Germany if they take all those millions against their will. That he wished they could know this. I tell you merely what he said to me; he promised to be very cautious and to avoid saying this in public; and I repeat it again and again, it was not our affair to object—but thought you and perhaps Fritz had better just know this.

From the Queen   WINDSOR CASTLE, FEBRUARY 19, 1871
I am sorry and not surprised that the Empress Queen is critical of the speech.[1] How can a neutral be warm? If I

---

[1] The Queen opened Parliament in person on 9 February, and the German Empress was doubtless displeased by the allusion to the belligerents as "two great and brave nations" and the formal reference to the new Emperor "I have offered my congratulations on an event which bears testimony to the solidity and independence of Germany."

had expressed greater satisfaction at the unity of Germany it would have implied satisfaction at the defeat of France which in my public position I cannot. I must say I think it very unreasonable but that is the fate of all neutrals.

20TH FEBRUARY

I could not finish my letter yesterday and therefore do so today. I must just say that I am so glad Fritz sees the speech in the right light. It shows his good sense. The excitement of both countries against each other seems to me like a shuttlecock which is tossed backwards and forwards.

From the Queen   WINDSOR CASTLE, FEBRUARY 19, 1871

I am very much pleased and relieved to see that you take the same view upon the whole as I do on the subject of a good reciprocal feeling and understanding between the highest and working classes. But I thought that the German was much more difficult to get on with than our people—especially than the Highlanders, who are out and out the most delightful to get on with from their high breeding, intelligence, and wonderful warmness of heart, hospitality and attachment. The English and especially the Southern English are much less easy to get on with—suspicious, not courteous or hospitable and stupid and far needier and greedier. Still with them even, one can after a time also get on much better by taking pains.

Valerie must be mad!! To refuse to marry when there is no difficulty about it—is totally inconceivable.

From the Queen   WINDSOR CASTLE, MARCH 1, 1871

The preliminaries of peace are declared but they are very hard. That was to be expected, and I fear that they may not be accepted. This march through Paris alarms us all very much. If only nothing untoward happens. The feeling here towards Prussia is as bitter as it can be. It is a great grief to me—and I can do nothing! You will have seen by Mr. Gladstone's excellent speech on Friday how difficult my path is!—distrusted and suspected on account of my relationships and feelings.[1] To see the enmity growing up between two nations—which I am bound to say began first in Prussia, and was most unjust and was fomented and encouraged by Bismarck—is a great sorrow and anxiety to me—and I cannot separate myself or allow myself to be separated from my own people. For it is alas! the people, who from being very German up to three months ago are now very French! I tell you this with a heavy heart but it is the fact. The only way is to leave matters as quiet as possible, and to let people quiet down. For me to attempt to do anything, beyond preaching neutrality and prudence would be useless. I can do nothing more.

As regards the dowry you must not dream of thinking you would have to restore it;[2] and as a proof I send you Lord Granville's letter to me about it. Please send it me back when copied.

This is a letter from Lord Granville to the Queen dated 2 March 1871.

Lord Granville congratulates your Majesty on the cessation of the dreadful war which has been a source of so much anxiety to your Majesty. It must be a great satisfaction to your Majesty that the Crown Prince should have distinguished himself not only by his military success, but by his humanity, his moderation and his large political views, while H.I.H.'s friendship for England, in spite of the atmosphere with which he has been surrounded, is invaluable for the future.

---

[1] The *Daily Telegraph* published a report that the Queen, the Prince of Wales and the Duke of Cambridge had congratulated the Crown Prince on the German victories. Asked about this in Parliament Gladstone denied that this compromised British neutrality and regretted the raising of questions personal to the Royal Family.

[2] A dowry of £40,000 and an annuity of £4,000 were voted by Parliament when the Crown Princess married. Lord Granville firmly rebutted the idea that the Crown Princess had any obligation to return the dowry, and the extract from his letter, which the Queen copied herself, shows the high hopes placed on the Crown Prince, and the confidence that he would before long reign in his father's stead.

This selection from the correspondence may fittingly close with this shadow which begins to loom over it—the mounting hostility between Germany and England. On 4 March 1871 the Crown Princess wrote:

A thousand most tender thanks for your dear and kind letter by messenger. I am sure it must give you who are so generous, kind and just, pain to think of the animosity growing in England against Germany, but it is no use shutting our eyes against facts, and that it is one I do not doubt. It makes your position often trying, I am sure; but I can understand what that position is; you must not in any way allow yourself to be separated from your own people— the first people in the world, for I may say so to you, and it is every day more my conviction. How much I have suffered from the feeling between the two nations I cannot say! How at times unkindly and unjustly I have been used! And how many tears I have shed!

The Queen replied from Windsor on 8 March 1871;

Beloved and darling Child, Your dear, affectionate and beautiful letter of the 4th. touched me deeply. We have indeed both had most painful and trying times to go through, and I fear have still to go through—but I rejoice to see that you understand my duties—cruel as they are. With time and patience and a wish to go on in a conciliatory line, I hope and trust that we shall yet see a good understanding return and finally be established between our nations.

INDEX

This index gives a brief description of only those people who are not already identified in the text, the footnotes, or the list of familiar names.

Austria, Archduke Charles Louis, 1833–96, father of Archduke Franz-Ferdinand, 258

Austria, Archduchess Charlotte of, later Empress of Mexico (1840–1927), daughter of Leopold I of the Belgians, 48, 102, 103, 104, 141, 144, 148, 170, 171, 203, 214, 230

Austria, Empress Elizabeth of (1837–98), 144

Austria, Emperor Francis Joseph of (1830–1916), 67, 95

Austria, Archduchess Gisela of, daughter of above, 278

Austria, Archduchess Sophie, mother of the Emperor of Austria, 155

Austria, Archduke Louis Victor of, son of above, 258

Austria, Archduke Maximilian of, later Emperor of Mexico (1832–67), death, 141, 148; funeral in Vienna, 170, 173

Austro-Prussian War — developments between Austria and Prussia over Schleswig-Holstein, 58; mediation by England sought by Prussia, 60–1; refused by Government, 62; withdrawal of Austrian troops from Bohemia, 65; conference between Austria and Prussia urged by Russia, 67, 72; Crown Prince in command of the Second or Silesian Army, 76; Austria defeated at Königgrätz or Sadowa, 79, 80; occupation by Prussia of the Kingdom of Hanover, 84, 87, 88, 135; Crown Princess visits the war victims, 92; and comments unfavourably on the Austria army compared with that of Prussia, 94–6; triumphant return of the Prussian army to Berlin, 97, 99; preliminary peace settlement signed at Nicolsburg, 132

BACOURT, Adolphe de, French diplomatist. Died 1865, 24

Baden, Princess William of (Maroussy), 147

Baden, Louise, Grand Duchess of (1838–1923), daughter of King William I of Prussia, 124, 128, 268

Baden, Princess Marie of, 107

Baden, Stephanie, Grand Duchess of (1789–1860), 283

Balfour, Lady Georgina, daughter of Lord Cawdor, wife of Colonel Balfour of Balbirnie, 244

Balfour, Miss, sister-in-law of above, 244

Bancroft, George, American Minister in London, 151

Barrington, Lady Caroline, 108, 109, 111, 168, 209, 239, 251, 257

Bassano, Duchesse de (1814–67), Lady of Honour to the Empress, 145

Bavaria, Ludwig II, King of (1845–86), 154–5, 249, 316

Beatrice, Princess (1857–1944), fifth daughter of Queen Victoria, 77, 123, 142, 217, 259, 275, 308

Beauchamp-Walker, General, 312

Beauharnais, Vicomte de, 283

Becker, Dr. E., German secretary to the Prince Consort, 248

Belgium, King Leopold I of (1790–1865), 22, 46, 48–9, 50, 74, 104, 123, 141

Belgium, King Leopold II of (1835–1909), formerly Duke of Brabant, 50, 102, 104, 129, 134, 144, 148, 170, 171, 195, 213, 214, 221, 230, 249, 286

Belgium, Queen Louise of, wife of Leopold I, 141

Belgium, Queen Marie of, formerly Duchess of Brabant, wife of Leopold II, 65, 102, 104, 141, 144, 170, 213, 214, 221

Bell, John (1811–95), sculptor. An iron copy of his Eagle-Slayer is at the entrance to South Kensington Museum, 227

France—attempt to annex Luxemburg, 126, 127, 128, 129, 131–2, 133, 134; resists election of Prince Leopold Hohenzollern to the throne of Spain, 282–3. See Franco-Prussian war

France—Empress Eugénie, 144, 145, 204, 295, 297, 298, 300, 301, 310, 311

France—Emperor Napoleon III, 72, 81, 102, 127, 131–2, 134, 136, 139, 286, 290–1, 293, 294, 295, 297, 299

France—Prince Napoleon (1822–91), son of Jerome Bonaparte and first cousin to the Emperor Napoleon III, 291

France—the Prince Imperial, 139–140, 292, 310

Franco-Prussian War—events leading up to, 285–6; France declares war, 286; draft treaty terms by Bismarck published in *The Times*, 289; French division routed at Wissemburg, 292; deterioration of the French position, 294–5; battle of Regonville–Gravelotte, 296; French defeat at Sedan and surrender of the Emperor, 285, 297; fall of Metz, 311; bombardment of Paris, 312, 315; three weeks' armistice signed, 316; terms of armistice, 318, 321

Frederick William, Crown Prince. See Prussia

Fuad Pasha (1814–69), 142

Fürstenstein, Count, 37, 169

GAINSBOROUGH, Lady, 4th wife of 1st Earl of Gainsborough, 211

Galitzine, Princess Alexandrine, 243

Gambetta, Leon (1838–82), French statesman — member of the Government of National Defence, 1870, 318

Gardiner, General Sir Robert (1781–1862)—served throughout the Napoleonic Wars.

Equerry to King Leopold on his marriage to Princess Charlotte; lived at Claremont, 162

Garibaldi, Guiseppi (1807–82), 157, 159

Garnier-Pagès, Louis Antoine (1808–78), French lawyer and politician, 134

Gastein Convention of August, in 1865, 41, 58, 61

Gathorne-Hardy, Gathorne (1814–1906), afterwards Earl of Cranbrook, 169

Geffcken, Frederick Heinrich (1830–96), 108, 140

Geneva Conference, 233

George, Prince, later King George V, 105, 211, 222

George I, King of the Hellenes. See Greece

George V, King of Hanover and Duke of Cumberland. See Hanover

Gerson, W., 128

Gisela, Archduchess of Austria. See Austria

Gladstone, William Ewart (1809–1898), Prime Minister, 35, 180, 189, 221, 226, 228, 231, 235, 248, 259, 261, 320, 321

Gleissner, Lewis, 279

Goltz, Count Robert von der (1817–69), Prussian Ambassador in Paris, 133, 291, 292–3

Goltz, Marie, formerly Countess Marie Lynar. Married Count Charles von der Goltz, 1860. Lady-in-Waiting to the Crown Princess before marriage, 170, 209, 256

Grafton, Duchess of, wife of 6th Duke, daughter of 3rd Lord Ashburton. Married 1858, died 1928, 254

Grant, John, head keeper at Balmoral, 22, 28, 29, 208

Granville, 2nd Lord (1815–91), Liberal statesman, 32, 212, 215, 261, 284, 288; succeeded Lord Clarendon as Foreign Secretary, 290, 291, 293, 322

English fireplace installed in the Neues Palais, 24; visit of the Grand Duke and Grand Duchess Michael of Russia, 27; Prince William is placed in the charge of his tutors, 28; expresses a hope of spending Christmas in England, 29; but has to give up the idea, 30–1; visit to Posen, 33–4; her love for England, 34–5; holiday at Wyke on the Isle of Fohr, 35–7; visit to Heligoland, 38; persuades the Queen to entertain the King of Prussia when visiting Darmstadt, 40; attends the autumn manœuvres at Mersburg, 42; visits Krupp's cannon foundry at Essen, 44; describes the wedding of Princess Alexandrine of Prussia to Duke William of Mecklenburg-Schwerin, 46–7; regrets that King Leopold is not to be buried at Windsor, 48–9; funeral attended by Crown Prince in Brussels, 50.
1866:
Grieves over the death of Count Blücher, 53; suggests John Charles Robinson as successor to Sir Charles Eastlake as Director of the National Gallery, 54–5; is alarmed at the growing threat of war with Austria, 58–59; which she blames on Bismarck, 60–1; is saddened by the confused policy of the King, 71; and upset by the excitability of the Queen, 73; Crown Prince takes command of the Second or Silesian army, 76; her profound grief at the death of Prince Sigismund, 77; regards the Prussian people as a superior race, 80; is anxious that the Crown Prince's part in the war should be fully recognised, 82; describes her lonely state during the illness and death of Prince Sigismund, 85; defends Princess Alice against the Queen's criticisms, 86; discusses the unfortunate position of those states who sided with Austria against Prussia, 87–8; wishes to instal a Lady Superintendent in her household, 88; visits the wounded in hospital, 92; compares the discipline and efficiency of the Prussian army with the chaotic conditions of the Austrian army, 94–6; agrees about the inadvisability of the King of Hanover settling in England, 97; describes the triumphal entry of the Prussian army into Berlin, 97–8; assures the Queen that the King of Hanover has been treated generously, 99–100; but has proved unco-operative; 101; reports the rumour that Charlotte, Empress of Mexico, is mentally deranged, 102; praises the qualities of Princess Alexandra, 106–7; suggests Prince Fritz Carl's eldest daughter as a possible wife for Prince Arthur, 109; visit of the Prince of Wales to Berlin, 110; asks the Queen to let Princess Alexandra be her sole companion on occasions, 111; expresses a belief in phrenology, 112.
1867:
Her deep interest in the cause of liberty and progress, 119–20; asks the Queen to send contributions for a bazaar in aid of war victims, 121, 122; complains of the Queen of Prussia's lack of interest in her grandchildren, 123–4; refers to the growing dispute between France and Germany over Luxemburg, 127; accuses France of aggression, and wishes to see her reduced to a second-rate power, 129; attends the wedding of Prince Philippe of Flanders and Princess Marie of Hohenzollern, 130–1; explains in more detail her attitude to the Luxemburg

Roman Catholic Church will only be broken when priests are allowed to marry, 247; refers to the strange behaviour of King Ludwig of Bavaria, 249; visit to the south of France, 250; is upset by the sudden departure of her lady-in-waiting Countess Valerie Hohenthal, 257.

Stanley, Augusta, daughter of 7th Lord Elgin, wife of the above, 254

Stanley, Edward Henry, afterwards 15th Earl of Derby. Foreign Secretary 1866–8, 150–151, 154

Star Spangled Banner, The, 122

Steinitz, General, Prussian Commander, 96

Stockmar, Baron Christian Frederick (1787–1863), 102, 125, 165, 194, 207, 273

Stockmar, Baron Ernest, secretary to the Crown Princess, 177; marriage, 224–5, 229, 268

Stowe, Harriet Beecher, author of *Lady Byron Vindicated*, 258

Stuart, William (1824–96), son of Lord Blantyre, 157

Suez Canal, opening of, 245; attended by the Crown Prince, 246

Sutherland, Duchess of, wife of 4th Duke, 254

Sutherland, Duchess of, wife of 3rd Duke. Married 1849. Died 1888, 232

Sutherland, Harriet, Duchess of (died 1868), wife of 2nd Duke, daughter of 6th Lord Carlisle, 75

Sweden, Princess Louise of, married King Frederick VIII of Denmark, 71, 106, 109

Talbot, Gerald Francis, 281

Tankerville, 6th Lord (1810–99), 143

Teck, Francis Duke of (1837–1900), 68, 69, 164, 221

Teck, Mary Duchess of, 41, 68, 76, 140, 164, 183, 211

Teck, Princess Mary of, later Queen Mary, 140, 164, 183

Tennyson, Alfred Lord, 254, 255, 257, 258

Thyra, Princess of Denmark (1853–1933), younger sister of the Princess of Wales, 181, 279

The Times, 262; denied the authenticity of correspondence alleged to have been written by the Prince of Wales and Prince Alfred, 279, 281–2; published the terms of a draft treaty agreed between Bismarck and the French Ambassador at the end of the Austro-Prussian War, 289

Treaty of Paris—denounced by the Russians, 308

Trench, William Steuart (1808–1872), 229, 235

Tresckow, M. de, 150

Turkey, Sultan Abdul-Hamid of, 143

Turkey, Sultan Abdoul Aziz (1830–1876), visits England, 140, 141, 143–4

Turkey, Sultan Mourad V, 143

Turnbull, John, 66

Üxküll, Count, 251, 257, 273, 275

Veitch, James, Exeter horticulturalist, father of Sir Harry Veitch: born 1840, 236

Victoria, Princess, the Princess Royal. See Prussia

Victoria, H.M. Queen (1819–1901) 1865:

Commends Lord Napier to the Crown Princess, 15; sends birthday wishes to Prince William, 16; speaks with regret of the departure of Countess Blücher, 17; refutes the accusation of 'hating babies', 18; reception of the Corps Diplomatique at Buckingham Palace, 18; expressed admiration of *Aurora Leigh*, 19; but does not share the Crown Princess's admiration of the novels of J. H. Michon, 20; appoints John Brown as her personal servant, 21–3; whom she finds an 'immense comfort', 23; Duchess of Atholl in waiting, 26; refers to the unselfish devotion of John Brown, 29;

Victoria, H.M. Queen (1819–1901)
—*continued*
1868:
Is gratified by the success of her book, 169, 171, 178; but reproaches the Crown Princess for her lack of interest, 173; resignation of Lord Derby as Prime Minister: is replaced by Benjamin Disraeli of whom the Queen approves, 174, 176; speaks highly of Princess Louise and her artistic talents, 178–9; praises the works of Mrs. Oliphant, 179; is against the move to disestablish the Irish Church, 180; is strongly opposed to child marriages, 181; illness of Sir James Clark, 183; attempted assassination of Prince Alfred when in Australia, 185; lays the first stone of St. Thomas's Hospital, 189; refers again to her uneasiness at the behaviour of Prince Alfred, 193; and reflects that children are more anxiety and sorrow than pleasure when they grow up, 193; is pleased to find Princess Alice 'kind, amiable and discreet', 197; but does not enjoy the large family party at Osborne, 200–1; visit to Switzerland, 204–6; warns the Crown Princess of the danger of pride in a Prince, 206; finds a great improvement in the behaviour of Prince Alfred, 207–8; expresses pity for the fate of Queen Isabella of Spain, 208, 209; hints at the resignation of Disraeli as Prime Minister, 212.
1869:
Meets and talks with John Bright, 215; death of the only son of the King and Queen of the Belgians, 221; decides not to open Parliament, 222; is anxious about the health of Prince Leopold, 225; sends good wishes to Baron Stockmar on his

marriage, 225; visits a number of sculptors' studios, 227; thinks that the Irish Church should be reformed, but not disestablished, 228; and reports that the second reading of the Irish Church Bill was passed by a large majority, 230; visit to St. Bartholomew's Hospital, 231; bestows a knighthood on Michael Costa, 232; feels that the Crown Princess does not understand the state of affairs in Ireland, 235–6; visit to Aldershot, 238; visit of the Grand Duchess Marie, widow of the Duke of Leuchtenberg, 241; feels that a marriage between Princess Louise and Prince Albrecht of Prussia is out of the question, 252.
1870:
Is distressed at, but does not condemn, the elopement of Countess Valerie Hohenthal, 253–41, 255; Duchess of Sutherland appointed lady-in-waiting, 254; feels that the position of unmarried ladies is untenable, 257; suggests that the Crown Princess visits Osborne in the summer, 261–2; is distressed at the Prince of Wales' connection with the Mordaunt divorce case, 262; returns to the subject of large families and the anxiety they cause, 263, 264; illness of Countess Blücher, 263; and death of, 267–8, 269, 270, 271; alarming illness of General Grey, 269; and death of, 272–3; Henry Ponsonby succeeds as Private Secretary to the Queen, 272, 275; is indignant at the supine attitude of the King of Portugal against the coup of the Duke of Saldanha, 280; is startled to hear of Prince Leopold Hohenzollern's election as King of Spain, 282; and relieved to hear of his withdrawal, 284; is indignant at the French

declaration of war on Prussia, 286; and feels that England must remain neutral, 287; denies the stories about the Prince of Wales circulated by Count Bernstorff, 287; and hopes for his removal as Prussian Ambassador to London, 288; is saddened at the deterioration of France, 295, 296; culminating with Sedan and the surrender of the Emperor, 297–8; sends a message to the Empress Eugénie, 298; asserts that English sympathies are pro-German, 299; recalls the Prince Consort's lack of confidence in the French Emperor, 299–300; sends a telegram to the King of Prussia urging clemency towards the enemy, 300; death of Baroness Lehzen, 301; has a changed opinion of Lord Lorne, 301; reaffirms the neutrality of England in the Franco–Prussian dispute, 301; announces the engagement of Princess Louise to Lord Lorne, 302–3, 304, 305; which she regards as a great link between the Royal Family and the country, 306; discusses the ill-feeling in Germany towards England which she largely attributes to the malicious reports of Count von Bernstorff, 307; explains to the Crown Princess why Princess Louise's marriage to Lord Lorne is preferable to a second Prussian alliance, 309–10; visit to Queen Eugénie at Camden Place, Chislehurst, 310; trusts that Alsace and Lorraine will not be another source of war between France and Germany, 311–12; is hurt at the bitterness of her half-sister, Princess Feodora, against England, 314; reports on the unfavourable reception in England of the Armistice terms, 318; stresses the necessity of people in high positions behaving with humility and kindness towards others, 318–20; is pleased that the Crown Princess reciprocates these sentiments, 321; speaks of a change in public opinion in favour of France, 322; assures the Crown Princess that she is under no obligation to return her dowry, 322; is glad to feel that the Crown Princess understands her position as Queen of England, and hopes for the final establishment of good understanding between 'our nations', 323.

Victoria Alexandra Olga Marie, Princess, second daughter of King Edward VII, 200, 211

Victoria Alberta, Princess (1863–1950), eldest daughter of Princess Alice, Grand Duchess of Hesse, 211

Voss, Countess, 203

Vyner, Frederick (1847–70), son of Henry Vyner and Mary, daughter of 1st Lord de Grey, 276

WAAGEN, G. F. (1794–1868), Professor of Art and History at Berlin University: author of *The Treasures of Art in Great Britain*, 55, 235

Wagner, Richard, author of *Jewish Influence in Music*, 232

Wakelin, Mrs., 249

Waldeck, Princess, daughter of the Duke of Nassau: married 1853 the Prince of Waldeck-Pyrmont. Their daughter married King William III of the Netherlands, 250

Wales, Albert Edward, Prince of (1841–1910)—sends the Queen an account of Prince Arthur's journey in the Admiralty yacht *Enchantress*, 24, 41, 42, 43; entertains the Crown Princess at Sandringham, 44–5; on amiable